Targeting

THE JOB

You Want

Third Edition

Kate Wendleton

**author of The Five O'Clock Club's
best-selling career development series**

with Wendy Alfus Rothman,
an authority on job-search research

http://www.FiveOClockClub.com

The
Five
O'Clock
Club®

Career Press / 2000

For my parents

who had the strength to impose their own terms upon life
—with generosity and caring

To order this title, please call toll-free 1-800-CAREER-1 (NJ and Canada: 201-848-0310) to order using VISA or Mastercard, or for information on books from Career Press.

The Career Press, Inc., 3 Tice Road, PO Box 687, Franklin Lakes, NJ 07417

Library of Congress Cataloging-in-Publication Data

Wendleton, Kate.
   Targeting the job you want: featuring special sections throughout on using the Internet to identify and reach your job targets / by Kate Wendleton.
     p.   cm.
   Includes bibliographical references and index.
   ISBN 1-56414-449-6 (pbk.)
   1. Job hunting   2. Internet (Computer network)   I. Title
HF5382.7 .W46   2000
     650.14--dc21   99-057231
                                 CIP

For information, address The Five O'Clock Club,
300 East 40th Street - Suite 6L - New York, New York 10016
http://www.FiveOClockClub.com

If you haven't the strength
to impose your own terms upon life,
then you must accept the terms it offers you.

T. S. Eliot,
The Confidential Clerk

Dear Member or Prospective Member of The Five O'Clock Club:

Have you ever asked yourself the question, "What should I be doing with my life?" This book will help you find the answer. It is the first in a four-part series for job hunters, career changers, freelancers and consultants who want some guidance about what to do in this changing economy. None of us can depend on our employers to help us through this—we have to figure it out for ourselves. And if we do, we will all be better off.

Learning how to manage our own careers is the only job security we can expect from now on. And this book will show you how to do it. *Targeting the Job You Want* is the most extensive and thorough book on the subject. It is important to do the exercises in this book. The results are the only things that will keep you calm and secure in this stormy market.

Taken together, the books in this series prepare you to deal with the continuous change we are all experiencing, figure out where you fit in, and help you to get what you want.

The books present the strategies we use at The Five O'Clock Club, our national job-search strategy program. *The Five O'Clock Club* series is the result of fourteen years of research into how successful people plan and manage their careers, and land the best jobs—whether on payroll or on assignment—at the best pay. These books provide the most sophisticated and most detailed explanation of the process:

- *Targeting the Job You Want* helps you figure out what to do with your professional life.
- *Getting Interviews* presents the targeted, strategic approach to career development and job search that we use at The Five O'Clock Club. It tells you how to get more interviews in your target areas and contains dozens of cover letters. It also tells you how to answer ads on the Internet.
- *Interviewing and Salary Negotiation* teaches you the consultative approach to job interviews, how to turn those interviews into offers, and how to get the best compensation package—whether for full-time, part-time, freelance or consulting work.
- *Building a Great Résumé* uses a case-study approach. You will find out why a perfectly good "before" résumé did not work for a job hunter. When you read about the situation that job hunter was facing, you will see why the "after" résumé was more effective. The index references the over 100 industries and professions reflected in the book.

Running The Five O'Clock Club is the most gratifying thing I do. Those who coach job hunters privately or at our branches agree that nothing gives them more satisfaction than helping someone figure out a career path, and then coaching that person to land a great job at a great salary.

Even those who have been unemployed a long time find help with us. Do not become discouraged if you have been in search a long time. You may be doing something wrong. Some of our best stories are about people who had been unemployed two years or longer, and found the job that was perfect for them at just the right salary. All of the case studies in this and our other books are of actual people.

All of this information is based on the highly successful methods used at The Five O'Clock Club, where the average, regularly attending member finds a job within ten weeks. For a packet of information on joining the Club and subscribing to *The Five O'Clock News*, call 1-800-538-6645 ext. 600, or see the Application Form in the last section of this book or on our website.

We are guided by the original Five O'Clock Club, where the leaders of Old Philadelphia met regularly to exchange ideas and have a good time. Today's members are the same—they exchange ideas at the Club or through our website, operate at a high level, brainstorm to help each other, and truly enjoy each other's company. In addition, they work closely with a Five O'Clock Club career counselor to find the best strategies for their search.

I hope these books will assist you as they have so many others. Thank you for supporting The Five O'Clock Club through your purchase of this book. Because of people like you, we can keep the program going and spread to new cities so we'll be there when you need us. Our goal is, and always has been, to provide the best affordable career advice. And—with you as our partners—we will continue to do this.

Cheers and good luck!

Kate Wendleton
New York City, 2000
www.FiveOClockClub.com

Acknowledgements

With appreciation to my husband, Richard, who was just a dream in my Forty-Year Vision, and to our children, Sara, Paul and Martin, for all that I have learned from them. They have become one of my top Seven Stories. To the entire Dobbs Family, of which I am the eldest, for being dependable cheerleaders.

I appreciate all of The Five O'Clock Club members, old and new, some of whose stories are contained herein: Members provide feedback on our techniques, which allows our approach to evolve continually with the changing job market. Members also give us information for our database, so we can track trends and know what is going on.

I thank our career counselors who are a highly trained and dedicated group and our branch heads, who have brought this high-quality program to other cities with enthusiasm and dedication to our members.

I thank the excellent staff of The Five O'Clock Club who keep our office running smoothly. Special mention to Wendy Alfus Rothman, who wrote the research and bibliography sections of this book, was one of the original Five O'Clock Club counselors and started two of our branches. In addition, I would like to acknowledge Patricia Kelly, whose artwork, *Fruytagie*, hangs in our offices and appears in our publications—including this one.

We are all especially proud of Workforce America, our not-for-profit operation which runs The Five O'Clock Club program in Harlem. After I started it and ran it for two years, it was taken over by Deborah Brown. When I met her six years ago, I knew Deborah was the ideal person to head up this program. She has proven herself to be an intelligent, refined, selfless leader who has shown initiative, dedication and persistence. Deborah's story is proof that planning works.

Since I came to New York in 1985, I have gotten a number of big breaks from people who believed in me. Edith Wurtzel at The New School for Social Research encouraged me to speak there. Three hundred and fifty people attended, and I later became director of their career center. Abe Fiss at Barnes & Noble agreed to carry my first self-published book in 1986, then my second, and kept reordering them for five years. Many, many others have befriended me, and have helped me to bring you what we have today.

K.W.
New York City, 2000

The
Five
O'Clock
Club®

Table of Contents

PART FOUR—Quick and Effective Research: How To Get on the Right Track

(Do not skip this step.)

PART FIVE—How to Manage Your Future

PART SIX—Career and Job-Search Bibliography

(Look at this part for help in researching a field or industry.)

PART SEVEN—What is The Five O'Clock Club?

"America's Premier Career Counseling Organization"

Targeting

THE JOB

You Want

Third Edition

PART ONE

THE CHANGING JOB MARKET

HOW IT WORKS TODAY

The
Five
O'Clock
Club®

You and the
New Job Market

I'm going to fight hard.
I'm going to give them hell.
Harry S. Truman
Remark on the presidential campaign,
August 1948

Your Employer Has Got to be Sharper—
and So Do You

In a growing but stable economy, the market favors the job hunter. There are more jobs than there are job applicants. Sloppy job-hunting techniques work "well enough." Organizations can hire more people than they need and hope someone will do the job right.

In today's ever-changing economy, job hunters face greater competition for the jobs that are available. Everyone has to be sharper. Just as your employer cannot be sloppy when competing in world markets, you cannot be sloppy when competing in job markets. Your prospective employers have to be more serious about every position they fill. You, too, must take your job hunt more seriously.

Don't Be Scared by the Headlines

Labor is the superior of capital, and
deserves much the higher consideration.
Abraham Lincoln

Job hunters are starting to realize that a large number of people may be laid off in one part of an organization, while different kinds of people are hired in other parts of the same organization. In the news, you will hear about the layoffs, but you will not hear about the hiring—the organization would be deluged with résumés.

Get used to the headlines. Organizations must react quickly to changing world circumstances, and they no longer have time to figure out where the laid-off people could fit into other parts of the same organization. Some organizations now allow laid-off employees to job-hunt both inside and outside the organization. It can be an efficient way for the organization to change direction, and save perhaps 10 percent of the laid-off employees who can fit into the new direction.

The laid-off employee is usually able to find a position outside more quickly because, by definition, there are more positions outside. No matter how big the old organization is, it is small compared to the outside world. A smart employee would devote 10 percent of his efforts to an inside search, and 90 percent outside.

Security is mostly a superstition. It does not exist in nature, nor do the children of men as a whole experience it. Avoiding danger is no safer in the long run than outright exposure. Life is either a daring adventure or nothing.

Helen Keller

A Changing Economy

Today, we know that doing a good job is not enough. Our career prospects can now change for reasons that have nothing to do with our personal job performance, but with the performance of our employers. It's a new economy—a world economy—and the changes are not going to slow down. Not only will things not return to the way they were, the amount of change will increase.

Government statistics show the impact of change on job hunters:

The average American has been in his or her job only four years.

The average American getting out of college today can expect to have five careers during his or her lifetime—that's not five jobs, but five separate careers!

We will probably have twelve to fifteen jobs in the course of those five careers.

Ten years from now, half the working population will be in jobs that have not yet been invented. Let's make that more personal: ten years from now, half the people reading this book will be in jobs that do not exist today. That's okay. We'll tell you where some of the new jobs are, but you'll have to do research as well.

Ten years from now, half the working population will be in non-traditional forms of employment. This means that half of us will not be working full-time, on payroll, for one employer—a wrenching change in our mindsets. Some of us may work two days a week on payroll for one employer, and three days a week for another. Or three days a week on payroll, with consulting or freelance work on the other days. Or we may be paid by one company that farms us out to another. The variations are endless—and changing.

The situation is unsettling—to say the least. However, we cannot fight it. In this time of dramatic change, few organizations really know where they are heading, but some are learning what kind of workers they need: flexible, self-aware ones who continually improve their skills. Gone are the days when it was good enough for employees to simply do their assigned jobs well. America wants and needs a new kind of workforce.

Employees too are learning that they must take care of themselves and remain marketable so they are not dependent on one employer. They are proactively figuring out what they bring to the party, while finding out—and fitting into—the new directions their organizations and industries are taking.

A few smart organizations have wisely embraced a process of helping employees take charge of their own careers. Most of us, however, will have to develop career plans on our own, and this book can help you do just that.

Continual Career Development —An Enlightened Approach

All of this fits in with what we have taught at The Five O'Clock Club since 1978: It is best for both the employee and the employer if "job hunting" is seen as a continual process—and not just something that happens when a person wants to change jobs. **Continual job search means continually being aware of market conditions both inside and outside of our present organizations, and continually learning what we have to offer—to both markets**.

With this approach, workers are safer because they are more likely to keep their present jobs longer: they learn to change and grow as the organization and industry do. And if they have to go elsewhere, they will be more marketable. Organizations are better off because employees who know what is going on outside their insular halls are smarter, more sophisticated and more proactive, and make the organization more competitive.

Every industry is going through dramatic change—and hence needs a more aware and flexible workforce. Regardless of the industries you are targeting, read our reports on the interactive job market: that industry may affect your job. Even as a consumer, you will be surprised and intrigued by what is happening.

The economy is changing too fast for you to use the same old career planning techniques or the

People are always blaming their circumstances for what they are.
I don't believe in circumstances. The people who get on in this world are the people
who get up and look for the circumstances they want, and if they can't find them, make them.
George Bernard Shaw

same old attitudes about job hunting.

Technology is the Most Pervasive

Probably no change will affect our careers more than technological change. It's not like a stock market crash, or tearing down the Berlin Wall. It doesn't make the headlines, because it's happening everywhere—every day. When you want money from a bank, you can go to a machine. The human—the middleman doing the drudgery—is no longer required in that job. People are required in *new* jobs—to design and make the machines, service them, sell them, and so on—jobs that did not exist a few years ago.

Computers are part of the reason organizations have been able to cut the ranks of middle management. Organizations no longer need layers of management to pass information up and down. The reports and studies and controls that were the domain of these managers are now that of computers.

As a result of technology, new industries are possible, such as direct marketing and the express-mail industry. Desktop publishing has affected the publishing, typesetting, and printing industries.

Professions are changing. Most artists now work at a computer keyboard instead of a drawing board. Their jobs did not exist ten years ago. Accountants are no longer needed to do compounded-growth rates and other complex calculations. Their jobs are changing. Salespeople are being replaced by computers and the UPC codes you see on packages. Musicians are being replaced by electronic synthesizers, which can replicate virtually every instrument. The Internet is a category by itself, so read our report on the Internet marketplace.

Whether you are talking about manufacturing or hospital technology, artists or accountants, salespeople or teachers—virtually every industry and profession has or will be affected. There are no secure jobs because the jobs themselves are changing. If you think your industry or profession is not being affected, think again.

The Good Old Days—People Were Stuck

I remember the "good old days"—the days of one employer and one career. It used to be that when you found a job, you had found a home. You expected to get in there, do what the organization wanted, learn to play the game, rise through the ranks, and eventually retire. People had secure jobs with large, stable employers.

People may have had job security, but the downside is that they were often stuck. Changing jobs was frowned upon. For every satisfied person, there was someone stifled, who knew he or she had made a dreadful mistake.

Today, many of us might fear losing our jobs—even from week to week—but *no one—absolutely* no one—needs to feel stifled, deadened, or stuck in a career they no longer find satisfying. *Everyone has an opportunity to do something that is better.*

What we see now is that many of the people pushed out of organizations after twenty years are actually relieved to get out of jobs they'd found deadening. Some decide to think about what they really want to do and make the second phase of their lives much more fulfilling than the first.

In this book you will learn how to take more control of your life, how to plan for your own future and not be at the mercy of others. Many people who are laid off say, "This will never happen to me again. I will never again be caught off guard and unprepared."

A New Definition of Job Hunting

Job hunting in our changing economy is a *continuous* process and requires a new definition. As I mentioned earlier, job hunting now means continually becoming aware of market conditions both inside and outside of our present organizations, and learning what we have to offer—to both markets. This new definition means we must develop new attitudes about our work lives, and new skills for doing well in a changing economy.

Today's economy requires job hunters to be more proactive, more sophisticated, and more willing to go through brick walls to get what they want. Employers no longer plan your career for you. You must look after yourself, and know what you want and how to get it.

Understanding How the Job-Hunting Market Works

Knowing why things work the way they do will give you flexibility and control over your job hunt. Knowing how the hiring system works will help you understand why things go right and why they go wrong—why certain things work and others don't. Then you can modify the system to fit your own needs, temperament, and the workings of the job market you are interested in.

It is overly simplistic to say that only one job hunting system works. The job selection process is more complicated than that. Employers can do what they want. You need to understand the process from their point of view. Then you can plan your own job hunt, in your own industry. You will learn how to compete in this market.

Always remember, the best jobs don't necessarily go to the most qualified people, but to the people who are the best job hunters. You'll increase your chances of finding the job you want by using a methodical job-hunting approach.

Even if you have worked for the same employer for many years, learn how to job-hunt in a changing economy. At first it will seem strange. It's a new skill, but one you can use for the rest of your life. For a while you may feel as though things will never be the same. And they won't. No job is secure. At the same time, we now know that no one has to be locked into one job, one boss, one employer. Skilled job hunters have a real ability to plan their careers.

The Only Port in This Storm: You

"They" cannot offer you job security. They cannot offer you loyalty in exchange for your own loyalty. The rules have changed very quickly, and they expect you to adapt very quickly.

If you don't plan your own path through all of this, you will continue to be thrown around by the turbulence. The better you understand yourself—your motivations, skills, and interests—the more solid your foundation will be.

In our world of revolving bosses—whether you are on payroll or not—you will come across a shallow, rough person who does not understand your value. But if you have done the exercises in this book—especially the Seven Stories—you will understand your own value, and your self-esteem is more likely to remain intact. You will keep yourself on course and continue to follow your plan.

The better you are at plotting out your own future, the more you will get out of each of your jobs or assignments. Each one will fit in with your long-term vision, and you will not get so ruffled by corporate politics and pettiness. You will be following your own vision.

They say we will all adapt to this new world, and I am sure we will. I must admit that Five O'Clock Clubbers are a heartier and more resilient bunch than I am sometimes. Every week, I see people land great new jobs and assignments in this exciting new world. They have created their own career paths, have let go of the old fields that they loved and had worked in for so long, and are having fun—sometimes even more fun—in the new fields. Like these other Five O'Clock Clubbers, you can do it too. You will have help from the head of The Five O'Clock Club branch in your area, as well as from the Five O'Clock Club counselor who heads your small group. You can read more about The Five O'Clock Club at the end of this book.

Changes Mean New Opportunities

The world is changing. What's hot today is not tomorrow. You can use these changes to your advantage. You can choose to head your career in the direction that's right for you.

You can impose your own terms upon life. You don't have to accept the terms it offers you. Read on, and see what others have done.

Alice said nothing: she had sat down with her face in her hands, wondering if anything would ever happen in a natural way again.
Lewis Carroll, *Alice in Wonderland*

If an idea, I realized, were really
a valuable one, there must be
some way of realizing it.
Elizabeth Blackwell
(the first woman to earn a medical degree)

When a large American steel company began closing
plants in the early 1980's, it offered to train the displaced
steelworkers for new jobs. But the training never "took;"
the workers drifted into unemployment and odd jobs
instead. Psychologists came in to find out why,
and found the steelworkers suffering from acute identity
crises. "How could I do anything else?"
asked the workers. "I am a lathe operator."
Peter Senge, *The Fifth Discipline*

T ed had spent ten years in marketing and finance with a large cosmetics company. His dream was to work in the casino industry. He selected two job targets: one aimed at the cosmetics industry, and one aimed at his dream.

All things being equal, finding a job similar to your old one is quicker. A career change will probably take more time. What's more, the job-hunting techniques are different for both.

Let's take Ted's case. The casino industry was small, focused in Atlantic City and Las Vegas. Everyone knew everyone else. The industry had its special jargon and personality. What chance did Ted have of breaking in?

Ted had another obstacle. His marketing and finance background made him difficult to categorize. His hard-won business skills became a problem.

It's Not Easy to Categorize Job Hunters

The easier it is to categorize you, the easier it is for others to see where you fit in their organizations, and for you to find a job. Search firms, for example, generally will not handle career changers. They can more easily market those who want to stay in the same function in the same industry. Search firms that handled the casino industry would not handle Ted.

You Must Offer Proof of
Your Interest and Competence

Civility is not a sign of weakness,
and sincerity is always subject to proof.
John F. Kennedy
Inaugural Address, January 20, 1961

Many job changers essentially say to a prospective employer, "Give me a chance. You won't be sorry." They expect the employer to hire them on faith, and that's unrealistic. The employer has a lot to lose. First, you may lose interest in the new area after you are hired. Second, you may know so little about the new area that it turns out not to be what you had imagined. Third, you may not bring enough knowledge and skill to the job and fail— even though your desire may be sincere.

The hiring manager should not have to take those risks. It is the job hunter's obligation to prove that he or she is truly interested and capable.

How You As a Career Changer Can Prove Your Interest and Capability

- Read the industry's trade journals.
- Get to know the people in that industry or field.
- Join its organizations; attend the meetings.
- Be persistent.
- Show how your skills can be transferred.
- Write proposals.
- Be persistent.
- Take relevant courses, part-time jobs, or do volunteer work related to the new industry or skill area.
- Be persistent!

Ted, as a career changer, had to offer proof to make up for his lack of experience. One proof was that he had read the industry's trade newspapers for more than ten years. When he met people in his search, he could truthfully tell them that he had followed their careers. He could also say he had hope for himself because he knew that so many of them had come from outside the industry.

Another proof of his interest was that he had sought out so many casino management people in Atlantic City and Las Vegas. After a while, he ran into people he had met on previous occasions. Employers want people who are sincerely interested in their industry, their company, and the function the new hire will fill. Sincerity and persistence count, but they are usually not enough.

Another proof Ted offered was that he figured out how to apply his experience to the casino industry and its problems. Writing proposals to show how you would handle the job is one way to prove you are knowledgeable and interested in an area new to you. Some people prove their interest by taking courses, finding part-time jobs, or doing volunteer work to learn the new area and build marketable skills.

Ted initially decided to "wing it," and took trips to Atlantic City and Las Vegas hoping someone would hire him on the spot. That didn't work and took two months and some money. Then he began a serious job hunt—following the system which will be explained in the pages that follow. He felt he was doing fine, but the hunt was taking many months and he was not sure it would result in an offer.

After searching in the casino industry for six months, Ted began a campaign in his old field—the cosmetics industry. Predictably, he landed a job there quickly. Ted took this as a sign that he didn't have a chance in the new field. He lost sight of the fact that a career change is more difficult and takes longer.

Ted accepted the cosmetics position, but his friends encouraged him to continue his pursuit of a career in the casino industry—a small industry with relatively few openings compared with the larger cosmetics industry.

Shortly after he accepted the new position, someone from Las Vegas called him for an interview, and he got the job of his dreams. His efforts paid off because he had done a thorough campaign in the casino industry. It just took time.

Ted was not unusual in giving up on a career change. It can take a long time, and sometimes the pressure to get a paycheck will force people to take inappropriate jobs. That's life. Sometimes we have to do things we don't want to. There's nothing wrong with that.

What *is* wrong is forgetting that you had a dream. What *is* wrong is expecting people to hire you on faith and hope, when what they deserve is proof that you're sincere and that hiring you has a good chance of working. *What is wrong is underestimating the effort it takes to make a career change.*

In the future, most people will have to change careers. Your future may hold an involuntary career change, as new technologies make old skills obsolete. Those same new technologies open up new career fields for those who are prepared—and ready to change. Know what you're up against. Don't take shortcuts. And don't give up too early. Major career changes are normal today and may prove desirable or essential tomorrow.

The Five O'Clock Club®

Job Hunting versus Career Planning

Most people say their main fault is a lack of discipline. On deeper thought, I believe that is not the case. The basic problem is that their priorities have not become deeply planted in their hearts and minds.
Stephen R. Covey,
The Seven Habits of Highly Effective People

*Afoot and light-hearted
I take to the open road,
Healthy, free, the world before me,
The long brown path before me,
leading wherever I choose.*
Walt Whitman,
Complete Poetry and Collected Prose

You are probably reading this because you want a job. But you will most likely have to find another job after that one, and maybe after that. After all, the average American has been in his or her job only four years. To make smoother transitions, learn to plan ahead.

If you have a vision and keep it in mind, you can continually "position" yourself for your long-range goal by taking jobs and assignments that lead you there. Then your next job will be more than just a job. It will be a stepping stone on the way to something bigger and better.

When faced with a choice, **select the job that fits best with your Forty-Year Vision—the job that positions you best for the long term.**

It takes less than an hour to make up a rudimentary Forty-Year Vision. But it is perhaps the single most important criterion for selecting jobs. Do the exercise quickly. Later, you can refine it and test it against reality. Do the Forty-Year Vision using the worksheet in this book. This is exactly what helped the people in the following case studies. **All of the people described are real people and what happened to them is true.**

CASE STUDY: BILL
Bypassing the "Ideal" Offer

For most of his working life, Bill had been a controller in a bank. He was proud of the progress he had made, given his modest education. Now he was almost fifty years old. It was the logical time to become a chief financial officer (CFO), the next step up, ideally in a company near home, since his family life was very important to him. At just this point, he lost his job.

Following The Five O'Clock Club method, Bill got three job offers:

1) as CFO for a bank only ten minutes from home —the job of his dreams.

2) as controller for a quickly growing bank in a neighboring area—still a long commute.

3) as controller for the health-care division of an insurance company—but it was 200 miles from home.

Bill wisely selected the job that would put him in the strongest position for the long term, and would look best in his next job search. He selected job #3 because it would allow him to include two new industries on his résumé. Health care was growing, and insurance would broaden his financial-services experience.

Bill wanted to hedge his bets, and not uproot his family. So he got an apartment close to the new company, and went home on weekends. After a year and a half, the company was taken over, an unpredictable event. The new management brought in their own people. He was out.

But this time, Bill was not worried. Since he now had valuable new experience on his résumé, he was sought after. He was offered and took a key post in a consulting firm that served the health-care and financial industries.

CASE STUDY: CHARLOTTE
Positioning over Money

Charlotte, a marketing manager, received three offers:

1) with a credit-card company in a staff marketing position dealing with international issues.

2) with a major music company as head of marketing for the classical-music division.

A man may not achieve everything he has dreamed,
but he will never achieve anything great without having dreamed it first.
William James

3) with a non-profit research organization as head of marketing.

The first two positions paid about the same, let's say $90,000. The position with the not-for-profit offered $75,000, and there was no room for moving the salary higher.

How did Charlotte decide which position to take? The music company was not a good fit for her: she was not compatible with the people, and she would probably have failed in that job. The credit-card job would have been easy but boring, and she would not have learned anything new.

Charlotte selected the not-for-profit position, the lowest-paid job. In her Forty-Year Vision, she saw herself as the head of a not-for-profit someday. Since she was only thirty-five, she did not now need a position with a not-for-profit. But she felt good when she interviewed there. So she took the job that best fit with her long-term vision.

Charlotte loved the people, and her position put her in contact with some of the most powerful business people in America. Top management listened to her ideas, and she had an impact on the organization.

After one and a half years, there was a reorganization. Charlotte was made manager of a larger department. She received a pay increase to match her new responsibilities, which brought her salary higher than the salaries of the other two job offers. But, best of all, Charlotte's job was a good fit for her, and made sense in light of her Forty-Year Vision.

CASE STUDY: HARRY
Stuck in a Lower-Level Job

Harry was a window-washer for the casinos, earning an excellent hourly salary. The pay was high because the building was slanted, making the job more dangerous.

Harry did a great job, was responsible and well-liked. He was offered a supervisory position, which could lead to other casino jobs. But the base pay was less than his current pay including overtime, and allowed for no overtime pay. Harry decided he could not afford to make the move and stayed as a window-washer paid by the hour. Today, several years later, he still cleans windows.

There's nothing wrong with washing windows, or any other occupation. But if you make this kind of choice based on short-term gain, be aware that you may be closing off certain options for your future. **Sometimes we have to make short-term sacrifices to get ahead—if indeed we *want* to get ahead.**

Selecting the Right Offer

Doing the exercises will give you some perspective when choosing among job offers. I hope that you will attempt to get six to ten job possibilities in the works (knowing that five will fall away through no fault of your own). Then most likely you will wind up with three offers at approximately the same time.

If you have three offers, the one to choose is the one that positions you best for the long run.

People Who Have Goals Do Better

A study of Harvard students, ten years after graduation, shows that **those who had specific goals made salaries three times greater than the salary of the average** Harvard graduate. **Those with *written* goals made ten times the average!**

Money is not the only measure of success. When you have a clear, long-term goal, it can affect everything: your hobbies and interests, what you read, the people to whom you are attracted. Those who have a vision do better at reaching their goals, no matter what those goals are. A vision gives you hope and direction. It lets you see that you have plenty of time—no matter how young or how old you are.

CASE STUDY: BILL CLINTON
A Clear Vision

Bill Clinton is a good example of the power of having a vision. A small-town boy, Bill decided in his teens that he wanted to become President. He developed his vision, and worked his entire life to make that dream come true.

The psychic task which a person can and must set for himself is not to feel secure, but to be able to tolerate insecurity, without panic and undue fear.

Erich Fromm, *The Sane Society*

Optimism Emerges as Best Predictor to Success in Life

"Hope has proven a powerful predictor of outcome in every study we've done so far," said Dr. Charles R. Snyder, a psychologist at the University of Kansas. . . . "Having hope means believing you have both the will and the way to accomplish your goals, whatever they may be. . . . It's not enough to just have the wish for something. You need the means, too. On the other hand, all the skills to solve a problem won't help if you don't have the willpower to do it."

Dr. Snyder found that people with high levels of hope share several attributes:

• Unlike people who are low in hope, they turn to friends for advice on how to achieve their goals.

• They tell themselves they can succeed at what they need to do.

• Even in a tight spot, they tell themselves things will get better as time goes on.

• They are flexible enough to find different ways to get to their goals.

• If hope for one goal fades, they aim for another. Those low on hope tend to become fixated on one goal, and persist even when they find themselves blocked. They just stay at it and get frustrated.

• They show an ability to break a formidable task into specific, achievable chunks. People low in hope see only the large goal, and not the small steps to it along the way.

People who get a high score on the hope scale have had as many hard times as those with low scores, but have learned to think about it in a hopeful way, seeing a setback as a challenge, not a failure.

Daniel Goleman,
The New York Times,
December 24, 1991

CASE STUDY: BRUCE
Plenty of Time

Bruce—young, gifted, and black—was doing little to advance his career. Like many aspiring actors, he worked at odd jobs to survive and auditioned for parts when he could.

But, in fact, Bruce spent little time auditioning or improving his craft because he was too busy trying to make ends meet. What's more, he had recently been devastated by a girlfriend.

Using The Five O'Clock Club assessment, Bruce realized he was going nowhere. His first reaction was to attempt to do everything at once: quit his part-time jobs, become a film and stage director, and patch things up with his girlfriend. With the help of the Forty-Year Vision, Bruce discovered that his current girlfriend was not right for him in the long run, and that he had plenty of time left in his life to act, direct, and raise a family.

Because of his vision, Bruce knew what to do next to get ahead. He was prompted to look for a good agent (just like a job hunt), and take other steps for his career. Six months later, Bruce landed a role in *Hamlet* on Broadway. He is on tour with another play now.

CASE STUDY: SOPHIE
Making Life Changes First

Sophie, age twenty-two, had a low-level office job, wanted a better one, and did the assessment.

She did her Forty-Year Vision, but was depressed by it. Like many who feel stuck, Sophie imagined the same uninspiring situation from year to year. It seemed her life would never change.

With encouragement and help, she did the exercise again, and let her dreams come out, no matter how implausible they seemed. She saw herself eventually in a different kind of life. Although she initially did the exercise because she wanted to change jobs, she saw she needed to change other things first.

She moved away from a bad situation at home, got her own apartment, broke up with the destructive boyfriend she had been seeing for eight years, and enrolled in night school. It took her two years to take these first steps.

She is now working toward her long-term goal of becoming a teacher and educational film maker. She says that she is off the treadmill and effortlessly making progress.

CASE STUDY: DAVE
A New Life at Sixty-two

After Dave had worked for his organization for over twenty-five years, they eliminated his job. He still had a lot of energy and a lot to offer, and he wanted to work. But he was depressed by his prospects until he did his Forty-Year Vision.

His dream for his new life included: working two days a week developing new business for a small organization, volunteering on the Board of a not-for-profit, heading a state commission, and consulting for an international not-for-profit. Instead of slowing down, Dave became busier and happier than he had been on his old job. He was able to quickly implement most of his vision.

CASE STUDY: BOB
Sticking With His Vision

Bob was feeling restless about his career. This prompted him to do a Forty-Year Vision. He wanted to end up at age eighty having done something significant for the community, and having earned a good living doing it. At age forty-three, he was offered a substantial promotion at his curent job—but it was at odds with his community-service goal. After much soul-searching, Bob turned down the promotion, and took steps to implement his plan. He ended up starting his own not-for-profit that eventually would impact communities across America.

CASE STUDY: KAREN
Our Values Change Over Time

Karen had been a high-powered executive, earning over $300,000 a year. When she took time off to have her first baby, she was surprised by how much she loved taking care of her daughter. After Karen had stayed at home for two years, her husband lost his job. She had to look for work.

At first, her vision was to "have it all." She assumed she needed another $300,000-a-year job to keep up their lifestyle, yet she also wanted time with her child. The assessment helped her see that she had never really enjoyed the grueling hours she had to work before, and she now imagined a better balance between work and family.

Karen received three offers: one for $300,000; one for $200,000, which required a lot of travel; and one for $125,000, which she knew fit into her Forty-Year Vision. Although she was at first embarrassed by having taken a lower-level position, she grew to love it and her new lifestyle.

Over time, our values change. As her daughter grow older, Karen may decide again that a higher-powered job is fine for her.

Men experience value changes too--easing up a little when they want to spend time with the kids, for example, and focusing more on their careers at other times.

CASE STUDY: HANK
Thinking Too Small

Hank, a senior executive who lost his job, chose a new field, just because it was lucrative. But the assessment showed it would not position him well for the job *after* that one.

Instead, Hank became a senior executive with a major organization in his old field. The quick route to financial success no longer appealed to him. He took a more sure road that would position him well for the future. In fact, the job he took paid well enough to make his family very comfortable.

Thinking Big; Thinking Small

A Forty-Year Vision gives you perspective. Without one, you may think too small or too big. Writing it down makes you more reasonable, more thoughtful, and more serious. **Having a vision also makes you less concerned about the progress of others because you know where *you* are going.**

CASE STUDY: JIM
Objective vs. Subjective

Jim had to choose between two job offers, one

For most of us, it is easier to think about how to get what we want than to know what exactly we should want.

Robert N. Bellah, et al., *Habits of the Heart*

paying $350,000 and another at $500,000. The thought process is the same regardless of salary. To prove it, let's pretend the positions were paying $35,000 and $50,000. Which should he take?

Jim's wife wanted him to take the $50,000 job. It paid more and had a better title.

Jim liked the people at the $35,000 job, and they appreciated him and listened to his suggestions. But they could pay no more than $35,000. He delayed the start date while we talked, and listed the pros and cons of each position. He *still* could not decide. After all, $15,000 is a big difference.

Finally, I said to Jim: "I'm going to make it easy for you. The $35,000 a year job no longer exists. Let's not talk about it. You will take the $50,000 a year job, have a very nice commute, make your wife happy, have a title you can be proud of, and make $50,000."

Jim sat in silence. Then he said: "The thought of going there depresses me. I think the job is not do-able. They may be offering me an impossible job."

Sometimes objective thinking alone is not enough. The exercise helped Jim find out what his gut was telling him. During the interview process, things had turned him off about the $50,000 organi-zation--but not enough to turn down the extra $15,000. It wasn't logical.

When Jim finally made up his mind to take the "$35,000" job, he was so happy, he bought presents for everyone. Even his wife was pleased. He had made the right choice.

Consider Objective and Subjective Information

If you tend to pay too much attention to subjec-tive information, balance it by asking: "What is the logical thing for me to do regardless of how I feel?"

If you tend to be too objective, ask: "I know the logical thing to do, but how do I really feel about it?"

CASE STUDY: DEAN
Expect to Be Paid Fairly

Dean had been making $60,000. He lost his job and uncovered two choices: one at $75,000 and one at $100,000. He asked to meet with me.

Dean was not worth $100,000 at this stage in his career, and I told him so. In addition, that organization was not a good fit for him.

The $75,000 job seemed just right for Dean. He had an engineering degree, and the work dealt with high-tech products.

Yet he took the $100,000 position. Within four months, he was fired.

Dean met with me again to discuss two more possibilities: another position for $100,000 and one at a much lower salary. Since he had most recently been making $100,000, interviewers thought perhaps he was worth it. Again, he opted for the $100,000 position--he liked making that kind of money. Again he could not live up to that salary, and again he was fired.

Life Skills, Not Just Job-Hunting Skills

A vision helps people see ahead, and realize that they can not only advance in their careers, but they can change their life circumstances--such as who their friends are and where they live.

Your career is not separate from your life. If you dream of living in a better place, you have to earn more money. If you would like to be with better types of people, you need to **become a better type of person yourself.**

The Forty-Year Vision cannot be done in a vacuum. **Research is the key to *achieving* your vision. Without research, it is difficult to imag-ine what might be out there, or to imagine dream situations**. Be sure to read the two chap-ters on research in this book.

Whatever your level, to get ahead you need:

- **exposure** to other possibilities and other dreams;
- **hard facts** about those possibilities and dreams (through networking and research);
- the **skills** required in today's job market;
- **job-search training** to help you get the work for which you are qualified.

In 1991, nearly 1 out of 3 American workers had been with their employer for less than a year, and almost 2 out of 3 for less than 5 years. The United States contingent workforce—consisting of roughly 45,000,000 temporaries, self-employed, part-timers, or consultants—has grown 57% since 1980. Going, if not yet gone, are the 9-5 workdays, lifetime jobs, predictable hierarchical relationships, corporate culture security blankets, and, for a large and growing sector of the workforce, the workplace itself (replaced by a cybernetics "workspace"). Constant training, retraining, job-hopping, and even career-hopping, will become the norm.

Mary O'Hara-Devereaux and Robert Johansen, *GlobalWork: Bridging Distance, Culture and Time*

Since 1983, the U.S. work world has added 25,000,000 computers. The number of cellular telephone subscribers has jumped from zero in 1983 to 16,000,000 by the end of 1993. Close to 19,000,000 people now carry pagers, and almost 12,000,000,000 messages were left in voice mailboxes in 1993 alone. Since 1987, homes and offices have added 10,000,000 fax machines, while E-mail addresses have increased by over 26,000,000. Communications technology is radically changing the speed, direction, and amount of information flow, even as it alters work roles all across organizations. As a case in point, the number of secretaries is down 521,000 just since 1987.

Rich Tetzeli, "Surviving Information Overload," *Fortune*, July 11, 1994

The Department of Labor estimates that by the year 2000 at least 44% of all workers will be in data services—for example, gathering, processing, retrieving, or analyzing information. As recently as the 1960's, almost one-half of all workers in the industrialized countries were involved in making (or helping to make) things. By the year 2000, however, no developed country will have more than one-sixth or one-eighth of its workforce involved in the traditional roles of making and moving goods. Already an estimated two-thirds of U.S. employees work in the services sector, and "knowledge" is becoming our most important "product." This calls for different organizations, as well as different kinds of workers.

Peter F. Drucker, *Post-Capitalist Society*

The factory of the future will have only two employees, a man and a dog. The man will be there to feed the dog. The dog will be there to keep the man from touching the equipment.

Warren Bennis

Less than half the workforce in the industrial world will be holding conventional jobs in organizations by the beginning of the 21st century. Those full-timers or insiders will be the new minority. Every year more and more people will be self-employed. Many will work temporary or part-time—sometimes because that's the way they want it, sometimes because that's all that is available.

John Handy, *The Age of Unreason*

Targeting the Jobs
of the Future

The time is not far off when you will be answering your television set and watching your telephone.
Raymond Smith, chairman and chief executive of the Bell Atlantic Corporation, *The New York Times*, February 21, 1993

There is guidance for each of us, and by lowly listening, we shall hear the right word.
Ralph Waldo Emerson

All our lives we are engaged in the process of accommodating ourselves to our surroundings; living is nothing else than this process of accommodation. When we fail a little, we are stupid. When we flagrantly fail, we are mad. A life will be successful or not, according as the power of accommodation is equal to or unequal to the strain of fusing and adjusting internal and external chances.
Samuel Butler, *The Way of All Flesh*

Note: In this article, fields and industries mentioned in the text are underlined to help you locate them later.

The Times are Changing

Ten years from now, half the working population will be in jobs that do not exist today.

Positions and industries will disappear almost completely—edged out by technological advances or new industries. When was the last time you saw a typewriter repairman? When was the last time you saw a typewriter? There are few TV or radio repair jobs either. They have been replaced by new jobs.

Some industries retrench—or downsize—slowly and trick us into thinking they are solid and dependable. At the turn of the last century, there were literally thousands of piano manufacturers. A few still remain, but that industry was affected by new industries: movies, TV, radio, and other forms of home entertainment, most recently, the Internet.

At the time, most people probably thought: "But we'll *always* need pianos." People today think the same way about the industries they are in.

Experts say the traditional advertising industry has permanently retrenched. Those who want to stay in that industry often must go to small U.S. cities or abroad. Or they work for corporations rather than advertising agencies.

Peter Drucker said: "Network television advertising is in a severe crisis. . . . None of the mass advertisers—Procter & Gamble, Coca-Cola—none of them knows what to do about it."

A study by Lee Hecht Harrison, a major outplacement firm (as reported by Patricia Kitchen in *The American Banker*, March 1993), showed that 47 percent of laid-off bankers found their next jobs outside the industry. They moved, for example, to the technology, health-care and not-for-profit industries. Banking is permanently retrenching—and changing at the same time because of technology and the international marketplace.

Being a bank teller, for example, used to be a good entry-level position. But many tellers have been replaced by ATMs. There is a new industry that has created jobs to manufacture, sell and

*If you succeed in judging yourself rightly,
then you are indeed a man of true wisdom.*
Antoine de Saint-Exupéry, *The Little Prince*

service these machines.

Some promising new industries don't last at all, so great is the impact of the ever-quickening pace of technological and global change. Data entry until very recently seemed like a relatively safe new field. However, some studies say that data-entry jobs will be virtually non-existent in the United States five years from now. Much of that work is now being farmed out to low-paying countries, such as Russia and India. Job seekers focusing on data-entry jobs in the United States will find it more difficult as time goes on.

Temporary Setbacks

Further, some industries and occupations ebb and flow with supply and demand. When there is a shortage in a well-paid field, such as nursing, engineering, or law, school enrollments increase, creating an excess. Then people stop entering these fields, creating a shortage. So sometimes it's easy to get jobs and sometimes it isn't.

The overall economy may also temporarily affect a field or industry. Real estate, for example, may suffer in a down economy and pick up in a strong one.

Ahead of the Market

When the Berlin Wall came down, there was a rush of companies wanting to capitalize on the potential market in Eastern Europe. Given all they were reading in the papers, job hunters thought it would be a good market for them to explore as well. They were ahead of the market. It took a few years before the market caught up with the concept. Now many people are employed in Eastern Europe or in servicing that market.

The same may be true for the area that you are in or are trying to get into: The market may not be there because it has not yet developed.

Another growth area is the "new media." This is such a rapidly changing area that it is hard to define. As of this writing, it can include cable stations, a number of which are devoted to home shopping; "imaging" of medical records and credit card receipts; supermarket scanners and other

devices that promote items or record what you buy; multi-media use of the computer (sound, motion and color instead of just text); virtual reality; interactive TV; telephone companies (with cable already going into every home); CD/ROM (compact disc containing "read-only memory") which puts materials such as games and encyclopedias on CD's; and the increasingly important Internet.

Two years ago, a client at The Five O'Clock Club believed that the "new media" would be in much demand in the industry she has long followed. But she believed the demand would not happen for a few years—she was then ahead of the market. So she found a job with a small company that was *developing* the new media (as opposed to using it).

She has worked for that company for two years. With this marketable experience under her belt, she plans to move on to the industry she is most interested in—it is now ready for her.

What About *Your* Industry or Profession?

Is your industry or field growing, permanently retrenching, or in a temporary decline because of supply and demand or other economic conditions? If you are lucky, your organization is ahead of the market, and the industry will pick up later. However, this is unlikely unless you are on the cutting edge of high tech.

Most people in permanently retrenching industries, including the leaders, incorrectly think the decline is temporary. You have to decide for yourself. You could perhaps gain insight and objectivity by researching what those outside your industry have to say.

It has been predicted that if things continue as they are going, there will soon be a great divide in America, with technologically and internationally aware workers making fine salaries, while the unaware and unskilled earn dramatically lower wages. (Even high-level executives can be unaware and unskilled, and thus face reductions in their salaries as they become less useful.) If this does come to pass, the best I can do as a career counselor is to encourage people to try to be on the winning side of that divide. You could hedge your bets, as Debbie did.

One doesn't discover new lands without consenting
to lose sight of the shore for a very long time.
André Gide

CASE STUDY: DEBBIE
Hedging Her Bets for the Future

Debbie had been an account manager in advertising for fifteen exciting years. She loved learning everything she could about her shampoo or detergent account, or whatever she was assigned. Debbie was reluctant to change industries despite some negatives: She had a long commute. (Those who want to stay in a retrenching industry often must commute long distances or relocate.) And her job was not as much fun as it used to be. (Companies that survive in retrenching industries tend to experience greater pressure on their bottom line; thus employees have to work longer hours with smaller rewards.) She decided to stay on, but took proactive steps to better insure her future in two ways:

1.) She asked to be assigned to a high-tech account. She knew that if she learned that business, she could someday get a job in the marketing or advertising department of a high-tech organization in an industry that is growing.

2.) In addition to proposing traditional advertising solutions for her clients' problems, she also began to investigate and propose that they take advantage of the new media, such as home shopping and the Internet. This would help her clients, but would also give Debbie experience in the way companies market their goods in the nineties, and give her an edge over those who know only traditional advertising.

Debbie continues to hold her own as her colleagues get squeezed out of advertising. Some are forced to commute longer distances or relocate just so they can stay in the industry. Although many have lost their jobs, or work for half what they used to, there are still enough people making good money to create the illusion that things are the same as they were.

Traditional advertising may revive and prove the doomsayers wrong, but at least Debbie has hedged her bets: she can either stay in the industry or be valuable outside.

You can be like Debbie: you can position yourself for the future by gaining new experience on the job you are now in, or by doing volunteer work or taking a course to learn the new skills you need to remain competitive.

Retrenching Markets Are All Alike

When an industry retrenches, the results are predictable. A retrenching market, by definition, has more job hunters than jobs. The more that market retrenches, the worse it gets.

Those who want to stay in the field have increasingly longer searches as more people chase fewer jobs. They will also tend to stay less time in their new jobs as companies in the retrenching industry continue to downsize or go out of business.

Profit margins get squeezed as companies compete for a slice of a shrinking pie. Those companies become less enjoyable to work for because there is less investment in training and development, research, internal communications, and the like. Of course, salaries are cut.

Most laid-off workers target only their current industry at the start of their search. They consider other targets only after they have difficulty getting another job in their present field. They would probably have found something faster if they had looked in other fields from the beginning.

Those in retrenching industries who also target new industries have a shorter search time.

Expanding Your Search Geographically; Targeting Small Companies

Census Bureau data show that more than 90 % of all new jobs in the 80s were created in the suburbs (a Harvard University study as reported by Leon E. Wynter in *The Wall Street Journal*, May 3, 1993). Oops! It's good to know the facts, because you can conduct your search accordingly. If you have been ignoring the suburbs, think about them.

Job growth has been in smaller companies. Large companies do most of the downsizing. In New York City, for example, there are 193,000 companies. Only 270 of them employ 1000 people or more. James Brown, economist for the Department of Labor, specializing in the New York City labor market, advised members of the mid-Manhattan Five O'Clock Club to look to the other

192,730 companies—those that employ fewer than 1,000 employees.

Think about your geographic area, and think about the companies you are targeting. Most jobs hunters naturally think about the big companies that are in the news, but perhaps you should think about the new "hidden job market": the suburbs, and companies with fewer than 1000 employees.

The Bad News Is Good News
—If You Are *FLEXIBLE*

Virtually every industry and field has been and will continue to be affected by technological changes. Whether you are in education, work for the Post Office, or sell books, your field will be affected. As Alice said about Wonderland: It takes all the running you can do to stay in the same place.

The good news is that many fields are much easier to enter today than they were in times when careers were more stable. There is room for you if you target properly and stay flexible. If you continue to learn in the field you are now in, and get to know the areas you are pursuing, you will be able to make changes as the world changes.

If your current industry or profession is retrenching (and you expect to be working more than five or ten more years), it makes sense to investigate some of the growing fields.

Even if you end up back in your old retrenching industry, the time you have spent exploring a new industry is not wasted, because you will probably have to search again.

Growth Industries and Occupations

The U.S. Census Bureau offers the most reliable and comprehensive employment data available. The bureau has projected *annual* rates of employment growth or shrinkage in major US **industries**: manufacturing (-0.2% shrinkage by 2006 compared to 1996 levels), mining (-2.5%), construction (0.9%),

service producing (1.7% growth), and agriculture (-0.1%). The US has moved from a primarily manufacturing economy to a service economy, and this is projected to continue well into the future.

Perhaps more important for the job seeker to know, the Bureau projects these **occupations** to have the fastest rate of growth: database administrators and computer support specialists (118% growth by 2006 over 1996 levels), computer engineers (109%), systems analysts (103%), personal and home care aides (85%), physical therapy aides (79%), medical assistants (74%), and desktop publishing specialists (74%). Given recent advancements in the microprocessor, the computer industry has and will continue to expand and create jobs as ever more applications for the technology are found.

The National Business Employment Weekly projected these employment opportunities, based on executive recruiting activity in managerial and professional areas:

- Consumer Goods: strong demand for senior marketing executives, especially with direct-mail experience.
- Retailing: need for merchandisers remains strong.
- Information systems and technology: demand is strong if your skills are current, and you have some business know-how.
- Publishing: is looking for business-oriented executives and database marketers.
- Insurance: needs senior-level marketers,

For workers, there are dark spots, but the overall picture is still far brighter than commonly believed. Real wages are starting to turn up, after years of decline. The old factory jobs are disappearing, but new jobs in other industries are being generated at an unprecedented rate. Rather than becoming a nation of hamburger flippers, we are becoming a nation of schoolteachers, computer programmers, and health-care managers. About 11 million new jobs have been created since 1989, and of those, approximately two-thirds are managerial and professional positions. There is a tremendous surge in creativity and new opportunities, ranging from new forms of entertainment to cheap global communications.

Michael Mandel, *The High-Risk Society*

especially with direct-mail experience.
- <u>Banking</u>: is looking for credit-card marketers, corporate and retail product specialists, senior relationship managers, and multi-discipline managers. International experience is a plus.
- <u>Pharmaceuticals</u>: no growth expected overall, but there is opportunity in small biotech firms that are partnering with big firms.
- <u>Health care</u>: demand for workers in hospitals is slowing, as managed care health systems emphasize outpatient and in-home care; home care and outpatient clinics will have growth.
- <u>Engineering</u>: continues to have problems in defense and export-related areas but opportunities are increasing in manufacturing related to the general increase in consumer demand. Opportunities continue to be good in software engineering.

The new fields are new to everyone. An outsider has a chance of becoming an insider.

Predictions 1995 to 2005

Harriet Greisser, director of Executive Employment Research for Right Associates, had this to say in *The Five O'Clock News:*

The Bureau of Labor Statistics predicts that service-producing jobs will account for 93% of all job growth during the period. Health services and business services (which includes computer and data processing services) will be among the fastest-growing areas. Education, child day-care, and residential care will also grow, driven primarily by demographics. Financial services, such as banking and insurance, will continue to lose jobs due to the consolidation of functions and increased productivity from the application of technology.

Manufacturing employment is projected to decline due to technology-based productivity increases, and the composition of manufacturing jobs will shift as production jobs decrease and managerial jobs increase. Construction is expected to increase substantially, and growth in agricultural services will help fuel modest growth in the agricultural, forestry and fishing sector.

Projections for occupational groups show the fastest growth rates for those requiring higher levels of education or training: 1) professional specialty; 2) technicians and related support; and 3) executive, administrative, and managerial. These occupational groups are also those that have the highest earnings.

Since demographics drives employment growth overall, the aging of the baby boomers over the 1995 to 2005 period will create a glut of highly experienced workers competing for the best jobs. On a regional basis, the U.S. Bureau of the Census projects that the West (24%) and the South (16%) will continue to be the fastest-growing regions, while the Midwest will grow 7% and the Northeast will grow only 3%.

Getting More Sophisticated

If you have been working awhile, think past the obvious and think more deeply about the changes that are occurring.

Listed below are a few of the industries business experts project will grow in the next decade. Try to discover other areas that may be affected by these or how your own job may be affected by growth in these areas. Each is huge and changing, and should be better defined by your investigation through networking, Internet and library research.

Here is the list of some of the industries expected to grow:

- <u>Computer software</u>, not hardware.
- <u>Anything high-tech</u>, or the high-tech aspect of whatever field or industry you are in.
- The <u>international</u> aspect of the field/industry you are in.
- The <u>environmental</u> area; <u>waste management.</u>
- <u>Telecommunications</u>, the <u>new media</u> and <u>global communications</u> (<u>movie studios, TV networks, cable companies, computer companies, consumer-electronics companies, and publishers</u>).

- Health care, or anything having to do with it. Even if health care's growth slows down, it will change dramatically, which means there will be room for new people. Health care is still considered a sure bet because of the aging population and the advances being made in medical technology.
- Education in the broadest sense (as opposed to the traditional classroom), including computer-assisted instruction. (Researchers have found that illiterates learn to read better with computer-assisted instruction than they do in a classroom.)

Because all of us will have to keep up-to-date in more areas in order to do our jobs well, technology will play an important part in our continuing education. Further, with America lagging so far behind other countries educationally, both the for-profit and not-for-profit sectors are working hard to revamp our educational system.

- The alternative means of distributing goods. Instead of retail stores, think not only about direct mail, which may already be a bit out-of-date, but about purchasing by TV—or the World Wide Web.
- Anything serving the aging population, both products and services.

In studying the preceding list, think of how you can combine different industries to come up with areas to pursue. For example: combine the aging population with education, or the aging population with telecommunications, or health care with education, and so on. The more you research, the more sophisticated your thoughts will get.

If you combine education with the new media, you will be thinking like many experts. They seem to agree that students in schools will soon learn from interactive multi-media presentations on computers—presentations that will be as exciting as computer games and MTV combined, and almost as up-to-date as the morning news (most textbooks are years out-of-date). Teachers will do what computers cannot do: facilitate the groups, encourage, reinforce learning.

The National Gallery of Art has put its entire collection of 2,600 works of American painting and sculpture on laser video disk for use in schools. 700 disks were distributed free to schools in poor neighborhoods. "Thanks to digitized computer imaging technology, the quality of the images is extremely sharp, perhaps 10 times clearer than pictures produced by the earlier video disks . . . approaching magazine quality. . . . In most cases, there are five or six detailed close-ups for children to study. Some of the detail pieces are so clear that brush strokes can be examined and the warps and weaves of the canvases are clearly visible." (Irvin Molotsky, The New York Times, June 6, 1993)

A computer-based approach can be used to train and update the knowledge of America's workers: employees can learn when they have the time and at their own pace, rather than having large numbers of workers leave their jobs to learn in a classroom situation.

When you read predications that there will be a huge growth in home health care workers, personal and home care aides, and medical assistants, medical secretaries, radiology technologists and technicians, and psychologists, you may think: "I don't want to be any of those." Think more creatively. Companies will have to spring up to supply and train those workers. (Some of the training could even be done on multi-media.) People will be needed to manage the companies, regulate the care given, coach patients on how to select and manage such workers, and so on.

When you read about the tremendous growth in the temporary help business, you may become a temporary worker yourself, or you could go to work running one of the temporary help companies.

Your Own Field or Industry

Think about the field you are in now, and how it is being affected by technology. People say: "Not my field. I'm a salesperson. They'll always need salespeople." Wrong. The sales-person's job has been affected by technology —the UPC bar codes on the sides of packages now allow computers to take inventory—something the salesperson used to do. Stores no longer need a salesperson to ask for the reorder.

Virtually every job and industry—whether it is

*When I examined myself and my methods of thought,
I came to the conclusion that the gift of fantasy has meant more to me
than my talent for absorbing positive knowledge.*
Albert Einstein

publishing, entertainment, manufacturing, financial services, or farming— is being impacted by technology, and by the global marketplace. If you are not aware , you will be blind-sided.

For example, a photographer noticed that digital imaging was affecting her industry, so she bought a computer. Now she can do digital imaging herself rather than being left out of the market. Musicians are learning to use electronic synthesizers; artists are drawing on computers.

Peter Drucker said: "I see the disappearance of the computer market as the computer becomes an accessory. That's already happening. Look at all the medical instrumentation that has become computerized. We are at the point where telecommunications, television, copying and computers are becoming incorporated into one instrument. You don't sell an automobile engine separately. This will soon be the same for computers." (*Forbes ASAP*, March, 1993)

Your Age: How Much Longer Do You Want to Work?

If you want to work only two more years, it may not be worth investing the time to learn a new area. (This is assuming you can get a job in your old area if it is retrenching.)

If you want to work another ten years, learn new things—if only to keep up with what is happening in your present field.

Some Areas Are Safer Bets

The rate of change is so fast that by the time this is published, some of the technologies discussed here will be replaced with new developments. However, some areas are safer bets than others. "Hard skills" are more marketable than "soft skills." For example, a person who wants to get a job as a general writer will have more difficulty than someone who can bring more to the party—such as doing layout on the Macintosh.

We publish *The Five O'Clock News*™ to keep you up-to-date on market information and changing techniques for managing your career. Look at the order form in the back of this book, and consider

becoming a member. We'll keep you informed.

Figure It Out

It's your job to figure out how your industry or field is being impacted by technology and global competition. Think where you fit into the future. Do research.

When I started out as a computer programmer in 1966, I believed I was on the ground floor of this amazing industry. Computers are still on the ground floor, and there's room for those who are interested. In fact, we are now on the ground floor of many industries, and at an exciting time for those who choose to take advantage of the revolutionary changes that are taking place.

Remember the new definition of job-hunting (which The Five O'Clock Club developed in 1978):

> **Job-hunting in a changing economy means continuously becoming aware of market conditions inside as well as outside your present organization, and learning more about what you have to offer—both inside and outside your organization.**

A New Way of Thinking

Any assignment (or job) you get, is a temporary one. You're doing work, but you don't have a permanent job. It's like an actor who lands a part. He or she does not really know how long it may last. Furthermore, actors tend to worry about whether or not a role will typecast them and potentially cause them to lose future roles. Or they may intentionally decide to be typecast, hoping it will increase their chances going forward. Actors understand that they will most likely have to land another role after this one, and they constantly think about how a certain role will position them going forward. And so must you. Your next job is only a temporary assignment.

Learning to Track Trends and Move into a New Market

I remember Chris Marentis's job search. At the beginning, he thought there would be no jobs at his senior level in the area that interested him: the new media. Chris had a terrific background in sports and publishing but no new media experience. He had barely touched a computer at this point.

Four months, 19 job possibilities in new media and nine job offers later, Chris protested to me: "I simply don't want any more offers. I get calls almost every day!" He had a tough decision to make among so many excellent offers, but Chris was finally swayed by the energy and excitement he felt about America Online. Chris became the Group General Manager of their Sports, Outdoors, Health and Fitness channels.

None of the Five O'Clock Clubbers in our interactive stories, which appear later in this book, had previous interactive experience, except for Patricia Raufer, one of our authors. The interactive marketplace is just like other growth areas: By definition, they must hire from outside the industry. Sure, job hunters have to learn the new field. Within two months, most people can learn what they need to know about a new industry: by joining associations, reading trade journals and really getting to know people in the new field (such as through The Five O'Clock Club website). Like other Five O'Clock Clubbers who want to change careers, some of those in this book gained experience by doing volunteer work or consulting.

In addition, the new media is accessible: A person can learn a lot by playing with the Internet. This is different from other growth fields; for example, you cannot learn about health care by hanging around an HMO.

You are not stuck in your present field or industry just because that's where you have your experience. You do not have to take a pay cut or start at the bottom to get into a new field. Trade off what you already know. Learn the new area. Become an insider. In this volatile market, where jobs are disappearing every day, new jobs are appearing. Select a field that will position you for the long run. The people in our stories are picking up skills and experience that will be transferable to other jobs—and they will be extremely marketable.

Virtually every industry is in turmoil. Read what experts write about the industries that interest you. Then think about—or research—the industry you are in now. What are the trends? What outside forces are affecting *your* industry? How might you be affected? How can you prepare for the future?

Reading about the Internet helps you to understand one industry—an industry that is affecting essentially every other industry. So it's worthwhile to know something about it.

If you are targeting other industries, research them to see how you fit in with their new directions. This research and planning will keep you more prepared—and more stable—in this unstable world.

I truly appreciate the generosity of the Five O'Clock Clubbers who have agreed to share their knowledge and experience in these chapters. As usual, we—and your fellow Five O'Clock Clubbers—are working to help you keep up with changes in our workplace.

The Five O'Clock Club®

So You Think Things Are Changing Fast?
Let's Have a Little Perspective

Note: This chapter appeared in *The Five O'Clock News* in 1998, a time when many were wondering whether the Internet was a fad. We wanted to help Five O'Clock Clubbers take the Internet seriously.

By the time I got my MBA in 1975, I was already a techno-nerd, having worked my way through college as a computer programmer. We were all in on the ground floor of this great adventure—and there was plenty of room for everyone. Naturally, I gave lots of lectures encouraging people to get into the field.

Today, with the success of the Internet, we have a new ground floor—and there's still room for virtually everyone, so to speak.

In the past few years, it has been exciting to watch Five O'Clock Clubbers brave the storm of this new development. Like all new technology, the Internet was filled initially with young techies—people just like me in the old days. Beginning in mid-1995, Five O'Clock Clubbers— brave, mature *adults*—got into the picture.

The first senior-level openings were primarily for marketing people: companies need customers. Marketers preceded content-developers, those with backgrounds in editing and the like. Next came the typical business functions one finds in any company: chief financial officers, project managers, and so on. Then large companies saw what was happening and jumped on board, creating even more jobs.

Entire industries will be changed. For example, experts expect every segment of financial services—from retail brokerage to initial public offerings—to be impacted.

The Attributes of a Growth Industry

By definition, growth industries must hire from outside: They don't have enough people inside the industry. The new industry attracts new competitors—many of whom will fail—and there is a shake-out. But if the industry is still growing, those who got in early are the most knowledgeable and valuable, and can command larger salaries. If the industry does *not* continue to grow, new entrants create a surplus of labor and salaries decrease.

The Open Window

So long as the industry continues to grow—as the Internet and related interactive areas will for some time—there is an open window: those outside the industry can get in. As the industry stabilizes, there will be plenty of experienced people, companies will want only those with direct experience, and the window will close.

To quote Five O'Clock Club member Bart Morrison, former chief financial officer of New Century Network, "I actually feel good about having a year-and-a-half experience as a CFO in a new media company. In the interactive world, that's significant. I'm not worried about going back out into the job market."

HMOs, cellular technology, for-profit schools—and the Internet— were essentially non-existent industries just five years ago.

But Only "Insiders" Get Jobs

The early entrants into the Internet had no experience at all—just raw skill and some hands-on time playing around with it. Today's entrants are expected to know more than their predecessors—there are now plenty of magazines to read, anyone can create a website or promote something on the Internet, and plenty of books analyze what's going on so the applicant is expected to have an opinion.

At some point—but not yet—companies will look only for people with full-time experience in the field. I believe that's a long way off.

Are you more likely to find stability in the old, retrenching industries, or in the uncertain industries of the future?

The Growth of the Web

A few years ago, the pace of technological change started to pick up: there was a confluence

The essence of the high-risk society is choice: the choice between
embracing uncertainty and running from it.
Michael Mandel, *The High-Risk Society*

of technological work in various arenas that began to bear fruit.

You may know that the Internet itself was envisioned in 1945—more than 50 years ago—by Vannevar Bush, an electrical engineer. Hypertext, the basis for interactivity on the Internet, was developed in 1965! The World Wide Web was created in 1989 using hypertext. HTML, the "HyperText Markup Language," was developed in 1990. Yet interactive business applications on desktop computers were in relatively wide commercial use by 1980.

Here's one way to look at it:
Radio → TV → Computers → Internet
Internet—not interactive as a category
—is the core medium.
It will affect every job and every person.

The long-accepted concept of computer-based interactivity, combined relatively recently with HTML and URLs, laid the groundwork for the surge we are experiencing today.

In the mid-1990s, we told concerned Five O'Clock Clubbers who were targeting Internet-related companies that even if the Internet didn't make it, their new skills would be transferable to whatever interactive technologies took its place. Clearly, "interactive" was here to stay: computer interactivity had been popular in business applications for over 20 years! But the Internet was not just another interactive medium, such as ATMs, interactive kiosks and telephones, or even CD-ROMs. The Internet was an international infrastructure for commerce and ideas, an intelligent medium that made people smarter and proactive. It was a core medium that would change everything.

Even if you don't want
a job having to do with the Internet,
learn it anyway.
It *will* affect your job.

Intranets

For many years companies have "networked" their internal PCs to their mainframes or servers. Today, they are sometimes referred to as Intranets.

Intranets are networked systems that are closed to the outside, such as those inside organizations, or password-protected Internet-sites. Extranets have parts available to the public and other parts that are password-protected.

Five O'Clock Clubber Paul Miller, who is knowledgeable about the Internet, says, "Organizations are starting to connect their computer systems to the Internet and Internet software protocols are becoming standardized on Intranets. This convergence will lead to broader use and many new applications."

Take hospitals, for example. Managers at Staten Island University Hospital realized that, "in addition to its own locations, the hospital would need to exchange data with medical practices which had formal business relationships with the hospital and others." (*Network Magazine*, March, 1998). Intranets are becoming commonplace, requiring technical people, but also trainers and writers.

The Same Development Pattern in Other Industries

The development of the Internet—a long gestation period followed by a "sudden" appearance on the market—happened concurrently in a number of unrelated industries, and the results added to the cataclysm. Probably half of the jobs that exist today did not exist ten years ago:

- HMOs and alternative medicine have changed the face of healthcare. Ask any physician.
- Telecom, with cellular phones and its international reach, looks nothing like it did only a few years ago.
- Education will be permanently changed by for-profit schools, the erosion of tenure, and the technological advances that are impacting

> *In this high-risk society, each person's main asset will be his or her willingness and ability to take intelligent risks. Those people best able to cope with uncertainty ... will fare better in the long run than those who cling to security.*
> Michael Mandel, *The High-Risk Society*

the industry—with or without the approval of powerful unions.

- "Retail" no longer necessarily means going into a store or even talking to a person. Alternative distribution methods have been in the works for decades—through direct mail and other means—and now through the Internet. People don't need stores to buy computers, travel agents to arrange travel or stockbrokers to purchase stocks. Automobiles are "sold" over the Internet, a new direct-marketing approach: showrooms are there so you can kick the tires.

Consequently, consumers—including my 73-year-old father—are gaining a more level playing field. Every intelligent purchase will be helped by using the Internet.

Who could have dreamed of today's situation just five years ago? But these changes created open windows in the new areas while traditional fields retrenched and revamped.

Interactive Applications Will Stay in Demand

Over the past 35 years, computers have plodded along—affecting virtually every industry and function. The computer industry in general is lobbying to increase the immigration quota for computer scientists and other information workers, so that foreigners can fill thousands of job openings in this country. Here we are, 35 years after computers became commercial, and there is more of a demand than ever.

Interactive applications will be the typical applications of the future, permeating every nook and cranny. The public—and corporations—will accept nothing less. Do we really think that the interactive job market is going to constrict soon? I don't think so.

And even if you don't want a job in an Internet-related field, understand the Internet because it *will* affect your job.

Computer Techies: Watch Out

However in demand techies are, they are quickly put out to pasture when they do not keep their skills up. Yes, techies are hot, but only those who know the hot areas. What's going to happen to those who are working on the Year 2000 projects—mostly maintenance applications—when those projects are done? Most of these programmers will not be learning the new technologies. A word of caution to those folks: take courses and freelance on the side so you develop new skills. Then jump off the Year 2000 project when you find something that can use your new skills.

Risk vs. Security

Should those looking for jobs or consulting assignments focus on the "stable" industries—such as banking ("I've been in banking for 15 years—obviously, I should find another job in banking"), hospitals, the traditional telephone companies, and the old retail? Some should.

But in retrospect—we're almost far enough removed to be able to look back on these "old" industries—the answer for many is "no." Those looking for another job or assignment cannot necessarily find stability by staying in the same field or industry: those areas have changed.

Do we really think that the interactive marketplace is going to constrict very soon? I don't think so.

Professions Also Get Outmoded Overnight

It used to be that once a person had found a profession, that was the source of stability. That is absolutely no longer the case: professions change overnight. Ask physicians or attorneys about their early visions of those professions and you will quickly hear how their fields have dramatically changed. Physicians in their 50s and 60s say they are lucky to have been part of the "golden age" of medicine—when doctors could see whoever they wanted, recommend whatever they felt was in their patients' best interests, get

Fighting futility is a waste of energy, Samantha.
Either do something or quit fretting.
Celebra Tueli

referrals from other physicians, and earn good money. Now, nothing is the same.

Ten years ago, we rarely saw an attorney at The Five O'Clock Club, and until a year ago, we had no physicians. Now, we have plenty of both—and computer programmers as well. Their professions have changed—quickly.

The High-Risk Society

One of my favorite books in 1996 was *The High-Risk Society* by Michael Mandel. The times are good, he says, but prosperity has come at a high price: more intense, more pervasive economic uncertainty than Americans have suffered at any time in the past 50 years.

Mr. Mandel points out that prosperity and security no longer go hand-in-hand. "Today, the very forces behind economic turbulence are also the world's greatest engines of growth. As a result, success hinges on your willingness to embrace risk—rather than flee from it."

Those who keep up and see where the future is heading—in both their professions and their industries—can benefit from the changes that are going to take place anyway. Five O'Clock Clubber Barbara Kerr, New Media Producer for Data Communications Magazine, notes that, "The technological pace will continue but become less intimidating."

I agree. After all, most Americans have been surprised by the sudden changes in diverse industries that have taken decades to develop—but which all appeared on the scene during the same three- to five-year period. It's been hard to take, but things will settle down. We've all been changed by this—even those who knew change was coming—because no one could know exactly what those changes would be.

Now, we all expect new developments and we expect uncertainty. We expect our fields and industries to change. This time, we're ready.

Our eyes are open now. We keep up-to-date. We stay in touch. We're thinking about our next move even before we start a new position. We

know that we have to take charge of our careers, and that doesn't seem so bad anymore. We've got perspective.

God bless you as you face the uncertain future. It's better than trying to stay in the non-existent past.

Ten years ago, we rarely saw an attorney or a computer programmer at The Five O'Clock Club. Until a year ago, we had no physicians. Now, we have plenty of all three. Their professions have changed dramatically.

When to See a Counselor Privately

Just as you have a doctor to help you with medical problems (or to prevent problems), consider developing a relationship with a counselor who gets to know you over the long term. Speak to your counselor when you have specific problems, such as those listed below, or for a "check-up" to make sure everything is okay. Schedule a private session to:

- Negotiate your severance package (get what you deserve and need)
- Solve present job problems (do a better job of managing up, down and across)
- Determine your career path (plan now; avoid the rush)

And when you are job hunting, to:

- Prepare your résumé
- Plan your marketing campaign
- Practice for an important interview
- Plan your salary negotiation

If you need help, visit the coaching section of our website: www.FiveOClockClub.com or call 1-800-538-6645, ext. 210.

When you become a member, we will refer you to two Five O'Clock Club-certified counselors. You can choose one to help you with job search and career planning.

Work today is not just doing;
it is, more than ever, thinking.
Today's corporation needs thinking, flexible,
proactive workers. It wants creative problem
solvers, workers smart and skilled enough
to move with new technologies and with the
ever-changing competitive environment.
It needs workers accustomed to collaborating
with co-workers, to participating in quality
circles, to dealing with people high and low.
Communication skills and people skills have
become parts of the necessary repertoire
of the modern worker.

Hedrick Smith, *Rethinking America*

The line between
the self-employed condition
and working for an "employer"
has become unclear:
Communications technology and flextime
arrangements allow official, full-time employees
to telecommute and to do their
forty hours a week without leaving home.
At the same time, self-employed people may get
contracts that not only require them to perform
the tasks that used to be done by a jobholder,
but also give them an in-house office,
membership on a task force within the
organization, and even a discount at the
employee store.

William Bridges, *JobShift: How to Prosper in a*
Workplace Without Jobs

Strangely enough, this is the past that somebody
in the future is longing to go back to.

Ashleigh Brilliant

Executives have often been hired
with contracts that specify some compensation
if the arrangement is terminated sooner than
planned, and such clauses will
become available to other workers as well.
All of us are going to move toward
some kind of contract with the organization
that pays for our services.

William Bridges, *JobShift: How to Prosper in a*
Workplace Without Jobs

Today's workers need to forget jobs
completely and look instead for work that needs
doing—and then set themselves up as the best
way to get that work done.

William Bridges, *Ibid.*

The trouble with the future is that it usually
arrives before we're ready for it.

Arnold H. Glasow

Enjoy yourself. If you can't enjoy yourself,
enjoy somebody else.

Jack Schaefer

I was going to buy a copy of The Power of
Positive Thinking, *and then I thought:*
What the hell good would that do?

Ronnie Shakes

Progress might have been all right once,
but it has gone on too long.

Ogden Nash

Case Studies: Targeting the Future

While your basic emotional temperament may not change much during your lifetime, you can make significant day-to-day adjustments in the way you perceive events and respond to them. When you face an emotionally trying situation, guard against exaggerating or over-generalizing, and focus instead on your specific options for taking direct action. Avoid putting yourself down by doing something that will exercise your good traits. And seek the company of others, whether it's to gather more rational views on the situation or simply to change your mood.

Jack Maguire,
Care and Feeding of the Brain

---

*The person who fears to try
is thus enslaved.*
Leonard E. Read

---

*Cato learned Greek at eighty; Sophocles
Wrote his grand Oedipus, and Simonides
Bore off the prize of verse from his compeers,
When each had numbered more than four-score years...
Chaucer, at Woodstock with the nightingales,
At sixty wrote the Chaucer Tales;
Goethe at Weimar, toiling to the last,
Completed Faust when eighty years were past.*
Henry Wadsworth Longfellow,
Morituri Salutamus

Within the next decades education will change more than it has changed since the modern school was created by the printed book over three hundred years ago. An economy in which knowledge is becoming the true capital and the premier wealth-producing resource makes new and stringent demands on the schools for education performance and educational responsibility . . . How we learn and how we teach are changing drastically and fast—the result, in part, of new theoretical understanding of the learning process, in part of new technology.
Peter Drucker, *The New Realities*

What About Your Field, Industry or Geographic Area?

A job target is "a clearly selected geographic area, an industry or organization size, and function or position within that industry." An accountant, for example, may target a certain industry (such as telecommunications or hospitals), or may see himself in the accounting function and may not care which industry he is in but prefer instead to focus on "organization size." This means he wants to target a small, medium, or large organization, regardless of industry.

Examine your target to see how each is doing. Perhaps, for example, your industry is okay, but the large organizations are not doing well, while smaller organizations are hiring. In this case, target the smaller organizations.

What changes are taking place in your industry or function? If you think your industry or function will continue to retrench, find a "new horse to ride": an industry or function that is on a growth curve, or one that will give you transferrable skills.

CASE STUDY: ED
The Benefit of Targeting

Ed and Steve were both administrative managers in the retail industry. Both had lost their jobs. Each had spent twenty years--their entire working lives--in retail. Both wanted to work in health care.

Steve actually had hands-on health-care experience. A few years earlier, his organization had lent him to a major hospital to serve as the interim administrative head for a full year. He loved that assignment, did very well at it, and swore he would get a job like that again someday.

But Steve decided to be "practical": "All my contacts are in retail, and I need a job *now*. It's true I would like to move into a growth area, but I don't have time to learn a new industry. I have no choice but to focus on the retail industry."

Ed, on the other hand, targeted health care, and had retail as a separate target. Ed joined health-care associations that dealt with administration, read all the health-care administration trade magazines, and became knowledgeable about the industry. He met with lots of people, largely through the associations. He was even willing to take a temp job doing data entry in the administrative area of hospitals so he could see what was happening from the inside. His ego did not get in the way.

A job came up: exactly the same hospital job Steve had worked in for a full year. Both Ed and Steve heard about the job, and interviewed extensively.

Who got the job? Ed did—because he sounded more believable, more committed to the industry. Even though he had never held a job in that industry, Ed had *proven* by all his activities that he was sincerely interested in health care.

Steve sounded like all the other job-hunters: He wanted this job just because there happened to be an opening.

He had nothing to talk about except the fact that he had held that job before and that they had liked him. Of course, he tried to maximize that experience. But what was noticed was that he had given no recent indication that he was committed to hospital work—he had not interviewed at other hospitals, etc.

This story is a vivid example of the benefits of thoroughly targeting an industry. It is also encouraging proof that people can enter new industries with no prior experience.

"People in that industry won't let me in."

Job-hunters always say it's hard to change from one industry to another. "Hiring managers don't believe I want to get into that field." I don't believe those job-hunters either because they never read anything about the field, and don't know anyone in the field who would serve as a reality check for them. How do you prove to the hiring managers that you are truly interested? As we say in the chapter "How to Change Careers:"

- Read the industry's trade journals.
- Get to know people in that industry or field.
- Join its organizations; attend its meetings.
- Be persistent.
- Write proposals.
- Be persistent.
- Take relevant courses, part-time jobs, or do volunteer work related to the new industry or skill area.
- Be persistent.

If you want to get into an industry or field, learn about it.

It's Time to Take Control of Your Own Career

Get in the habit of reading the papers and noticing what news may affect the industry or field you are in. Learn about some of the industries of the future.

Even if all you want is a job right now, instead of a career, do the exercises in the next section. Be sure to include at least the Seven Stories Exercise, Interests, Values, and Forty-Year Vision. They won't take a long time to do, and they will shorten the length of your search.

CASE STUDY: SCOTT
What Should I Be When I Grow Up?

Scott is thirty-eight, a lawyer with a varied background. He had worked for the DA's office, a stock exchange, and writing for a magazine. With his diverse past, he didn't know what to do next.

I know only one way to figure out what a person should be, and it's to use the methodology in this book. So that's what I did with Scott—a shortened version of the exercises.

Seven Stories Exercise

First, we did The Seven Stories Exercise. I said: "Tell me something you've done that you really enjoyed doing, know you did well, and felt a sense of accomplishment about. It doesn't matter what other people thought, how old you were, whether or not you earned money doing it. You may want to start with: 'There was the time when I . . .'"

Scott said: "There was the time when I argued my first case before a jury."

I asked him to tell me the details and what he enjoyed about it.

"I liked being independent, I was calling the shots. I had to plan the whole thing myself . . ."

I asked for another story.

Scott said: "I wrote an exposé for a magazine."

I asked Scott to tell me more. He said he enjoyed the same things: being independent, calling the shots, etc. Seemingly, the only time Scott enjoyed a bureaucratic environment was when he broke away from it.

Scott thought that he had a scattered background, and that everything was different. To my mind, those two stories were alike, so I had enough to go on. (If the stories had been in conflict, I would have asked him for as many as seven stories.)

Values Exercise

"Scott, tell me the things that are important to you." He replied, "Money is important, and independence."

Interests Exercise

"Scott, what are your interests?" Languages were very important to him; he had command of a few. The international area was central to his interests.

Scott's exercise results will serve as a template. He can make sure that his next job will allow him to be independent, to earn the money he wants, to enjoy the international area, and so on.

The Forty-Year Vision

Then I guided him through an abbreviated version of the Forty-Year Vision. I don't know how to help people unless I know where they are heading. If all I know is their past, their future will be more of the same. We spent only five minutes on this exercise.

I start with the present to get people grounded in the present. If I simply ask: What do you want to be? it doesn't work. They have nothing to base it on.

"Tell me what your life is like right now. What is your relationship with your family, however you define family? Where do you live? What is it physically like? What are your hobbies and interests? How is your health? What do you do for exercise? How would you describe the job you have right now? And tell me anything else you want to about your life today.

Next, I asked Scott to tell me about his life at age forty-three. Then I asked about his life at age fifty-three. In part, he said:

"I am living in the suburbs. I have a wife and four kids. The oldest is sixteen; the youngest is nine. (It is helpful to put down how old your kids are at each stage so you feel yourself getting older.) I have a small consulting firm, with perhaps four employees who do research and support me in what I am doing. I do a lot of business in Europe. Whatever I am doing is 'at the center of the world'—I feel I'm on top of the important things that are happening."

From my point-of-view, there were no conflicts in the results of his exercises. They all showed him in an independent situation.

Scott seemed to me to be the stereotypical entrepreneur. I do think he should have his own business, but not right now. Having people work for him sounded right because he seemed disorganized. As he himself suggested, one person could keep him in line and clean up after him. His business might have to do with international business, and also with high-tech. He wants to be at the center of what's happening.

Scott needs to *focus* on something that is a growth area and also satisfies his other needs. There are lots of areas that could fulfill him. The danger is that he may spend twenty years never selecting something to focus on. If a person like Scott is always exploring, it may be best to just arbitrarily pick something because there is no one correct answer. Other people, who are in a rut, may need to spend more time exploring.

Scott happens to have contacts in the telecommunications industry. If he can get into the telecommunications field, he should try to learn what he can, and develop a business plan while he is there.

Scott now has a vision. He can follow the vision, or not. If he continues to try out every field he comes across, he will be in constant turmoil. He will simply go from job to job, and wind up in his sixties with a lot of experiences but no career, and never reach his dream.

It's the same for you. Figure out the things you enjoy doing and also do well. Do your Forty-Year

Vision. These exercises will serve as your anchor as well as your guide. You won't get as irritated in your next job, because you'll know what you're getting out of it. You will keep up your research and your knowledge of the field. You will gain the skills you need to go forward.

Retraining Is For Everybody
—Even Executives

When people talk about retraining in America, they are usually talking about lower-level workers who don't have computer skills. Retraining is necessary at all levels. Do research to learn the terminology of the industry you want to enter so you can be an insider, not an outsider.

By definition, new industries must hire people from outside the industry. If a job-hunter studies the field, and develops a sincere interest in it, he or she has a good chance of being hired.

Careful research is a critical component, and will become a central part of every sophisticated person's job search.

If you just think off the top of your head about the areas you should be targeting, your ideas will probably be superficial—and outdated.

The Rate of Change

Change is happening at an increasingly faster rate. Industries disappear, and new ones spring up quickly. Instead of simply hunting for the next job, think about your long-range career.

You can pick the "right horse to ride" into your future rather than hanging on for dear life in a declining market. If you pick the right horse, you'll have a much easier ride.

Achieving Stability in a Changing World

How can you keep yourself stable in a constantly changing economy? If the world is being battered, and organizations are being battered, and even CEO's cannot keep their jobs, what are you going to do?

The benefit of doing the following exercises is that they give you confidence and a sense of stability in a changing world. You will learn to know yourself and become sure of exactly what you can take with you wherever you go.

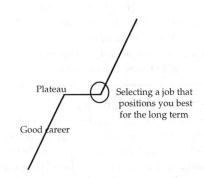

Plateau — Selecting a job that positions you best for the long term

Good career

The Result of Assessment Is Job Targets

If you go through an assessment with a career counselor or vocational testing center, and do not wind up with tentative job targets, the assessment has not helped you very much. You must go one more step, and decide what to *do* with this information.

The Result of Assessment Is Power

The more you know about yourself, the more power you have to envision a job that will suit you. The exercises give you power.

People find it hard to believe that I went through a period of about thirty years when I was painfully shy. In graduate school, I was afraid when they took roll because I obsessed with whether I should answer "here" or "present." When I had to give a presentation, the best I could do was read the key words from my index cards. (Today, my throat is actually hoarse from all the public speaking I do.) I will be forever grateful for the kindness of strangers who told me I did well when I knew I was awful.

The only thing that ultimately saved me was doing the Seven Stories Exercise. When I was little, I had led groups of kids in the neighborhood, and I did it well. It gave me strength to know that I was inherently a group leader regardless of how I was behaving now. (I was in my thirties at the time.) **The Seven Stories Exercise grounds you, and the Forty-Year Vision guides you**. When people said: "Would you like to lead groups?" I said to myself, "Well, I led groups when I was ten. Maybe I can do it again." The transition was painful, and took many years, but my Seven Stories Exercise kept me going. And my Forty-Year Vision let me know there was plenty of time in which to do it.

What Longevity Means to Your Career

by Lydia Bronte, author of *The Longevity Factor*

*"When I was fifty, I thought my life was over...
Little did I know that the best years of my life
were still ahead of me."*
Evelyn Nef, 80-year-old psychotherapist
who trained in her 60's

In every era there have been a few people who lived to be unusually old, but who kept working—and were still good at what they did. We all know that Pablo Picasso and Marc Chagall continued to paint until their deaths at 92 and 97 respectively; and that classical cellist Pablo Casals remained a master musician until his death at 96, despite arthritis.

Usually we rationalize the accomplishments of people like these by calling them exceptions— implying that perhaps their genius was also responsible for their lasting productivity.

But we won't be able to dismiss such late-life achievements as rarities much longer. One of the most astonishing changes that has ever taken place in human life occurred during the 20th century, although it went relatively unnoticed until a few years ago: people are living a lot longer.

The average life expectancy today in the United States is 29 years longer than it was in 1900. These years have been added to middle age, not old age.

Recently we have begun to focus upon one aspect of this change—aging—because of the growing numbers of older people in our society. The big news, however, is not aging. It is longevity. And as it turns out, although we tend to confuse them, they are two quite different things.

Galloping Longevity

How many times do you say to yourself, "If only I had more time"? Chances are that you'll have it: up to thirty years' worth of extra time, and maybe more. **Longevity has increased during the last 100 years more dramatically than at any other time in recorded human history.**

In less than one hundred years, the length of adult life has doubled. We've gone from an average life expectancy of 47 to one of 76, and still climbing.

Something that happens over the span of one century may seem ploddingly slow in terms of an individual's day-to-day experience. By ordinary statistical standards, however, this change has taken place with the speed of a moon rocket.

Consider: from A.D. 1 to A.D. 1900, human beings gained about **1 1/2 years** of average life expectancy per century. By contrast, from 1900 to 1994, we added **29 years**—almost three decades—to average life expectancy.

This is a stunning change. What is even more stunning is that it is continuing; in both 1993 and 1994, average life expectancy gained one year in the U.S.A. **We are nearing the point where we may add as much average life expectancy every year as former generations added in an entire century!**

The extra time starts to click in at around the age of 50. And to make it even better, even though you will live to an older chronological age, for reasons scientists don't yet understand, that extra time for most is **not** time spent in old age.

The Second Middle Age

As lifetimes have lengthened, the physical aging process has been slowed down or postponed. The three extra decades gained through longevity have really been added to the **middle** of our lives. It amounts to a "second middle age" between the end of the old-style "first middle age," 35 to 50, and the age at which we become physically old, which varies according to the individual.

The Long Careers Study

From 1987 to 1993, I conducted detailed life-history interviews with 150 people who continued to be active and to work during the second middle age and beyond the age of 65. Their ages ranged between 65 and 102, with the majority in

"If you can feel growth and development, you don't feel old. It's when you feel you can't learn anything or do anything new that it's the end of the road."
Shirley Brussell, Founder of Operation Able
at age 55 (now 74 and still its executive director)

their 70's and 80's. These long-lived Americans can be considered the pathfinder generation for those of us in our 30's, 40's, and 50's.

We have had an image of adult life based on the lives of our parents and grandparents, assuming a relatively short lifetime. Relying on this outdated notion is a little like trying to drive across the U.S.A. using a road map that was printed in 1930: the highway system isn't the same and even the landscape is different. Today we need a new "map" when thinking about adult life.

The Long Careers Study suggests that in order to make good use of this new life stage, all of us need to change radically the way we think about work.

There's no question that the length of your life has a connection to your career. The more you know now, the better you will be able to plan ahead for your worklife. If you've followed The Five O'Clock Club's suggestion and made a Forty-Year Vision, you may live to see every aspect of it come true—even if you're 50 right now.

New Horizons in Growth

As a result of this study, I am convinced that the developmental patterns of a long lifetime are different in many respects from those of a short lifetime. And the patterns of a long career are different from those of a short one.

Americans have a widespread belief that youth and the "first middle age" are the most creative periods of one's life and career.

For many years we have been told that the most vigorous and productive period is between 30 and 45. This idea was publicized around 1950 by Harvey Lehman, a scientist who calculated creative output in scientists, philosophers, artists, writers, and musicians—without, however, taking into account the possibility that the automatic ceiling of a short lifetime might have skewed the results.

The examples cited below are drawn from the careers of well-known people because of their recognition value. But the patterns hold true for average people too.

Multiple Career Peaks

The Long Careers Study participants showed astonishing differences in their periods of high achievement. Some of them did have early peaks of achievement, while others blossomed later or several times. For example: Dr. Linus Pauling made a discovery in his early 30's for which he subsequently won a Nobel Prize; Dr. Jonas Salk invented the polio vaccine in his late 30's to early 40's.

However, most of the people who had early peaks subsequently went on to have second and third peaks later in life. Pauling, for example, went on to make other scientific discoveries, and then in his late 40's took ten years to go around the world speaking on behalf of world peace, an effort for which he won a second Nobel Prize.

Next, Pauling began his path-breaking research on human nutrition and vitamins. Ultimately he played a key role both in educating the public about the value of vitamin and mineral supplements, and in persuading government agencies to acknowledge the importance of nutrition to health and to sponsor more research on the subject.

Early Sustained Peaks

The exceptions to the multiple-peak pattern were people who stayed in the same career and turned an early peak into a lifelong high plateau, like science fiction writer Isaac Asimov. Beginning with his first successes in his early 30's, Asimov built a career which helped shape the genre itself, developing science fiction into one of the most popular forms of contemporary literature. His productivity continued unabated until shortly before his death of heart failure at 72.

The Age-50 Gateway

There was another group of participants who began an extraordinary period of productivity at about the age of 50. **Almost half of the Study participants had a major career peak after age 50.**

This was a completely unexpected finding. In this pattern, the individual seems to be serving a kind of apprenticeship during the first thirty years of working life—accumulating experience in a way that leads to a massive upward shift in achievement around 50.

Culinary expert Julia Child is a striking example. Forced to abandon her first career because she married a fellow civil servant, Paul Child, she searched for several years to find another field. Finally she discovered French cooking by chance, when her husband was assigned to France as a USIA officer.

Starting at about the age of 35, Child trained as a chef, founded her own cooking school, and worked on a cookbook, *Mastering the Art of French Cooking*. In 1960, when Child was almost 50, the couple moved back to the U.S.A., where the book was published. A chance publicity appearance on television led to her famous TV series. The peak of Child's career has lasted into her early 80's, and shows no signs of slowing down.

A slightly different pattern was that of John W. Gardner, who was president of Carnegie Corporation of New York. When he was in his late 40's, he was stimulated by the discussions of an education commission of which he was a member. Gardner started writing down his ideas. He eventually developed them into a small book, *Excellence: Can We Be Excellent and Equal Too?* Decades later the book still forms the basis for many popular business books, by Tom Peters and others.

Gardner went on to make another leap by leaving his comfortable Carnegie position in his 50's to become Secretary of HEW in Washington. Next he founded two public-interest organizations. He made his most recent career change at 79 when he accepted a professorship at the Stanford University Business School. Now in his early 80's, he is teaching students more than half a century younger than he is.

The Age-65 Gateway

<u>About one-third of the participants had major career peaks after age 65</u>; 5 percent had their <u>highest</u> peak of achievement after age 65.

Most of these people found their real vocation later in life. They had no intention or expectation of becoming prominent; they were simply following their own developmental pattern.

Take, for example, Maggie Kuhn, who had a stable and respectable career as a church organizer. What changed her life was her mandatory retirement at the age of 65. Several other women she knew were also forced out of their careers.

Kuhn and her friends were furious at the discrimination they had experienced. They felt that if they had been men, they undoubtedly would have been offered several more years of full-time work, or consulting contracts. But as women they were simply ushered out unceremoniously.

They decided to form a discussion group to figure out what to do with the rest of their lives. By a series of fortuitous circumstances, their little association ended up becoming the Gray Panthers, a nationwide activist organization.

The Long Growth Curve

Finally, there was a group of people who had "long growth curves." This means that they moved upward at a relatively steady pace throughout the first 30 or 40 years of their worklives. The progression ended in a pinnacle of achievement after age 50 or after 65.

The late Norman Cousins, for example, served for decades as the well-known and greatly loved editor of *The Saturday Review of Literature*. In his 50's he had an almost-fatal illness which stimulated him to write a book, *Anatomy of an Illness* (1979). Its tremendous popularity led him to a major career change at the age of 64: he became an adjunct professor of medicine at the UCLA Medical School.

Until his death at the age of 76, Cousins helped design experiments on the relationship of the mind to physical health. His brilliant work with his medical colleagues at UCLA laid a solid scientific foundation for mind-body health research.

Cousins' career had a steady ascent, with new periods of growth triggered by his response to experience. This proactive stance towards one's own life was displayed by most of the Study participants.

Progressive Patterns

Finally, there were other types of progressions in the careers of some Study participants. Many participants progressed from being employees, to becoming managers or administrators, to becoming entrepreneurs. This pattern suggests increased learning about administrative functions, and the growing desire to shape the course of an organization, culminating in the creation of one's own organization.

Another progression was a change in geographical order of magnitude: moving from local concerns, to state or regional, then to national and finally to an international level of interest. Esther Peterson, former advisor on consumer affairs to Presidents Johnson and Carter, started her career as a local union organizer, moved up to state and regional positions, worked on a national level, and at 87 is now the Consumer's Union's international representative to the U.N.

What About the Future?

In a long-lived society, inevitably more people will make career changes during the course of a lifetime, simply because they have more time available in which they can master and grow beyond a given job or career. Of course, not everyone will have multiple careers; some will still stay in the same career all their lives.

A cause for real concern is the paradox that at a time when human beings are living longer than ever—and remaining youthful and in good health—American corporations and businesses are going in the opposite direction. They are downsizing and early-retiring people out of the workforce in their 50's or even their late 40's.

This is a dysfunctional trend in a society where there are so many people who may want to continue working even beyond the conventional retirement age, and who have much skill, experience, and knowledge to contribute.

It also raises the question of how effective a company can be if a large segment of our population is over 50, while the majority of the company's employees are under 50. A workforce that is predominantly younger may not understand or be able to serve effectively the needs of a mature consumer group.

It seems to me that there must be some correction in the negative attitude of corporations towards maturity if companies wish to remain viable. The research of University of Pennsylvania psychologist Frank Landy has shown that mature workers play roles that are different from those of younger workers, and that a workforce with a broad spectrum of ages functions better than a workforce with a narrow age spectrum.

Another related change is the disappearance of the longstanding "psychological contract" of loyalty between the worker and the corporation, which so long was a foundation for American worklife.

For the most part, **the people in the Long Careers Study who were able to continue doing work that they loved at older ages had made themselves independent**. Their identity as workers did not depend on a company but on their own skills and expertise. Frequently they had an individual practice—as a lawyer, artist, doctor, writer, etc.—or they formed their own business.

In a long-lived society, until the prevailing age prejudice has diminished or disappeared, every one of us should have as a goal to achieve the kind of professional, psychological, and financial independence that will enable us to continue working for as long (or short) a time as we choose.

Then perhaps we will be able to say—as Norman Cousins remarked when he was in his early 70's—"I find that now I'm using everything I've ever learned—all of it together at the same time, and more effectively than I could ever have done at any earlier time in my life."

Lydia Bronte, Ph.D., is the author of
*The Longevity Factor: The New Reality of Long Careers
and How They Are Leading to Richer Lives,*
Harper/Collins. This piece originally appeared in
The Five O'Clock News

PART TWO

DECIDING WHAT YOU WANT

START BY UNDERSTANDING YOURSELF

The
Five
O'Clock
Club®

How to Find
Your Place in the World

*You are a child of the universe no less than the trees
and the stars; you have a right to be here.
And whether or not it is clear to you, no doubt the
universe is unfolding as it should.*
Desiderata

Change As Opportunity

Don't expect to hold on to the way things
have worked for you in the past. Get on
with the new way the world is operating.
You cannot stop the changes, but you *can* choose
the way you will respond. You can see change as a
threat to resist—or an opportunity to move forward.

Change represents danger to you when you
choose to resist it. While your energy goes into
trying to keep your situation the same, you will
become more dissatisfied as you see others taking
advantage of changes.

You can use change to your advantage if you
decide to see it as a source of opportunity. Then, it
won't be so threatening. You will reduce your
chances of being run over. You will be running
your own life.

To look at change as a source of opportunity,
become more aware of the changes taking place
around you— the events that can affect you and
your job. Decide which are best for you and how to
take advantage of those that interest you. The pace
of change in today's economy can be overwhelming—unless you can assess changes more objectively. In doing so, you will have more control *over
the way you respond.*

An Internal Reference Point

How can you make the most of changes? How
can you decide which ones bode well for you and
which ones bode ill? You need a stable, internal
point of reference—a clear picture of what you need
to feel satisfied with your job and with your life.
You can measure a changing situation against your
list of the *elements* you require, to decide if a change
is in your favor or not. You can perhaps alter the

situation to suit you, or get out of there at the
earliest point.

To feel in control and actually to *be* in control of
your life, make choices based on your inner direction. With so many changes swirling around, the
only stabilizing point must be inside of you. Nothing outside can be your anchor. This book has
exercises to help you determine your inner direction.

A Career Counselor Cannot Decide For You

*We can help one another find out the meaning of life. . . .
But in the last analysis, each is responsible
for "finding himself."*
Thomas Merton
No Man Is an Island

Let's be practical about it: a career counselor
cannot possibly know all the options out there for
you. There are so many choices and the world is
changing so fast, how *could* one person know the
answer that is right for you? And when things
change again, as they will, will you expect a career
counselor to tell you what to do then?

What you do with your life is *your* decision. A
counselor cannot decide for you, but can only *help*
you decide. Blaming someone else for your lack of
progress can be a reflection of your attitude about
life. Do you basically feel you control what happens
to you? Or do you feel what happens is essentially
in the hands of others? When you blame others, you
give up your power. You are saying that someone
else is deciding what will happen to you. When you
do not blame others, you have more power: you are
taking control over your own life.

Those who take responsibility for their own
lives do better than those who expect others to solve
their problems.

Accepting responsibility means, generally, not
blaming others for your situation. You accept that
your choices have gotten you where you are. You
are in control. You can make new choices to head
your life where you want.

When written in Chinese, the word "crisis" is composed of two characters
—one represents danger and the other represents opportunity.
John F. Kennedy, Address, United Negro College Fund Convocation, April 12, 1959

Why Use a Career Coach?

Nobody owns a job, nobody owns a market,
nobody owns a product. Somebody out there
can always take it away from you.
Ronald E. Compton, president/chairman, Aetna, as
quoted in *The New York Times*, March 1, 1992

In this changing marketplace, increasingly we all have to be out there selling ourselves. This is causing people a great deal of understandable stress. Most of us would rather just do our jobs and trust that we will be treated fairly. Since we cannot depend on this, some people have made a career coach a normal part of their lives—as normal as having a regular tune-up on your car or an annual physical. They go to their coach not only when they are conducting a job search or when they have problems, but perhaps once or twice a year for a checkup.

An important component of the career assessment
process is to help clients accept themselves:
their strengths as well as what
does not come naturally to them.
Barry Lustig
Director of The Professional Development Institute,
Federation Employment and Guidance Services, N.Y.

Clients working with a career coach learn what works for them personally and what does not, come to better understand the kinds of environments in which they should be working (bosses, corporate cultures, pace, and so on), learn how to be more effective in their work relationships (bosses, peers, subordinates, clients), learn how to balance their lives more effectively, and also lay the groundwork for the next career move they may have to make. They talk about their long-term career goals and the steps they need to take to reach them—or perhaps simply to stay even. They make sure they are doing what they must to develop their careers as the economy changes, such as getting specific experience, taking courses, or joining organizations.

Over time, your coach gets to know you, just as your family doctor gets to know you, and can warn you against things that may cause you problems, or advise you about things you could be doing next.

Just as a family doctor would want to give you a complete physical if you are to become his patient, so, too, your coach would want to give you an assessment to find out as much as possible about you. I tell clients that if I don't know enough about them, it is as if they were someone on the street coming up to me to ask advice. I need to know something about them so I can be a real coach.

If you decide to use a private coach, use someone who charges by the hour. Do not pay a huge up-front fee. After you have worked with the counselor a number of times, assess your relationship with that person. There should be a good personality fit between you and your counselor. For example, some counselors are very intense, while others have a softer approach. If the relationship is not good, or if the meetings damage your sense of self-worth, go to someone else.

For your part, make sure you are willing to make the necessary commitment. If you go only for one hour to have the counselor handle an emergency you are facing, do not expect that counselor to come to know very much about you. If you decide to use a counselor, you are likely to learn more about the wonderful person you are, so you can figure out how you fit into this changing world. You will have increased self-esteem and increased effectiveness.

One of the most important aptitudes we all
have to offer is our personality.
Barry Lustig

Develop a Vision; Make a Commitment

The field cannot well be seen from within the field.
Ralph Waldo Emerson

Take a stand. Decide where you want to head, and go for it. You'll be happier because you'll have a goal and you'll work toward it. Work will no longer be "work," but an activity that brings pleasure, pride, and a sense of accomplishment, and that carries out your vision.

When you know yourself and make a commit-

You can never enslave somebody who knows who he is.
Alex Haley

ment, things become clearer. You act more decisively, have less stress, and cope better with the progress of your career and the changes around you. Negative things will not bother you as much. The direction will not be coming from someone else, but from inside you.

Without commitment, we are wanderers without roots in a rapidly changing world. We feel a lack of meaning in our lives.

Commitment means accepting that you are responsible for your own career direction. It means *choosing* what you want to do in this changing society without losing your inner bearings.

Looking for Where You Fit In

For I know the plans I have for you, declares the Lord,
plans to prosper you and not to harm you,
plans to give you a hope and a future.
Jeremiah 29:11

We each fit in. What you're looking for is *where* you fit in. As you learn more about what is inside you, as well as what is outside, you will progressively change your situation to suit yourself better, and so you will also fit better into the world.

To grow with the world, know what you want and what you want to offer. Knowing yourself, in the context of career development, means knowing how you prefer to operate, what you like to do, and what you can do well. Knowing what you want to offer means stepping outside yourself to see what the world values. Take what you want to offer and market it.

Don't be *too* specific about what you want. If you are open to new opportunities, surprising things can happen. A large number of jobs are created with a certain person in mind. A job created with you in mind would probably be more satisfying than one in which you would have to mold yourself to fit a rigid job description. You would enjoy your job more and do better because you would be doing what you want.

What are the chances of having a job created to suit you? If you don't know what would suit you, chances are slim. Having definite ideas increases

your chances of finding such a job, or even of changing your present job to better suit your goals. Opportunities come along all the time. You won't recognize them unless you know what you are looking for.

We change the world and the world changes us. As we grow, we are developing ourselves—in relation to the world. We are each trying to know what we want and how to get it, while we are also trying to understand and fit into a changing world. It is a lifelong process, but a happy one. It is a process of seeing change as an opportunity while accepting the limitations of the world.

CASE STUDY: HENRY
Aiming Too Low

Henry, an executive of about forty-five, had just been fired, and I was asked to be his counselor. Henry said he already had a clear idea of what he wanted to do next—something that was quite in demand—loan workouts (when loans go bad, he would try to salvage them). Henry could certainly get a job like that, and quickly, but I felt as though I didn't know him at all, so I asked if we could do a few exercises. If I understood him better, I would be in a better position to coach him.

In his Seven Stories (an exercise you will do in this book), Henry stated that he was proud that he had grown up in a tiny Midwestern town (there were only sixty people in his entire high school), had gotten into Harvard, and graduated very high in his class.

Where was that little boy now? What had caused him to settle for a loan workout position that would have been right for lots of *other* people? I told Henry that I thought he could do better than that. I asked him to aim to find a job that would make him so proud it would wind up on his *future* Seven Stories list.

Within two and a half months, Henry had landed a job that was better than anything he had ever dreamed possible. At an excellent salary, he became a very senior executive in a major corporation. Henry was so proud, he beamed. He's still

*It is the first of all problems for a man to find out what kind of work
he is to do in this universe.*
Thomas Carlyle, *Sartor Resartus*

there now and doing very well.

You Need Information
—Out in the World

You need information about yourself and about the changing world of work. Find an optimal fit by matching what you learn about yourself against what you learn about the world.

If you're like most people, at least part of your career plan was decided by someone else. If that decision was not best for you, something has to change. You must either change to fit the job, or you must change the job to fit you. If you have often changed yourself to suit the job you were in, you may not know what you want. Soon we will help you figure out what you would enjoy doing in a job.

You cannot find out about yourself in a vacuum. Go out and test your ideas about yourself against what others think of you. That's the only healthy way. With more knowledge about the world, and with a clearer sense of our place in it, options will appear that we never noticed before.

The Steps to Finding Your Place

The basic steps to finding your place are covered in greater detail in the other chapters in this section. Spend as much or as little time as you want on each. The process can go on forever. Do what you want now, and do more later.

Step 1: Determine what you want. Develop a long-term view of yourself—a guiding light that can see you through a number of jobs. In fact, you could develop a view that will see you through your entire life.

Step 2: Decide what you want to offer. Notice that I say what you *want* to offer—not what you *have to* offer. You may be tempted to offer what you have been offering all along. Although a pragmatic choice may see you through a job transition, it is more important to decide what you *want* to offer. If you offer things you do not want to do, you increase your chances of *doing* things you do not want to do.

I looked at a secretary's résumé. It mentioned

heavy phone work as one of her duties. When I asked her if she liked phone work, she responded, "I hate phone work." I advised her to remove it from her résumé, or someone would say, "That's just what we need: someone who can do heavy phone work."

Of course, every job has parts you don't like. In fact, you may decide to offer such an aspect as one of your strong skills until you develop yourself in the areas on which you want to focus. That's often a good approach.

I'll use my own life as an example. I started out in computers as a way of working my way through school. After learning so much about them, I have always used computers to my advantage even though working with them was not central on my list of life goals. Sometimes the fact that I knew computers gave me an edge over other job hunters. While I didn't want working with computers to be a central part of my job, the skill has been a handy one to offer.

In this step you will develop a menu of everything you have to offer, and then you can decide to offer what you want.

Step 3: A combination of the results of Steps 1 and 2. You'll do best in a job that relies on some of your strengths and experiences, but also provides you with some growth toward your goals. Bring something to the job. This book will help you select a job target that considers both.

CASE STUDY: AARON
Knowing Where He Wants to End Up

*Having gifts that differ according to the
grace given to us, let us use them.*
Romans 12:6

Aaron has been in corporate marketing for eight years. Through the Seven Stories exercise and his Forty-Year Vision (which you will see in the next chapter), he developed a long-term view of himself: the head of a five-hundred-person public-sector-related agency or organization, such as the World Wildlife Fund.

Now that he knows where he wants to end up,

he can work backward to figure out how he could get there. To head up such a large organization, he has two choices: he can start it from scratch, or he can take over an existing organization. Aaron decided that five years from now, he would prefer to become the head of an existing fifty-person organization and expand it to a five-hundred-person organization.

But how can he go from where he is now to becoming the head of a fifty-person organization? What he has to offer is his corporate marketing background. Therefore, his next logical step is to try to get a marketing job in a not-for-profit organization that is similar to the one he would eventually like to head up. That way, his next job will be one that positions him well for the moves after that, and increases his chance of getting where he wants to go.

The Benefits of Knowing What You Want

As I have stressed so far, you are responsible for your own career development. Decide what you want, rather than hoping someone will think about it for you. The next chapter will get you started.

How to Decide
What You Want

Let me listen to me and not to them.
Gertrude Stein

What seems different in yourself;
that's the rare thing you possess.
The one thing that gives each of us his worth,
and that's just what we try to suppress.
And we claim to love life.
André Gide

Looking Ahead
—A Career Instead of a Job

If you don't decide where you want to go, you may wind up drifting from one organization to another whenever you're dissatisfied, with pretty much the same job each time. Even if you decide that you want to continue doing what you're doing right now, that's a goal in itself and may be difficult to achieve.

The first step in career management is goal setting. There are a lot of processes involved in the goal-setting area. But the one considered most central is that by which a person examines his or her past accomplishments, looking at the strongest and most enjoyable skills.

This process is not only the one favored by counselors, it is also the one most often used by successful people. In reading the biographies of such people, I see again and again how they established their goals by identifying those things they enjoy doing and also do well. This process of identifying your "enjoyable accomplishments" is the most important one you can go through.

What Successful People Do

When Steven Jobs, the founder of Apple Computers, was fired by John Sculley, the man he had brought in to run the company, he felt as though he had lost everything. Apple had been his life. Now he had lost not only his job, but his company. People no longer felt the need to return his phone calls. He did what a lot of us would do. He got depressed. But then:

Confused about what to do next . . . he [Jobs] put himself through an exercise that management psychologists employ with clients unsure about their life goals. It was a little thing, really. It was just a list. A list of all the things that mattered most to Jobs during his ten years at Apple. "Three things jumped off that piece of paper, three things that were really important to me," says Jobs.

Michael Meyer, *The Alexander Complex*

The exercise Steven Jobs went through is essen-

Make no little plans; they have no magic to stir men's blood and probably
themselves will not be realized. Make big plans; aim high in hope and work.
Daniel Burnham

tially what you will do in the Seven Stories exercise. The threads that ran through his stories formed the impetus for his next great drive: the formation of NeXT computers. If the Seven Stories exercise is good enough for Steven Jobs, maybe it's good enough for you.

"Successful managers," says Charles Garfield, head of Performance Services, Inc., in Berkeley, California, "go with their preferences." They search for work that is important to them, and when they find it they pursue it with a passion.

Lester Korn, Chairman of Korn, Ferry, notes in his book *The Success Profile:* "Few executives know, or can know, exactly what they aspire to until they have been in the work force for a couple of years. It takes that long to learn enough about yourself to know what you can do well and what will make you happy. The trick is to merge the two into a goal, then set off in pursuit of it."

This book will help you decide what you want to do in your next job as well as in the long run. You will become more clear about the experiences you have enjoyed most and may like to repeat. You will also examine your interests and values, and look at past positions to analyze what satisfied you and what did not. In addition, you will look farther ahead (through your Forty-Year Vision) to see if some driving dream may influence what you will want to do in the short term. I did my Forty-Year Vision about fifteen years ago, and the vision I had of my future still drives me today.

Knowing where you would like to wind up broadens the kinds of jobs you would be interested in today.

Look at it this way:

A B   C

The line represents your life. Right now, you are at A. Your next job is B. If you look only at your past to decide what to do next, your next job is limited by what you have already done. For example, if you have been in finance and accounting for the past fifteen years, and you base your next move on your past, your next job is likely to be in finance or accounting.

If you know that at C you would like to wind up as vice president of finance and administration, new possibilities open up. Think of all the areas you would manage:

Finance	Operations
Administration	Personnel
Accounting	Computers

Experience in any one of these would advance your career in the right direction. For example, you may decide to get some computer experience.

Without the benefit of a Forty-Year Vision, a move to computers might look like the start of a career in computers, but *you* know it's just one more assignment that leads to your long-term goal. You'll keep your vision in mind and take jobs and assignments that will continually position you for the long run. For example, in the computer area, you may focus on personnel or administrative systems, two areas that fit your goal. Then your computer job will be more than a job. You will work hard for your employer, but you will also know why you are there—you are using your job as a stepping stone to something bigger and better.

Happy in Your Work

People are happy when they are working toward their goals. When they get diverted—or don't know what their goals are—they are unhappy. Many people are unhappy in their jobs because they don't know where they are going. People without goals are more irked by petty daily problems than are those with goals.

To control your life, know where you are going, and be ready for your next move—in case the ax falls on you. When you take that next job, continue to manage your career. Companies rarely build career paths for their employees any more. Make your own way. There are plenty of jobs for those who are willing to learn and to change with the times.

Deciding What You Want:
Selecting Your Job Targets

It may sound surprising when I say, on the basis of my own clinical experience as well as that of my psychological and psychiatric colleagues, "that the chief problem of people in the middle decade of the twentieth century is emptiness." By that I mean not only that many people do not know what they want; they often do not have any clear idea of what they feel.
Rollo May, *Man's Search for Himself*

In the Nazi death camps where Victor Frankl learned the principle of proactivity, he also learned the importance of purpose, of meaning in life. The essence of "logotherapy," the philosophy he later developed and taught, is that many so-called mental and emotional illnesses are really symptoms of an underlying sense of meaninglessness or emptiness. Logotherapy eliminates the emptiness by helping the individual to detect his unique meaning, his mission in life.
Once you have that sense of mission, you have the essence of your own proactivity. You have the vision and the values which direct your life.
You have the basic direction from which you set long- and short-term goals.
Stephen R. Covey,
The Seven Habits of Highly Effective People

To have a great purpose to work for, a purpose larger than ourselves, is one of the secrets of making life significant; for then the meaning and worth of the individual overflow his personal borders, and survive his death.
Will Durant

Studies have shown that up to 85 percent of all American workers are unhappy in their jobs. They feel that they would be happier elsewhere, but they don't know where. After going through an evaluation process (assessment), many decide that their present situation is not so bad after all, and that no change is required. Some may find that a small change is all that is needed. On the other hand, some may want to make a major career change.

The exercises in this book will help you assess your work life so that you can better understand the situations in which you perform your best and are happiest. And, since we will *all* have to change jobs—and probably even careers—more often in the future, we should get to know ourselves better.

Assessment is helpful even if you do not want to change jobs. You will learn more about the way you operate and how to improve the situation where you are currently working.

Getting Started

The following exercises help you identify the aspects of your jobs that have been satisfying and dissatisfying. You will know which parts need to be changed and which parts need to stay the same.

You may do certain exercises and skip others. But don't skip the Seven Stories Exercise, and try to do the Forty-Year Vision. If you have had problems with bosses, you need to discover what those problems were and analyze them. Or perhaps examining your values may be an issue at this time. Your insights about yourself from the Seven Stories Exercise will be the primary source for your accomplishment statements, help you interview better, and serve as a template for selecting the right job.

After you do the exercises, brainstorm a number of possible job targets. Then research each target to find out what the job possibilities are for someone like you.

This workbook will guide you through the entire process.

Consider Your History

If you have enjoyed certain jobs, attempt to understand exactly what about them you enjoyed. This will increase your chances of replicating the

. . . and then I decided that to turn your life around
you had to start from the inside.
Ethan Canin, *Emperor of the Air*

enjoyable aspects.

For example, an accounting manager will probably not be happy in just any accounting-management job. If what he really enjoyed was helping the business manager make the business profitable, and if this thread of helping reappears in his enjoyable experiences (Seven Stories Exercise), then he would be unhappy in a job where he was *not* helping.

If, however, his enjoyment repeatedly came from resolving messy situations, then he needs a job that has messes to be resolved and the promise of more messes to come.

Furthermore, if he wants to do again those things he enjoyed, he can state them in the summary on his résumé. For instance:

Accounting Manager
Serve as right-hand to Business Manager, consistently improving organization's profitability.

or

Accounting Manager
A troubleshooter and turn-around manager.

The Results of Assessment:
Job Targets—*then* a Résumé

A job target contains three elements:
- industry or organization size (small, medium or large organization);
- position or function; and
- geographic location.

If a change is required, a change in any one of these may be enough.

Geographic Location

Let's take Joseph, for example. Joseph had been in Trusts and Estates for twenty-five years, and had taken early retirement. He didn't know what he wanted to do next, but he knew that it had to be "completely different."

Joseph did all of the exercises in this section. I also gave him a personality test, and did "confidential phone calls" on his behalf—a process by which I called people who know him well and asked them about him. I assured them that I would compile the results and not tell him who said what.

Based on all of this information, we developed a number of targets for him to investigate. We also developed a résumé that positioned him for these new targets.

Joseph conducted a campaign to get interviews in each of his three target areas. However, once he clearly looked at these new fields, his old field began to look more appealing. (This happened to me years ago when I desperately wanted museum work—until I actually looked into it and found it wasn't for me.)

Joseph decided to stay in his old field—but on the West Coast rather than the East—because he is bothered by the climate in the East and because many of his old friends had moved West. This change in location would get him out of the old rut and give him a new lease on life. But it was a relatively minor change compared with what he originally had in mind.

Industry or Organization Size

Many unhappy people may be in essentially the right position but in the wrong industry. A minor adjustment may be all that is needed.

A person could be a lawyer, but it makes a great deal of difference whether that person is a lawyer in a corporation, in a stuffy law firm, or in a not-for-profit organization. A change in industry may end the dissatisfaction.

By the same token, moving from a large organization to a small one—or vice versa—could increase your satisfaction.

Position or Function

On the other hand, a new field may be what is called for. My own career is a case in point. I had a successful career in computers, advertising and the financial end of business, with a respectable amount of prestige and money. However, when I did the Seven Stories Exercise (to identify those things I enjoyed doing and also did well), I discovered that only one of my "stories" related to my work life. The message was clear: my true enjoyment was coming from those things I was doing on the outside, such as running The Five O'Clock Club and other entrepreneurial ventures. I had a choice to make:

- I could stay in the lucrative field I was in, and continue to do on the side those things that gave me the most satisfaction; or
- I could move my career in the direction of those things I found most satisfying.

Being risk-averse, I was reluctant to give up the twenty-plus years I had invested in a business career for a profession that might have proved to be financially or otherwise unsatisfying. I decided to hedge my bets. I took a job as the chief financial officer of a major outplacement firm, and *also* headed up one of their career counseling offices. That way, I could slide into the new career, or go back into the old one if I was unhappy.

Many major career changes are made this way. A person *somehow* gets some experience in the new field while holding on to the old one. In general, it is relatively easy to get experience in the new field if you really want it.

Looking Ahead—A Career Instead of a Job

Assessment will help you decide what you want to do in your next job as well as in the long run. You will become clearer about the kind of boss you work best with and about all the other things that are important to you in a job.

Through your Forty-Year Vision, you will have the opportunity to look ahead to see whether there is some hidden dream that may dramatically influence what you will want to do in both the short and long run. I did my own Forty-Year Vision about fifteen years ago, and the idea I had about my future still drives me today, even though that vision was actually rather vague at the time. Knowing where you would like to wind up in ten, twenty, thirty, or forty years can broaden your ideas about the kinds of jobs you would be interested in today.

The Forty-Year Vision is a powerful exercise. It will help you think long-term and put things into perspective.

The Seven Stories Exercise is equally powerful. Without it, many job hunters develop stilted descriptions of what they have accomplished. But the exercise frees you up to brag a little, and express things very differently. The results will add life to your résumé and your interviews, and also dra-matically increase your self-confidence.

No Easy Way

It would be nice if you could simply take a test that would tell you what you should be. Unfortunately there is no such sure-fire test. But fortunately, in today's rapidly changing world, we are allowed to be many things: we can be a doctor, a lawyer *and* an Indian chief. We have an abundance of choices.

A Clear Direction

People are happy when they are working toward their goals. When they get diverted from their goals, they are unhappy. Businesses are the same. When they get diverted from their goals (for instance, because of a major litigation or a threatened hostile takeover), they too are unhappy. Life has a way of sneaking up and distracting both individuals and businesses. Many people are unhappy in their jobs because they don't know where they are going.

A happy person going toward his or her goal.

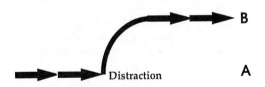

An unhappy person being deflected from his or her goal.

People without goals are more irked by petty problems on their jobs. Those with goals are less bothered because they have bigger plans. To control your life, you have to know where you are going, and be ready for your next move—in case the ax falls on you.

Even after you take that next job, continue to manage your career. Organizations rarely build career paths for their employees any more. Make your own way.

Your health is bound to be affected if, day after day, you say the opposite of what you feel, if you grovel before what you dislike and rejoice at what brings you nothing but misfortune.   Boris Pasternak, *Dr. Zhivago*

Wherever I went, I couldn't help noticing, the place fell apart. Not that I was ever a big enough wheel in the machine to precipitate its destruction on my own. But that they let me—and other drifters like me— in the door at all was an early warning signal. Alarm bells should have rung.   Michael Lewis, *Liar's Poker*

My illness helped me to see that what was missing in a society is what was missing in me: a little heart, a lot of brotherhood.

The 80's were about acquiring wealth, power, prestige. I acquired more . . . than most. But you can acquire all you want and still feel empty. . . . I don't know who will lead us through the 90's, but they must be made to speak to this spiritual vacuum at the heart of American society, this tumor of the soul.
Lee Atwater, formerly of the Republican National Committee, shortly before he died, *Life* magazine, February, 1991

I've never been poor, only broke.
Being poor is a frame of mind.
Being broke is only a temporary situation.
Mike Todd

Natural talent, intelligence, a wonderful education— none of these guarantees success. Something else is needed: the sensitivity to understand what other people want and the willingness to give it to them. Worldly success depends on pleasing others. No one is going to win fame, recognition, or advancement just because he or she thinks it's deserved. Someone else has to think so too.
John Luther

Aim so High You'll Never Be Bored

The greatest waste of our natural resources is the number of people who never achieve their potential. Get out of that slow lane. Shift into that fast lane. If you think you can't, you won't. If you think you can, there's a good chance you will. Even making the effort will make you feel like a new person. Reputations are made by searching for things that can't be done and doing them. Aim low: boring. Aim high: soaring.

(c) United Technologies Corporation, June 1981.

The
Five
O'Clock
Club®

Exercises to Analyze Your Past and Present: The Seven Stories Exercise

In this exercise, you will examine your accomplishments, looking at your strongest and most enjoyable skills. The core of most counseling exercises is some version of the Seven Stories exercise. A counselor may give you lots of tests and exercises, but this one requires *work* on your part and will yield the most important results. An interest or personality test is not enough. There is no easy way. Remember, busy executives take the time to complete this exercise—if it's good enough for them, it's good enough for you.

Do not skip the Seven Stories exercise. It will provide you with information for your career direction, your résumé, and your interviews. After you do the exercise, brainstorm about a number of possible job targets. Then research each target to find out what the job possibilities are for someone like you.

If you're like most people, you have never taken the time to sort out the things you're good at and also are motivated to accomplish. As a result, you probably don't use these talents as completely or as effectively as you could. Too often, we do things to please someone else or to survive in a job. Then we get stuck in a rut—that is, we're *always* trying to please someone else or are *always* trying to survive in a job. We lose sight of what could satisfy us, and work becomes drudgery rather than fun. When we become so enmeshed in survival or in trying to please others, it may be difficult to figure out what we would rather be doing.

When you uncover your motivated skills, you'll be better able to identify jobs that allow you to use them, and recognize other jobs that don't quite fit the bill. "Motivated skills" are patterns that run through our lives. Since they are skills from which we get satisfaction, we'll find ways to do them even if we don't get to do them at work. We still might not know what these skills are—for us, they're just something we do, and we take them for granted.

Tracking down these patterns takes some thought. The payoff is that our motivated skills do not change. They run throughout our lives and indicate what will keep us motivated for the rest of our lives.

*One's prime is elusive.... You must be on the alert to recognize your prime
at whatever time of life it may occur.*
Muriel Spark, *The Prime of Miss Jean Brodie*

The Seven Stories Approach: Background

This technique for identifying what people do well and enjoy doing has its roots in the work of Bernard Haldane, who, in his job with the U.S. government forty-five years ago, helped to determine assignments for executives entering the armed forces. The Seven Stories (or enjoyable accomplishments) approach, now quite common, was taught to me by George Hafner, who used to work for Haldane.

The exercise is this: make a list of all the enjoyable accomplishments of your life, those things you enjoyed doing *and also* did well. List at least twenty-five enjoyable accomplishments from all parts of your life: work, from your early career up to the present, volunteering, hobbies; your school years. It doesn't matter how old you were or what other people thought about these accomplishments, and it doesn't matter whether you got paid for doing them.

Examine those episodes that gave you a sense of accomplishment. Episodes from your childhood are important, too, because they took place when you were less influenced by trying to please others.

You are asked to name twenty-five accomplishments so you will not be too judgmental—just list anything that occurs to you. Expect this exercise to take you four or five days. Most people carry around a piece of paper so they can jot down things as they occur to them. When you have twenty-five, select the seven that are most important to you by however you define important. Then rank them: list the most important first, and so on.

Starting with your first story, write a paragraph about each accomplishment. Then find out what your accomplishments have in common. If you are having trouble doing the exercises, ask a friend to help you talk them through. Friends tend to be more objective and will probably point out strengths you never realized.

You will probably be surprised. For example, you may be especially good interacting with people, but it's something you've always done and therefore take for granted. This may be a thread that runs through your life and may be one of your motivated skills. It *may* be that you'll be unhappy in a job that doesn't allow you to deal with people.

When I did the Seven Stories exercise, one of the first stories I listed was from when I was ten years old, when I wrote a play to be put on by the kids in the neighborhood. I rehearsed everyone, sold tickets to the adults for two cents apiece, and served cookies and milk with the proceeds. You might say that my direction as a "general manager"—running the whole show, thinking things up, getting everybody working together—was set in the fourth grade. I saw these traits over and over again in each of my stories.

After I saw those threads running through my life, it became easy for me to see what elements a job must have to satisfy me. When I interview for a job, I can find out in short order whether it addresses my motivated skills. If it doesn't, I won't be as happy as I could be, even though I *may decide to take the job as an interim step toward a long-term goal.* The fact is, people won't do as well in the long run in jobs that don't satisfy their motivated skills.

Sometimes I don't pay attention to my own motivated skills, and I wind up doing things I regret. For example, in high school I scored the highest in the state in math. I was as surprised as everyone else, but I felt I finally had some direction in my life. I felt I had to use it to do something constructive. When I went to college, I majored in math. I almost flunked because I was bored with it. The fact is that I didn't enjoy math, I was simply good at it.

There are lots of things we're good at, but they may not be the same things we really enjoy. The trick is to find those things we are good at, enjoy doing, and feel a sense of accomplishment from doing.

To sum up: Discovering your motivated skills is the first step in career planning. I was a general manager when I was ten, but I didn't realize it. I'm a general manager now, and I love it. In between, I've done some things that have helped me toward my long-range goals, and other things that have not helped at all.

. . . be patient toward all that is unsolved in your heart and try to love the questions
themselves like locked rooms and like books that are written in a foreign tongue.
Rainer Maria Rilke, *Letters to a Young Poet*

Revealing *What to Look For* in a Job

It is important to realize that the Seven Stories exercise will *not* tell you exactly which job you should have, but the *elements* to look for in a job that you will find satisfying. You'll have a range of jobs to consider, and you'll know the elements the jobs must have to keep you happy. Once you've selected a few job categories that might satisfy you, talk to people in those fields to find out if a particular job is really what you want, and the job possibilities for someone with your experience. That's one way to test if your aspirations are realistic.

After you have narrowed your choices down to a few fields with some job possibilities that will satisfy your motivated skills, the next step is to figure out how to get there. That topic will be covered in our book *Getting Interviews.*

A Demonstration of the Seven Stories Exercise

To get clients started, I sometimes walk them through two or three of their achievement stories, and tell them the patterns I see. They can then go off and think of the seven or eight accomplishments they enjoyed the most and also performed well. This final list is ranked and analyzed in depth to get a more accurate picture of the person's motivated skills. I spend the most time analyzing those accomplishments a client sees as most important. Some accomplishments are more obvious than others. But all stories can be analyzed.

Here is Suzanne, as an example: "When I was nine years old, I was living with my three sisters. There was a fire in our house and our cat had hidden under the bed. We were all outside, but I decided to run back in and save the cat. And I did it."

No matter what the story is, I probe a little by asking these two questions: What gave you the sense of accomplishment? and What about that made you proud? These questions give me a quick fix on the person.

The full exercise is a little more involved than this. Suzanne said at first: "I was proud because I did what I thought was right." I probed a little, and she added: "I had a sense of accomplishment because I was able to make an instant decision

under pressure. I was proud because I overcame my fear."

I asked Suzanne for a second story; I wanted to see what patterns might emerge when we put the two together:

"Ten years ago, I was laid off from a large company where I had worked for nine years. I soon got a job as a secretary in a Wall Street company. I loved the excitement and loved that job. Six weeks later, a position opened up on the trading floor, but I didn't get it at first. I eventually was one of three finalists, and they tried to discourage me from taking the job. I wanted to be given a chance. So I sold myself because I was determined to get that job. I went back for three interviews, said all the right things, and eventually got it."

What was the accomplishment? What made her proud?

- "I fought to win."
- "I was able to sell myself. I was able to overcome their objections."
- "I was interviewed by three people at once. I amazed myself by saying, 'I know I can do this job.'"
- "I determined who the real decision-maker was, and said things that would make him want to hire me."
- "I loved that job—loved the energy, the upness, the fun."

Here it was, ten years later, and that job still stood out as a highlight in her life. Since then she'd been miserable and bored, and that's why she came to me.

Normally after a client tells two stories, we can quickly name the patterns we see in both stories. What were Suzanne's patterns?

Suzanne showed that she was good at making decisions in tense situations—both when saving the cat and when interviewing for that job. She showed a good intuitive sense (such as when she determined who the decision-maker was and how to win him over). She's decisive and likes fast-paced, energetic situations. She likes it when she overcomes her own fears as well as the objections of others.

We needed more than two stories to see if these patterns ran throughout Suzanne's life and to see what other patterns might emerge. After the full exercise, Suzanne felt for sure that she wanted excitement in her jobs, a sense of urgency—that she wanted to be in a position where she had a chance to be decisive and operate intuitively. Those are the conditions she enjoys and under which she operates the best. Armed with this information, Suzanne can confidently say in an interview that she thrives on excitement, high pressure, and quick decision-making. And, she'll probably make more money than she would in "safe" jobs. She can move her life in a different direction—whenever she is ready.

Pay attention to those stories that were most important to you. The elements in these stories may be worth repeating. If none of your enjoyable accomplishments were work-related, it may take great courage to eventually move into a field where you will be happier. Or you may decide to continue to have your enjoyment outside of work.

People have to be ready to change. Fifteen years ago, when I first examined my own motivated skills, I saw possibilities I was not ready to handle. Although I suffered from extreme shyness, my stories—especially those that occurred when I was young—gave me hope. As I emerged from my shyness, I was eventually able to act on what my stories said was true about me.

People sometimes take immediate steps after learning what their motivated skills are. Or sometimes this new knowledge can work inside them until they are ready to take action—maybe ten years later. All the while internal changes can be happening, and people can eventually blossom.

Motivated Skills—
Your Anchor in a Changing World

Your motivated skills are your anchor in a world of uncertainty. The world will change, but your motivated skills remain constant.

Write them down. Save the list. Over the years, refer to them to make sure you are still on target—doing things that you do well and are motivated to do. As you refer to them, they will influence your life. Five years from now, an opportunity may present itself. In reviewing your list, you will have every confidence that this opportunity is right for you. After all, you have been doing these things since you were a child, you know that you enjoy them, and you do them well!

Knowing our patterns gives us a sense of stability and helps us understand what we have done so far. It also gives us the freedom to try new things regardless of risk or of what others may say, because we can be absolutely sure that this is the way we are. Knowing your patterns gives you both security and flexibility—and you need both to cope in this changing world.

Now think about your own stories. Write down everything that occurs to you.

The Ugly Duckling was so happy and in some way he was glad that he had experienced so much hardship and misery; for now he could fully appreciate his tremendous luck and the great beauty that greeted him.
. . . And he rustled his feathers, held his long neck high, and with deep emotion he said: "I never dreamt of so much happiness, when I was the Ugly Duckling!"
Hans Christian Anderson, *The Ugly Duckling*

The Seven Stories
Exercise™ Worksheet

This exercise is an opportunity to examine the most satisfying experiences of your life and to discover those skills you will want to use as you go forward. You will be looking at the times when you feel you did something particularly well that you also enjoyed doing. It doesn't matter what other people thought, whether or not you were paid, or when in your life the experiences took place. **All that matters is that you felt happy about doing whatever it was, thought you did it well, and experienced a sense of accomplishment.** You can even go back to childhood. When I did my own Seven Stories Exercise, I remembered the time when I was ten years old and led a group of kids in the neighborhood, enjoyed it, and did it well.

This exercise usually takes a few days to complete. Many people review different life phases in order to capture the full scope of these experiences. Most carry around a piece of paper to jot down ideas as they think of them.

SECTION I:

Briefly outline below *all* the work/personal/life experiences which meet the above definition. Come up with at least twenty. We ask for twenty stories so you won't be too selective. Just write down anything that occurs to you, no matter how trivial it may seem. Try to **think of concrete examples, situations and tasks, not generalized skills or abilities**. It may be helpful if you say to yourself, **"There was the time when I . . ."**

RIGHT	WRONG
• Got extensive media coverage for a new product launch.	• Writing press releases.
• Delivered speech to get German business.	• Delivering speeches.
• Coordinated blood drive for division.	• Coordinating.
• Came in third in the Nassau Bike Race.	• Cycling.
• Made a basket in second grade.	• Working on projects alone.

1. _____

2. _____

3. _____

4. _____

5. _____

6. _____

7. _____

8. _____

9. _____

10. _____

11. _____

12. _____

13. _____

14. _____

15. _____

16. _____

17. _____

18. _____

19. _____

20. _____

21. _____

22. _____

23. _____

24. _____

25. _____

SECTION II:

Choose the seven experiences from the above which you enjoyed the most and felt the most sense of accomplishment about. (Be sure to include non-job-related experiences also.) Then **rank them**. Then, for each accomplishment, describe what *you* did. Be specific, listing each step in detail. Notice the role you played and your relationship with others, the subject matter, the skills you used, and so on. Use a separate sheet of paper for each.

If your highest-ranking accomplishments also happen to be work-related, you may want them to appear prominently on your résumé. After all, those were the things that you enjoyed and did well. And those are probably the experiences you will want to repeat again in your new job.

Here's how you might begin:

Experience #1: Planned product launch that resulted in 450 letters of intent from 1500 participants.

    a. Worked with president and product managers to discuss product potential and details.

    b. Developed promotional plan.

    c. Conducted five-week direct-mail campaign prior to the conference to create an aura of excitement about the product.

    d. Trained all product demonstrators to make sure they each presented our product in the same way.

    e. Had a great product booth built; rented the best suite to entertain prospects; conducted campaign at the conference by having teasers put under everyone's door every day of the conference. Most people wanted to come to our booth.

—and so on—

Analyzing Your Seven Stories

Now it is time to analyze your stories. You are trying to look for the threads that run through them so that you will know the things you do well that also give you satisfaction. Some of the questions below sound similar. That's okay. They are a catalyst to make you think more deeply about the experience. The questions don't have any hidden psychological significance.

If your accomplishments happen to be mostly work-related, this exercise will form the basis for your "positioning" or summary statement in your résumé, and also for your two-minute pitch.

If these accomplishments are mostly not work-related, they will still give you some idea of how you may want to slant your résumé, and they may give you an idea of how you will want your career to go in the long run.

For now, simply go through each story without trying to force it to come out any particular way. Just think hard about yourself. And be as honest as you can. When you have completed this analysis, the words in the next exercise may help you think of additional things. **Do this page first.**

Story #1. _____

What was the *main accomplishment* for you? _____

What about it did you *enjoy most*? _____

What did you *do best*? _____

What was your *key motivator*? _____

What *led up to your getting involved*? (e.g., assigned to do it, thought it up myself, etc.) _____

What was your *relationship with others*? (e.g., leader, worked alone, inspired others, team member, etc.) _

Describe the *environment* in which you performed. _____

What was the *subject matter*? (e.g., music, mechanics, trees, budgets, etc.) _____

Story #2. _____
Main accomplishment? _____
Enjoyed most? _____
Did best? _____
Key motivator? _____
What led up to it? _____
Your role? _____
The environment? _____
The subject matter? _____

We are here to be excited from youth to old age, to have an insatiable curiosity about the world . . . . We are also here to help others by practicing a friendly attitude. And every person is born for a purpose. Everyone has a God-given potential, in essence, built into them. And if we are to live life to its fullest, we must realize that potential.

Norman Vincent Peale

Story #3. _____
Main accomplishment? _____
Enjoyed most? _____
Did best? _____
Key motivator? _____
What led up to it? _____
Your role? _____
The environment? _____
The subject matter? _____

Story #4. _____
Main accomplishment? _____
Enjoyed most? _____
Did best? _____
Key motivator? _____
What led up to it? _____
Your role? _____
The environment? _____
The subject matter? _____

Story #5. _____
Main accomplishment? _____
Enjoyed most? _____
Did best? _____
Key motivator? _____
What led up to it? _____
Your role? _____
The environment? _____
The subject matter? _____

Story #6. _____
Main accomplishment? _____
Enjoyed most? _____
Did best? _____
Key motivator? _____
What led up to it? _____
Your role? _____
The environment? _____
The subject matter? _____

Story #7. _____
Main accomplishment? _____
Enjoyed most? _____
Did best? _____
Key motivator? _____
What led up to it? _____
Your role? _____
The environment? _____
The subject matter? _____

The
Five
O'Clock
Club®

Skills From Your Seven Stories

The numbers across the top represent each of your seven stories. Start with story #1 and check off all of your specialized skills that appear in that story. When you've checked off the skills for all seven stories, total them.

Story #	1	2	3	4	5	6	7	Total
Administration				✓			✓	1
Advising/Consulting		✓				✓		2
Analytical Skills		✓		✓				2
Artistic Ability								
Budgetary Skills	✓			✓				2
Client Relations	✓		✓	✓		✓		4
Communication	✓		✓	✓		✓	✓	5
Community Relations								
Contract Negotiation	✓							1
Control				✓				1
Coordination	✓	✓	✓	✓		✓		5
Creativity	✓	✓			✓			3
Decisiveness	✓			✓				2
Design		✓						1
Development								
Financial Skills	✓			✓				2
Foresight	✓							1
Frugality								
Fund Raising								
Human Relations				✓		✓		2
Information Mgmt.	✓			✓				2
Imagination		✓			✓			2
Individualism						✓		
Initiative	✓		✓	✓		✓	✓	5
Inventiveness								
Leadership	✓		✓	✓				3
Liaison			✓	✓		✓		3
Logic								
Management				✓				1
Marketing								
Mathematical Skills								
Mechanical Skills								
Motivational Skills		✓			✓		✓	
Negotiation	✓		✓	✓	✓			4
Observation								
Organization			✓	✓	✓	✓		4
Other Talents: Logistics				✓				

Story #	1	2	3	4	5	6	7	Total
Operations Mgmt.			✓	✓		✓		3
Org. Design/Devel.	✓					✓		2
Ownership								
Perceptiveness						✓		1
Perseverance				✓				1
Persuasiveness	✓					✓		2
Planning	✓			✓		✓	✓	4
Policy-Making								
Practicality						✓		1
Presentation Skills			✓			✓	✓	3
Problem-Solving			✓	✓		✓	✓	4
Procedures Design				✓				1
Production								
Program Concept						✓		1
Program Design						✓		1
Project Management		✓	✓	✓				3
Promotion								
Public Relations						✓		1
Public Speaking		✓						1
Quality Assessment								
Research	✓	✓	✓	✓	✓	✓		6
Resourcefulness	✓	✓		✓		✓	✓	5
Sales Ability								
Service	✓							1
Showmanship								
Speaking Skills						✓		1
Staff Dev./Mgmt.				✓		✓		2
Strategic Planning	✓	✓	✓			✓	✓	5
Stress Tolerance				✓				1
Systems	✓			✓				2
Teamwork		✓	✓			✓		4
Tenacity		✓		✓				4
Training			✓	✓		✓	✓	4
Travel	✓		✓				✓	4
Troubleshooting							✓	1
Writing	✓				✓	✓	✓	4
Other Talents: Hands on						✓		1

Note: Job hunters enjoy exercises like this because they are simple. But your experiences are more complex than the words on this page. These words alone do not reflect the richness of what you have to offer. So combine these words with the more in-depth answers you came up with on the preceding page, and continue to analyze your stories throughout your life. You will find deeper and deeper answers about yourself.

Top Six or Seven Specialized Skills, according to which had the most check marks:
1. Research (6)
2. Communication (5)
3. Coordination (5)
4. Initiative (5)
5. Resourcefulness (5)
6. Strategic Planning (5)
7. _____

Your Current
Work-Related Values

What is important to you? Your values change as you grow and change, so they need to be reassessed continually. At various stages in your career, you may value money, or leisure time, or independence on the job, or working for something you believe in. See what is important to you *now*. This will help you not to be upset if, for instance, a job provides you with the freedom you wanted, but not the kind of money your friends are making.

Sometimes we are not aware of our own values. It may be that, at this stage of our life, time with our family is most important to us. For some people, money or power is most important, but they may be reluctant to admit it—even to themselves.

Values are the driving force behind what we do. It is important to truthfully understand what we value, and we will increase our chances of getting what we want.

Look at the list of values below . Think of each in terms of your overall career objectives. Rate the degree of importance that you would assign to each for yourself, using this scale:

1—Not at all important in my choice of job
2—Not very but somewhat important

3—Reasonably important
4—Very important

Add other values that don't appear on the list or to substitute wording you are more comfortable with.

3	the chance to advance	4	artistic or other creativity
1	work on frontiers of knowledge	4	learning
3	having authority (responsibility)	4	location of the work place
2	helping society	2	tranquility
3	helping others	3	money earned
4	meeting challenges	4	change and variety
3	working for something I believe in	4	having time for personal life
2	public contact	2	fast pace
4	enjoyable colleagues	2	power
2	competition	2	adventure/risk taking
3	ease (freedom from worry)	2	prestige
2	influencing people	2	moral fulfillment
4	enjoyable work tasks	3	recognition from superiors, society, peers
2	working alone	3	security (stability)
3	being an expert	2	physical work environment
4	personal growth and development	4	chance to make an impact
4	independence	1	clear expectations and procedures

Of those you marked "4," circle the 5 **most** important to you today:

- If forced to compromise on any of these, which one would you give up? _location_

- Which one would you be most reluctant to give up? _meeting challenges_

Describe in ten or twenty words what you want most in your life and/or career.
Renewable challenges with resources + flexibility them, balanced with flexibility to meet the needs of my family. A creative environment, working with capable people with whom I can team up + make an impact. respect

Other Exercises:
Interests, Satisfiers, and Bosses

CASE STUDY: LAURA
Using Her Special Interests

For many people, interests should stay as interests—things they do on the side. For others, their interests may be a clue to the kinds of jobs they should do next or in the long run. Laura had food as her special interest. She had spent her life as a marketing manager in cosmetics, but she assured me that food was *very* important to her.

We redid her résumé to downplay the cosmetics background. Next, Laura visited a well-known specialty food store. She spoke to the store manager, a junior person, asked about the way the company was organized, and found that there were three partners, one of whom was the president. Laura said to the store manager, "Please give my résumé to the president, and I will call him in a few days." We prepared for her meeting with the president, in which she would find out the company's long-term plans, and so on. At the meeting, he said he wanted to increase revenues from $4 million to $40 million. Laura and I met again to decide how she could help the business grow through her marketing efforts, and to decide what kind of compensation she would want, including equity in the company. She met with the president again, and got the job!

It was the Interests exercise that prompted her to get into that field. Remember, all you need to do is make a list of your interests. Laura simply wrote "food." Other people list twenty things. Here is the exercise:

Interests Exercise

List all the things you really like to do. List anything that makes you feel good and gives you satisfaction. List those areas where you have developed a relatively in-depth knowledge or expertise. For ideas, think back over your day, your week, the seasons of the year, places, people, work, courses, roles, leisure time, family, etc. These areas need not be work-related. Think of how you spend your discretionary time.

If you cannot think of what your interests may be, think about the books you read, the magazines you subscribe to, the section of the newspaper you turn to first. Think about the knowledge you've built up simply because you're interested in a particular subject. Think about the volunteer work you do—what are the recurring assignments you tend to get and enjoy? Think about your hobbies—are there one or two you have become so involved in that you have built up a lot of expertise/information in those areas? What are the things you find yourself doing—and enjoying—all the time, things you don't *have* to do.

Your interests may be a clue to what you would like in a job. Rob was a partner in a law firm, but loved everything about wine. He left the law firm to become general counsel in a wine company. Most people's interests should stay as interests, but you never know until you think about it.

Satisfiers and Dissatisfiers Exercise

Simply list every job you have ever had. List what was satisfying and dissatisfying about each job. Some people are surprised to find that they were sometimes most satisfied by the vacation, pay, title, and other perks, but were not satisfied with the job itself.

Bosses Exercise

Simply examine those bosses you have had a good relationship with and those you have not, and determine what you need in your future relationship with bosses. If you have had a lot of problems with bosses, discuss this with your counselor.

For many people, interests should stay as interests—things they do on the side. For others, their interests may be a clue to the kinds of jobs they should do next or in the long run. Only you can decide whether your interests should become part of your work life.

List all the things you really like to do—anything that makes you feel good and gives you satisfaction. List those areas in which you have developed a relatively in-depth knowledge or expertise. For ideas, think of your day, your week, the seasons of the year, places, people, work, courses, roles, leisure time, friends, family, etc. Think of how you spend your discretionary time.

- Think about the books you read, the magazines you subscribe to, the section of the newspaper you turn to.
- Think about knowledge you've built up simply because you're interested in it.
- Think about the volunteer work you do--what are the recurring assignments you tend to get and enjoy?
- Think about your hobbies—are there one or two you have become so involved in that you have built up a lot of expertise/information in those areas?
- What are the things you find yourself doing all the time and enjoying, even though you don't have to do them?

reading
writing
scrapbooking
cooking

The
Five
O'Clock
Club®

Satisfiers and Dissatisfiers in Past Jobs

For each job you have held in the past, describe as fully as possible those factors which made that job especially exciting or rewarding (satisfiers) and those which made that job especially boring or frustrating (dissatisfiers). **Be as specific as possible** (See the example below, which shows that sometimes the satisfiers can be the perks, while the dissatisfiers can be the job itself).

JOB	SATISFIERS	DISSATISFIERS
VP of Mfg., ABC Co.	1. Status—large office, staff of 23, Exec. Dining Room 2. Fringes—4 weeks' vacation, travel allowance time for outside activities.	1. Manager —cold and aloof. Too little structure and feedback; no organizational credibility. 2. Limited promotional opportunities —none laterally, only straight line.
JOB	SATISFIERS	DISSATISFIERS

The
Five
O'Clock
Club®

Your Relationship with Bosses

1. Make a list of all the "bosses" you have ever had in work situations. Use a very broad definition. They don't have to have been "bosses" in the strictest sense of the word. Include bosses from part-time jobs, summer jobs, and even professors with whom you worked closely in your student days.

_____   _____
_____   _____
_____   _____
_____   _____
_____   _____
_____   _____

2. Divide the names from above into three lists: those people with whom you had no problems, those with whom you had some problems, and those with whom you had severe problems.

NO PROBLEMS	SOME PROBLEMS	SEVERE PROBLEMS

3. Look for factors that might help explain why you had some problems or severe problems with some bosses and not with others (or why you have never had problems). For example, consider:

- the type of people involved: age, sex, personality, etc.
- the structure of your relationship with the people: how much and what type of power they had over you.
- the broader contexts: the kind of work involved, the type of organizations involved, etc.

   Think about it. Do you see any patterns . . .

   . . . regarding the type of people?

_____
_____
_____

   . . . regarding the structure of the relationship?

_____
_____
_____
_____

   . . . regarding the contexts?

_____
_____
_____

This exercise is based on lectures given by John P. Kotter in his classes in power dynamics at the Harvard Business School.

Looking Into Your Future

A study was made of alumni ten years out of Harvard to find out how many were achieving their goals.
An astounding 83 percent had no goals at all. Fourteen percent had specific goals, but they were not written down.
Their average earnings were three times what those in the
83 percent group were earning.
However, the 3 percent who had written goals were earning ten times that of the 83 percent group.

Forrest H. Patton, *Force of Persuasion*,
as quoted by Ronald W. Miller,
Planning for Success

Your motivated skills tell you the *elements* you need to make you happy, your Values exercise tells you the values that are important to you right now, and the Interests exercise may give you a clue to other fields or industries to explore. But none of them give you a feel for the *scope* of what may lie ahead.

Dreams and goals can be great driving forces in our lives. We feel satisfied when we are working toward them—even if we never reach them. People who have dreams or goals do better than people who don't.

Setting goals will make a difference in your life, and this makes sense. Every day we make dozens of choices. People with dreams make choices that advance them in the right direction. People without dreams also make choices—but their choices are strictly present-oriented with little thought of the future. When you are aware of your current situation, and you also know where you want to go, a natural tension leads you forward faster.

When you find a believable dream that excites you, don't forget it. In the heat of our day-to-day living, our dreams slip out of our minds. In some respects this is good, because it means we're absorbed by the daily events of our lives. If we focused *only on the future*, we'd all be very upset and worried people. We each should be appropriately challenged and involved in what we're doing in the present, with a reminder every once in a while of where we want to go. Happy people keep an eye on the future as well as the present.

"Freeing-Up" Exercises

This next group of exercises may help you imagine broader dreams for yourself—dreams to inspire you and move you forward, add meaning to your everyday life, and give it some long-term purpose.

It's okay if you never reach your dreams. In fact, it can be better to have some dreams that you will probably never reach, so long as you enjoy the *process* of trying to reach them. For

In my practice as a psychiatrist, I have found that helping people to develop personal goals has proved to be the most effective way to help them cope with problems.
Ari Kiev, M.D., *A Strategy for Daily Living*

example, a real estate developer may dream of owning all the real estate in Phoenix. He may wind up owning much more than if he did not have that dream. If he enjoys the *process* of acquiring real estate, that's all that matters.

Exercise #1-—Write Your Obituary

Every now and then I think about my own death, and I think about my own funeral. . . . I ask myself, "What is it that I would want said?"

Say I was a drum major for justice; say that I was a drum major for peace; say that I was a drum major for righteousness. And all of the other shallow things will not matter. I won't have any money to leave behind. I won't have the fine and luxurious things of life to leave behind. But I just want to leave a committed life behind.
Martin Luther King, Jr.

Martin Luther King, Jr. knew how he wanted to be remembered. He had a dream, and it drove his life. Write out what you would want the newspapers to say about you when you die. Alfred Nobel had a chance to *rewrite* his obituary. The story goes that his cousin, who was also named Alfred, died. The newspapers, hearing of the death of Alfred Nobel, printed the prepared obituary—for the wrong man. Alfred read it the day after his cousin's death. He was upset by what the obituary said because it starkly showed him how he would be remembered: as the well-known inventor of a cheap explosive called dynamite.

Alfred resolved to change his life. Today, he's remembered as the Swedish chemist and inventor who provided for the Nobel Prizes.

Write your obituary as you want to be remembered after your death. It should also include parts that are *not* related to your job. If you don't like the way your life seems to be headed, change it—just as Alfred Nobel did. Some people do this exercise every five or ten years. It keeps them on track and moving

forward. Write your own obituary, and *then make a list of the things you need to do to get there.*

Exercise #2—Invent a Job

If you could have any job in the world, what would it be? Don't worry about the possibility of ever finding that job—make it up! Invent it. Write it out. It may spark you to think of how to create that job in real life.

Exercise #3—If You Had a Million

If you had a million dollars (or maybe ten million) but still had to work, what would you do?

When I asked myself this question some time ago, I decided I'd like to continue doing what I was doing at work, but would like to write a book on job hunting because I felt I had something to say. I did write that book—and I've gone on to write others!

People often erroneously see a lack of money as a stumbling block to their goals. Think about it: is there some way you could do what you want without a million dollars? Then do it!

Exercise#4—Your Forty-Year Vision

Take a look at this very important exercise, which starts on the next page.

There are more things in heaven and earth, Horatio, than are dreamt of in your philosophy.
Shakespeare, *Hamlet*

Your Forty-Year Vision®

If you could imagine your ideal life five years from now, what would it be like? How would it be different from the way it is now? If you made new friends during the next five years, what would they be like? Where would you be living? What would your hobbies and interests be? How about ten years from now? Twenty? Thirty? Forty? Think about it!

Some people feel locked in by their present circumstances. Many say it is too late for them. But a lot can happen in five, ten, twenty, thirty or forty years. Martin Luther King, Jr. had a dream. His dream helped all of us, but his dream helped him too. He was living according to a vision (which he thought was God's plan for him). *It gave him a purpose in life.* Most successful people have a vision.

A lot can happen to you over the next few decades—and most of what happens is up to you. If you see the rest of your life as boring, I'm sure you will be right. Some people pick the "sensible" route or the one that fits with how others see them, rather than the one that is best for them.

On the other hand, you can come up with a few scenarios of how your life could unfold. In that case, you will have to do a lot of thinking and a lot of research to figure out which path makes most sense for you and will make you happiest.

When a person finds a vision that is right, the most common reaction is fear. It is often safer to *wish* a better life than to actually go after it.

I know what that's like. It took me two years of thinking and research to figure out the right path for myself—one that included my motivated abilities (Seven Stories Exercise) as well as the sketchy vision I had for myself. Then it took *ten more years* to finally take the plunge and commit to that path—running The Five O'Clock Club. I was forty years old when I finally took a baby step in the right direction, and I was terrified.

You may be lucky and find it easy to write out your vision of your future. Or you may be more like me: it may take a while and a lot of hard work. You can speed up the process by reviewing your assessment results with a Five O'Clock Club career counselor. He or she will guide you along. Remember,

when I was struggling, the country didn't *have* Five O'Clock Club counselors or even these exercises to guide us.

Test your vision and see if that path seems right for you. Plunge in by researching it and meeting with people in the field. If it is what you want, chances are you will find some way to make it happen. If it is not exactly right, you can modify it later—after you have gathered more information and perhaps gotten more experience.

Start With the Present

Write down, in the present tense, the way your life is right now, and the way you see yourself at each of the time frames listed above. **This exercise should take no more than one hour**. Allow your unconscious to tell you what you will be doing in the future. Just quickly comment on each of the questions listed on the following page, and then move on to the next. If you kill yourself off too early (say, at age sixty), push it ten more years to see what would have happened if you had lived. Then push it another ten, just for fun.

When you have finished the exercise, ask yourself how you feel about your entire life as you laid it out in your vision. Some people feel depressed when they see on paper how their lives are going, and they cannot think of a way out. But they feel better when a good friend or a Five O'Clock Club counselor helps them think of a better future to work toward. If you don't like your vision, you are allowed to change it—it's your life. Do what you want with it. Pick the kind of life you want.

Start the exercise with the way things are now so you will be realistic about your future. Now, relax and have a good time going through the years. Don't think too hard. Let's see where you wind up. You have plenty of time to get things done.

Final note:
The fifteen-year mark proves to be the most important for most people. It's far enough away from the present to allow you to dream.

Your Forty-Year Vision® Worksheet

1. The year is **xxxx** (current year). 2004
    You are ___48___ years old right now.
➤ Tell me what your life is like right now.
    (Say anything you want about your life as it is now.)
➤ Who are your friends? What do they do for a living?
➤ What is your relationship with your family,
    however you define "family"?
➤ Are you married? Single? Children? (List ages.)
➤ Where are you living? What does it look like?
➤ What are your hobbies and interests?
➤ What do you do for exercise?
➤ How is your health?
➤ How do you take care of your spiritual needs?
➤ What kind of work are you doing?
➤ What else would you like to note about your life
    right now?

Year: 2004   Your Age 48

Busy with teen kids. No job (just quit Nissho)
Parents independant. In discovery period.

No strong friends from Nissho.
Connie/Ins. Lori/Mary Kay. Judy/PHd. Anne/teacher.
Open, good, communicative. Help each other
out.
Married. kids age 13 + 15.
Oregon City. Countryside, working on house + lot.
Reading, writing, cooking, gardening
Walking periodically.
Good
Not much.
Considering what I want to do.
Larry NS is in control. Important to
see results from projects/steps.
Financially living on severance.

Don't worry if you don't like everything about your life right now. Most people do this exercise because they want to improve themselves. They want to *change* something. What do *you* want to change? **Please continue.**

2. The year is **xxxx** (current year + 5). 2009
    You are ___53___ years old. (Add 5 to present age.)
    Things are going well for you.
➤ What is your life like now at this age?
    (Say anything you want about your life as it is now.)
➤ Who are your friends? What do they do for a living?
➤ What is your relationship with your "family"?
➤ Married? Single? Children? (List their ages now.)
➤ Where are you living? What does it look like?
➤ What are your hobbies and interests?
➤ What do you do for exercise?
➤ How is your health?
➤ How do you take care of your spiritual needs?
➤ What kind of work are you doing?
➤ What else would you like to note about your life
    right now?

Year: 2009   Your Age 53

Kids are ready to leave nest (or have left) so
am empty-nester. Parents are transitioning to
new place (smaller). Working at fulfilling jobs.
Friends now also include people from work

68

3. The year is **xxxx** (current year + 15). 2019   Year: 2019   Your Age 63
   You are _63_ years old. (Current age plus 15.)

➤ What is your life like now at this age?
   (Say anything you want about your life as it is now.)
➤ Who are your friends? What do they do for a living?
➤ What is your relationship with your "family"?
➤ Married? Single? Children? (List their ages now.)
➤ Where are you living? What does it look like?
➤ What are your hobbies and interests?
➤ What do you do for exercise?
➤ How is your health?
➤ How do you take care of your spiritual needs?
➤ What kind of work are you doing?
➤ What else would you like to note about your life
   right now?

The fifteen-year mark is an especially important one. This age is far enough away from the present that people often loosen up a bit. It's so far away that it's not threatening. Imagine *your* ideal life. What is it like? Why were you put here on this earth? What were you meant to do here? What kind of life were you meant to live? Give it a try and see what you come up with. If you can't think of anything now, try it again in a week or so.

4. The year is **xxxx** (current year + 25). You are _____ years old! (Current age plus 25)	Year: 2029 Your Age 73 Using a blank piece of paper, answer all of the questions for this stage of your life.
5. The year is **xxxx** (current year + 35). You are _____ years old! (Current age plus 35)	2039 83 Repeat.
6. The year is **xxxx** (current year + 45). You are _____ years old! (Current age plus 45)	Repeat.
7. The year is **xxxx** (current year + 55). You are _____ years old! (Current age plus 55)	Keep going. How do you feel about your life? You are allowed to change the parts you don't like.
(Keep going—don't die until you are past 80!)	

You have plenty of time to get done everything you want to do. Imagine wonderful things for yourself. You have plenty of time. Get rid of any "negative programming." For example, if you imagine yourself having poor health because your parents suffered from poor health, see what you can do about that. If you imagine yourself dying early because that runs in your family, see what would have happened had you lived longer. It's your life—your only one. As they say, "This is the real thing. It's not a dress rehearsal."

The
Five
O'Clock
Club®

Your Forty-Year Vision™
. . . It's (Almost) Never Too Late
How to Create Your Future Five Years at a Time

by David Madison, Ph.D.

When my daughter was a month old, I started writing a daily diary to preserve memories of her growing up. She's now 30 and I haven't missed a day since. Now well past the 11,000 page mark—and with my daughter living in California with her husband—I sometimes wonder why I continue writing it. But recently someone sent me a ten-year-old photo of friends and I was able to find the occasion, the day and even the hour in the diary; what a triumph! An even bigger triumph: I was able to tell my daughter what she was doing (building a snowman with me) on the day her husband was born.

Whenever I go digging in the old diaries, I am usually astounded: This happened 15 years ago!? The clichés turn out to be so true: "It seems like only yesterday," or "where did the years go?" It's only when we look ahead that we feel that the future is so far away. Ten or fifteen years out seems impossibly far away, but September 2010 and April 2020 will one day be a reality.

And that's why, in our roles as career counselors, we try to overcome the skepticism or even ridicule that some people express when they hear about the Forty-Year Vision. We commonly hear, "I have trouble planning next week. Forty years? Give me a break!"

But we're not asking you to predict 40 years out, much less guess the distant future: This is not supposed to be an exercise in crystal-ball gazing. The career counselor who urges you to do the Forty-Year Vision is asking you to imagine, fantasize, strategize, as the first steps in trying to create the future on your terms.

On a recent consulting assignment I worked with 17 people who had been downsized by a small bank. As a way of getting them to see the value of the Forty-Year Vision, I asked them what their "dream" careers were. Did they simply want to move to other banks and continue processing financial transactions? Most were emphatic: No! And their aspirations were across the board: One wanted to get into filmmaking, another, physical therapy; another, the hospitality

industry, and yet another wanted to teach ballroom dancing.

But guess what: No one had seriously considered trying to make such career moves because it was easier and safer to drift along in their current jobs, month after month, year after year. Their aspirations were just unfocused dreams that never moved beyond the "wouldn't it be nice" stage, precisely because they had never made any attempt to structure the dream; they had never thought of making serious and realistic plans, and wishing upon a star won't make it happen!

The Forty-Year Vision will help fire your imagination.

Doing the Forty-Year Vision, however, is a first step in turning unfocused dreams into reality, and it won't seem nearly so intimidating or scary if you bear five things in mind:

(1) You don't start at the 40-year mark! We're the first to admit that this would be too much to wrap your mind around. The first notch in the Forty-Year Vision is the five-year mark. And that's totally realistic: What do you want your life and career to be like in five short years? That's only 60 months out. And 10 years out won't seem so farfetched or daunting if the five-year mark has been given some form and content. The 15- and 20- year marks then allow you to do some really creative thinking and wondering; you can develop general scenarios to strive for.

(2) Don't be fooled by the simple wisdom that "we can't predict the future." Of course we can't; but not being able to predict the future doesn't stop you from having kids, buying a 20-year CD to pay for college or committing to a mortgage. Why let it stop you from seriously plotting your career? There's a commercial on

TV right now with the line, "If it can be imagined, it can be done." That's not necessarily so, as Bob Dole or Walter Mondale would tell you. Not everything that can be imagined can be done, but nothing will be done unless it is imagined. Goals are born in the imagination, and the Forty-Year Vision is a tool to help get the imagination firing at maximum capacity—and to give you the motivation to do the necessary planning and strategizing.

(3) Don't despair because you're "too old." Sitting down at the kitchen table on your 50th birthday to write a Forty-Year Vision may strike most people as silly. But don't forget the lament of one senior citizen: "If I had known I was going to live so long, I would have taken better care of myself." Precisely because we can't predict the future, the Forty-Year Vision is a good idea. If you do make it to 85 or 90 or beyond, don't you want those years to be fruitful, exciting and purposeful? We're living longer; the age 65 cutoff for productive years is becoming meaningless! So the 50th or even 60th birthday is as good a time as any to let yourself imagine and plan for a long future.

(4) Remember that the Forty-Year Vision is always subject to change. You're not chained down to anything; you're the one in charge. The Forty-Year Vision is a pact you make with yourself. There is no Federal Bureau for Monitoring Forty-Year Visions! As you grow and learn more about yourself and the realistic options that you face, the Forty-Year Vision evolves too; course corrections or even radical changes are part of the process.

(5) The Forty-Year Vision is meant to be fun: It's not a term paper, it's not a test. Sure, it's serious business, but let your mind go and imagine all the possibilities you can create. As time goes by and events unfold you'll need to do reality checks, but try to catch the excitement of imagining all the things you can accomplish.

Whether you choose to walk down memory lane with a diary or home movies, photo albums or scrap books, you know that nothing you do now can change what happened 10 years ago. But your daily routine in ten or fifteen years does depend largely on the visions and strategies you develop now. So give the Forty-Year Vision the benefit of the doubt. It could change your life.

David Madison is the Director of The Five O'Clock Club Guild of Career Counselors.

Steve Jobs, the legendary founder of Apple Computer, has had his share of ups and downs, but he is known for staying the course. After he was ousted from Apple (by John Sculley, whom he brought in to head the company), Jobs labored for seven years on his new company, NeXT Computers, and then founded Pixar, which made him a billionaire. Later, he sold NeXT to Apple, while serving as a consultant to that company. What is the secret of his success?

There are very few people who have a vision and stick to it. Steve (Jobs) does.
Keith Benjamin, quoted in *Success*,
July/August, 1996

You need a lot more than vision —you need stubbornness, tenacity, belief and patience to stay the course.
Edwin Pixar, co-founder of Pixar, on Steve Jobs.
As quoted in *The New York Times Magazine*,
January 12, 1997

Asked what he wants to pass on to his children, Job answers: "Just to try to be as good a father to them as my father was to me. I think about that every day of my life."
Steve Lohr, "Creating Jobs,"
The New York Times Magazine, ibid
(Steve Jobs was adopted.)

The
Five
O'Clock
Club®

The Ideal Scene

*Every great personal victory was
preceded by a personal goal or dream.*
Dennis R. Webb

From *The Art of the Long View*
by Peter Schwartz:

---

*In order to make effective decisions, you must
articulate them to begin with. Consider, for example,
the choice of a career in biotechnology.
A scenario-planner would tackle the decision
differently. It depends, he or she might argue, on
another set of questions: What is the future of the
biotechnology industry? (That in turn depends on:)
What is the path of development in the biotech
industry? (Moreover:) What skills will have enduring
value? (And:) Where will be a good place to begin?
The hardest questions will be the most important.
What is it that interests you about biotechnology in
the first place? What sorts of things about yourself
might lead you to make a decision with poor results?
What could lead you to change your mind?*

---

*Scenarious are <u>not</u> predictions. It is simply not
possible to predict the future with certainty.*

---

*For individuals and small businesses, scenarios are a
way to help develop their own gut feeling and assure
that they have been comprehensive, both realistic and
imaginative, in covering all important bases.*

---

*If you look at yourself on the level of historical time, as
a tiny but influential part of a century-long process,
then at least you can begin to know your own address.
You can begin to sense the greater pattern, and feel
where you are within it, and your acts take on
meaning.* Michael Ventura, quoted by P. Schwartz

This is another exercise to help you imagine
your future. Relax for a while. Arrange a
time when you will not be distracted. Set
aside about an hour. Sit by yourself, have a cup of
tea, take out a pad of paper, and imagine yourself
five, ten, fifteen, or twenty years from now—at a
phase in your life when all is going well. Just pick
one of these time frames.

Imagine in very general terms the kind of life
you were meant to have. Start writing—it's important to write it down, rather than just thinking
about it.

What is your ideal life like? Describe a typical
day. What do you do when you get up in the morning? Where are you living? Who are your friends?

If you are working, what is it like there? What
kind of people do you work with? How do they
dress? What kind of work are they doing? What is
the atmosphere (relaxed? frantic?)? What is your
role in all of this? Describe it in greater and greater
detail.

In addition to describing your work situation,
think about the other parts of your life. Remember:
we each have twenty-four hours a day. How do
you want to spend your twenty-four hours? Where
are you living? What do you do for exercise? How
is your health? What is your social life like? Your
family life? What are your hobbies and interests?
What do you do for spiritual nourishment? What
are you contributing to the world? Describe all of
these in as much detail as possible. But don't worry
if you are not able to identify seemingly important
things, such as the city in which you are living, and
the field in which you are working.

Keep on writing—include as many details as
you can—and develop a good feel for that life.
Work on your Ideal Scene for a while, take a break,
and then go back and write some more. Change the
parts you don't like, and include all the things you
really enjoy doing or see yourself doing at this
imaginary time frame in the future.

CASE STUDY: MAX
Identifying His Future Career

Max, age forty, is a lawyer. A temporary placement firm sends him on assignments to various organizations. He imagined working in a suburban office of six casually-dressed people who were on the phones all day talking excitedly to people all over the world. He had a partner in this business. His own role was one of making contacts with prospective customers. He also saw himself writing about the topic they were engaged in, and becoming relatively well-known within their small segment of the industry.

Max's Ideal Scene may seem general, but it contains a lot of information. It appears that he would like to be in his own small but hectic business, operating on an international level. It would be a niche business where he could develop an expertise and become known to his small marketplace.

The international element was strong in this exercise. It was also evident in his Seven Stories Exercise and his Forty-Year Vision. It was clear that an international focus had to be central in his future.

You Can Develop Multiple Scenarios for Your Future

If you simply do the exercise up to this point, you will have done more than most people. You will have developed one scenario for your future. Some people develop multiple scenarios and think about the various possible futures they could have. Then they decide which they would like best, and which they think is do-able.

It all starts with describing an Ideal Scene, but it takes a lot more than that. Writing down the scene makes it more serious, and is the start of a more concrete vision. The written vision and the plan are a lot of work, so you can see why most people do not develop visions—and therefore may tend to drift. But those who write down their visions usually find that they have a lot of fun doing it, and those who keep going realize that their future is, in large part, up to them.

Some people become less self-conscious and braver when they think not of what *they* would like to do, but what they think God has in mind for them. They try to discern God's plan for them, and it is this that motivates and inspires them. Whatever technique or inspiration you use to develop your vision, you will be better off for having done it.

The Next Step: Define It Better and Research It

Some people are more ambitious, and want to go on to the next step: they want to flesh out their vision and then test it against reality. In Max's case, he had to figure out what kind of international business he could go into that would rely on his skills and support his values. He came up with a few ideas that excited him. Now he needs to investigate the potential for the various ideas, come up with a plan, develop new skills in the areas where he may be lacking, and take other steps toward fulfilling that vision.

You too will need to flesh out your bare-bones idea and then check it against reality. But be aware that other people will almost always tells you that it's not do-able. Conduct enough research so that you can decide for yourself.

Then, if you are serious about achieving the kind of life that you have envisioned, think of what you need to do to succeed. Take a few little steps immediately to help you advance towards your goal.

Encountering Roadblocks

Remember that this is not a sprint; it is a long-distance run. Do not become discouraged the first time you venture out. You will come up against lots of roadblocks along the way. That's life. Say to yourself, "Isn't this interesting? Another roadblock. I'll take a short breather (and perhaps even allow myself to feel a tingle of discouragement for a little while) and then I'll think of how I can get around this barrier."

Ask yourself what you have learned from the experience, because these experiences are here to teach us something. "What is the lesson for me in this setback?" And then get moving again.

My Forty-Year Vision

My own Ideal Scene evolved from the Forty-

Year Vision I did twenty years ago. I imagined myself at age eighty in a beautiful living space with a housekeeper. I had a strong visual image of someone from the community coming to the door to ask my advice. What this "vision" meant to me was that I had lived my life in such a way that I had had a great impact on the community—people were asking my advice even when I was old. However, I wasn't poverty-stricken because of my devotion to the community.

In my Forty-Year Vision I hadn't yet thought of The Five O'Clock Club or even considered a life in career counseling. But the image that came to me, and which I later developed, served as a template for my ideas and my research. My Seven Stories Exercise told me I had better be working with groups, and perhaps writing and lecturing. My Forty-Year Vision eliminated other interests of mine which would not have helped the community as much as career counseling.

It took many years to develop the concept and the focus of The Five O'Clock Club. For years, I continually used the Seven Stories Exercise and the Forty-Year Vision as my template. If an idea fit in with my vision and abilities, I considered it. If an idea didn't fit, I rejected it. I spent many long hours doing library and other research to select the field I wanted to be in. All of this finally evolved into the concept of The Five O'Clock Club.

As you can see, the Forty-Year Vision is simply a vision of your future. By studying it, along with the Ideal Scene, you can get at unconscious desires you may have. Making your desires conscious increases your chances of being able to do something about them.

First, write out your Ideal Scene. Then in the next section, follow Howard step by step as he uncovers his dream.

The Ideal Scene Worksheet

Imagine yourself five, ten, fifteen, or twenty years from now—at a phase in your life when all is going well. Just pick one of these time frames. Imagine in very general terms the kind of life you were meant to have. Start writing—it's important to write it down, rather than just thinking about it.

What is your ideal life like? Describe a typical day. _____

_____

_____

_____

_____

_____

What do you do when you get up in the morning? Where are you living? _____

_____

_____

_____

Who are your friends? _____

_____

_____

If you are working, what is it like there? _____

_____

_____

What kind of people do you work with? How do they dress?_____

_____

What kind of work are they doing? _____

_____

What is the atmosphere (relaxed or frantic)?_____

_____

What is your role in all of this? _____

_____

_____

Use another sheet of paper to describe it in greater and greater detail.

I mean if you're gonna do it—go and do it. You can't let anything stop you.
But he gave up and lived that "What if. . . . " life.
Bruce Faulk, *You Still Got to Come Home to That*

In addition to describing your work situation, think about the other parts of your life. How do you want to spend your twenty-four hours?

Where are you living? _____

What do you do for exercise? _____

How is your health? _____

What is your social life like? _____

Your family life? _____

What are your hobbies and interests? _____

What do you do for spiritual nourishment? _____

What are you contributing to the world? _____

Describe all of these in as much detail as possible. But don't worry if you are not able to identify seemingly important things, such as the city in which you are living, and the field in which you are working.

Keep on writing—include as many details as you can—and develop a good feel for that life. Work on your Ideal Scene for a while, take a break, and then go back and write some more. Change the parts you don't like, and include all the things you really enjoy doing or see yourself doing at this imaginary time frame in the future. _____

_____

_____

_____

_____

_____

_____

Howard:
Developing a Vision

We live in an age when art and the things of the spirit
come last. The truth still holds, however, that through
dedication and devotion one achieves another kind of
victory. I mean the ability to overcome one's problems
and meet them head on.

"Serve life and you will be sustained." That is a truth
which reveals itself at every turn in the road.

I speak with inner conviction because I have been
through the struggle. What I am trying to emphasize is
that, whatever the nature of the problem, it can only be
tackled creatively. There is no book of "openings," as in
chess lore, to be studied. To find an opening one has to
make a breach in the wall—and the wall is almost always
in one's own mind. If you have the vision and the urge to
undertake great tasks, then you will discover in yourself
the virtues and the capabilities required for their accom-
plishment. When everything fails, pray! Perhaps only
when you have come to the end of your resources will the
light dawn. It is only when we admit our limitations that
we find there are no limitations.
Henry Miller, *Big Sur and the Oranges of*
Hieronymous Bosch

HAPPY: All I can do now is wait for the merchandise
manager to die. And suppose I get to be merchandise
manager? He's a good friend of mine, and he just
build a terrific estate on Long Island. And he lived
there about two months and sold it, and now he's
building another one. He can't enjoy it once it's
finished. And I know that's just what I would do. I
don't know what the hell I'm workin' for.
Arthur Miller, *Death of a Salesman*

Howard came to one of the branches of The
Five O'Clock Club that specializes in
helping people who are not yet in profes-
sional-level jobs. He had done the Seven Stories
and other exercises, and had tried to do the Forty-
Year Vision. Like most people, he had left out
important parts, such as what he would be doing
for a living. That's okay. I asked him if he would
mind doing it in the small-discussion group.

At the time, Howard was thirty-five years old
and worked in a lower-level job in the advertising
industry. He wanted to advance in his career by
getting another job in advertising. Based on our
research into the jobs of the future, which showed
that his current industry was a shaky choice, we
asked him to postpone selecting an industry while
we helped him complete his Forty-Year Vision.

Filling in His Forty-Year Vision

Kate: "Howard, you're thirty-five years old right
now. Tell me: who are your friends and what
do they do for a living?"

Howard: "John is a messenger; Keith minds the
kids while his wife works; and Greg delivers
food."

Kate: "What do you do for a living?"

Howard: "I work in the media department of an
advertising agency."

Kate: "Okay. Now, let's go out a few years. You're
forty years old, and you've made a number of
new friends in the past five years. Who are
these people? What are they doing for a living?"

Howard: "One friend is a medical doctor; another
works in finance or for the stock exchange; and
a third is in a management position in the
advertising industry."

Kate: "That's fine. Now, let's go out further. You're
fifty years old, and you have made a lot of new
friends. What are they doing for a living?"

Howard: "One is an executive managing one to
two hundred people in a corporation and is
very well respected; a second one is in education—he's the principal or the administrator of
an experimental high school and gets written
up in the newspapers all the time; a third is a

vice president in finance or banking."

Kate: "Those are important-sounding friends you have, Howard. But who are you and what are you doing that these people are associating with you?"

Howard: "I'm not sure."

Kate: "Well, how much money are you making at age fifty in today's dollars?"

Howard: "I'm making $150,000 a year."

Kate: "I'm impressed. What are you doing to earn that kind of money, Howard? What kind of place are you working in? Remember, you don't *have* to be specific about the industry or field you're in. For example, how do you dress for work?"

Howard: "I wear a suit and tie every day. I have a staff of sixty people working for me: six departments, with ten people in each department."

Kate: "And what are those people doing all day?"

Howard: "They're doing paperwork, or computer work."

Kate: "That's great, Howard. We now have a pretty good idea of what you'll be doing in the future. We just need to fill in some details."

I said to the group: "Perhaps Howard won't be making $150,000, but he'll certainly be making a lot by his own standards. And maybe it won't be sixty people, but it will certainly be a good-sized staff. What Howard is talking about here is a concept. The details may be wrong, but the concept is correct."

Howard said: "But I'm not sure if that's what I really want to do."

Kate: "It may not be exactly what you want to do, Howard, but it's in the right direction and contains the elements you really want. What you just said fits in with your Seven Stories Exercise (one story was about your work with computers; another was about an administrative accomplishment). Think about it for next week, but I'll tell you this: You won't decide you want to be a dress designer, like Roxanne here. Nor will you say you want to sell insurance, like Barry. What you will do will be very close to

what you just described.

"If you come back next week and say that you've decided to sell ice cream, for example, I'll tell you that you simply became afraid. Fear often keeps people from pursuing their dreams. Over the week, read about the jobs of the future [which is included in this book] and let me know the industries you may want to investigate for your future career. It's usually better to pick growth industries rather than declining ones. You stand a better chance of rising with the tide."

The Next Week

When it was Howard's turn in the group the next week, he announced that he had selected health care as the industry he wanted to investigate. That sounded good because it is a growth field and because there will be plenty of need for someone to manage a group of people working on computers.

We brainstormed the areas within health care that Howard could research. He could work in a hospital, an HMO, a health-care association, and so on. He could learn about the field by reading the trade magazines having to do with health-care administration, and he could start networking by meeting with someone else in the group who had already worked in a hospital.

Week #3

Howard met with the other person in the group and got a feel for what it was like to work in a hospital. He also got a few names of people he could talk to—people at his level who could give him basic information. He had spent some time in a library reading trade magazines having to do with health-care administration.

Howard needed to do a lot more research before he would be ready to meet with higher-level people—those in a position to hire him.

Week #4

Howard announced to the group that he had done more research, which helped him figure out

If I see what I want real good in my mind, I don't notice any pain in getting it.
George Foreman, former heavyweight boxing champion of the world

---

that he should start in the purchasing area of a hospital, as opposed to the financial area, for example. In previous jobs, he had worked both as a buyer and as a salesman, so he knew both sides of the picture. He would spend some time researching the purchasing aspect of health care. That could be his entry point, and he could make other moves after he got into the field.

Week #5

Today Howard is ready to meet with higher-level people in the health-care field. As he networks around, he will learn even more about the field, and select the job and the organization that will position him best for the long run—the situation that fits in best with his Forty-Year Vision.

After Howard gets his next job, he will occasionally come to the group to ask the others to help him think about his career and make moves within the organization. He will be successful in living his vision if he continues to do what needs to be done, never taking his eye off the ball.

If Howard sticks with his vision, he will make good money, and live in the kind of place in which he wants to live. Like many people who develop written plans, Howard has the opportunity to have his dream come true.

You Can Do It Too

The group that Howard attended was Workforce America®, our program in Harlem. In Harlem, there is a large professional and executive population, but Workforce America works mostly with adults who are not yet in the professional or managerial ranks, and helps them get into professional-track jobs. For example:

Emlyn, a thirty-five-year-old former baby-sitter, embarked on and completed a program to become a nurse's aide. This is her first step toward becoming an R.N., her ultimate career goal.

Calvin, who suffers from severe rheumatoid arthritis, hadn't worked in ten years. Within five weeks of starting at Workforce America, he got a job as a consumer advocate with a center for the disabled, and has a full caseload. Workforce

America is continuing to work with him.

These ambitious, hard-working people did it, and so can you. It's not easy, but what else are you doing with your twenty-four hours a day? Follow the motto of Workforce America: "Have a dream. Make a plan. Take a step. Keep on climbing."

You can complain that you haven't gotten lucky breaks, but Howard, Emlyn, and Calvin didn't either. They made their own breaks, attended a branch of The Five O'Clock Club, and kept plugging ahead despite difficulties. If they can do it, you can do it too.

You can either say the universe is totally random and it's just molecules colliding all the time and it's totally chaos and our job is to make sense of that chaos, or you can say sometimes things happen for a reason and your job is to discover the reason.
But either way, I do see it meaning an opportunity and that has made all the difference.
Christopher Reeve, former star of *Superman*, in an interview with Barbara Walters.
Reeve became a quadriplegic after a horseback-riding accident.

This is a real test of the wedding vows. He's my partner. He's my other half, literally. It's not within the realm of my imagination to do anything less than what I'm doing.
Mrs. Christopher Reeve (Dana), in that same interview

The
Five
O'Clock
Club®

Self-Assessment
Summary

Summarize the results of all of the exercises. This information will help define the kind of environment that suits you best, and will also help you brainstorm some possible job targets. Finally, it can be used as a checklist against job possibilities. When you are about to receive a job offer, use this list to help you analyze it objectively.

1. What I need in my relationship with bosses:

_____

2. Job satisfiers/dissatisfiers:
    Satisfiers: _____
    Dissatisfiers: _____

3. Most important work-related values:

_____

4. Special interests:

_____

5. The threads running through the Seven Stories analysis:
    Main accomplishments:_____
    Key motivators: _____
    Enjoyed most; Did best:_____
    My role: _____
    The environment: _____
    The subject matter: _____

6. The top six or seven specialized skills:

    _____
    _____
    _____
    _____
    _____
    _____

7. From the Forty-Year Vision:
    Where I see myself in the long run:

_____

    What I need to get there:

_____

8. My basic personality and the kinds of work cultures it will fit:

_____

For deep in our hearts
We do believe
That we shall overcome someday.
"We Shall Overcome"
African-American freedom song

Resolve to be thyself and know that
he who finds himself loses his misery.
Matthew Arnold

To repeat part of a quote we included earlier:

OPTIMISM EMERGES AS BEST PREDICTOR TO SUCCESS IN LIFE

"Hope has proven a powerful predictor of outcome in
every study we've done so far," said Dr. Charles R.
Snyder, a psychologist at the University of Kansas.
Having hope means believing you have both the will
and the way to accomplish your goals, whatever they
may be. . . . It's not enough to just have the wish for
something. You need the means, too. On the other
hand, all the skills to solve a problem won't help if you
don't have the willpower to do it.
Daniel Goleman,*The New York Times*,
December 24, 1991

How many cares one loses when one decides not to be
something but to be someone.
Coco Chanel

You move from obsessing about why me and
it's not fair and when will I move again and all of those
things into well, what is the potential?
And now, four months down the line, I see potential I
wasn't capable of seeing. . . So I really sense
being on a journey that's very interesting.
Christopher Reeve, former star of *Superman*,
in an interview with Barbara Walters.
Reeve became a quadriplegic
after a horseback-riding accident.

Sometimes we get so caught up in the path we are on that we think we have no choice. We forget what we would rather be doing. It is easy to lose sight of what would make us happy. We forget we have made choices that have brought us to where we are.

Approach career planning and job hunting with an open mind—be open to the possibilities available to you. It is only by going out into the world and testing your ideas that the possibilities present themselves. Explore. Don't rush to take a job just because it is something well-known to you.

The purpose of knowledge, and especially historical
knowledge, is understanding rather than certainty.
John Lukacs, A History of the Cold War

Although your motivated skills do not change, keep reexamining them so you can see how they fit into various situations in your changing world. You will always fit in because your motivated skills adapt themselves to new situations and new possibilities.

Expect to be surprised. And think of surprise as a pleasant thing, because it adds interest to your life. Every move you make will open a new range of possibilities.

The step you are now taking is one that can alter the direction of your life. If you are aware, it can have as much or as little effect as you want it to have. If it turns out to be a mistake, you can move on.

This is not the last step: it is a transition. The next step is a preparation for the one after that. In the future, it will rarely be possible to say, in concrete terms, "I want to be this for the rest of my life." The past is over and is subject to a new interpretation depending on the situation you are now in and where you want to go from here. It's your story, and it is a story you make up as you go along. You don't know how the story will end, and the ending really doesn't matter. What matters is that you are living your life, enjoying the process of living. It's a journey, not a battle.

PART THREE

HOW TO SELECT
YOUR JOB TARGETS

BRAINSTORMING POSSIBLE JOBS

Brainstorming
Possible Jobs

But when the family continued to struggle, and when Steve Ross was a teenager, he was summoned to his father's deathbed to learn that his sole inheritance consisted of this advice: There are those who work all day, those who dream all day, and those who spend an hour dreaming before setting to work to fulfill those dreams.
"Go into the third category," his father said, "because there's virtually no competition."
Obituary of Steven J. Ross, creator of Time Warner,
The New York Times, December 21, 1992

I've got peace like a river ina my soul.
African-American spiritual

It is never too late to be
what you might have been.
George Eliot

CHARLEY: *Yeah. He was a happy man with a batch of cement.*
LINDA: *He was so wonderful with his hands.*
BIFF: *He had the wrong dreams. All, all, wrong.*
HAPPY, almost ready to fight Biff: *Don't say that!*
BIFF: *He never knew who he was.*
Arthur Miller, *Death of a Salesman*

U se the worksheet on the next page to help you brainstorm possible jobs that you can then explore.

1. **Across the top of the page**, list the following elements as they apply to you. Use as many columns as you need for each category.
- Your Basic Personality
- Interests
- Values
- Specialized Skills
- From the Seven Stories Exercise:
  - the role you played
  - the environment in which you worked
  - the various subject matters in your stories
- Long-range Goals
- Education
- Work Experience
- Areas of Expertise

Here is one person's list of column headings across the top:
- Personality: <u>outgoing</u>;
- Interests: <u>environment</u>, <u>computers</u>, <u>world travel</u> (three different interests—takes three columns);
- Values: <u>a decent wage</u> so I can support a family;
- Specialized Skills: <u>use of PC</u>;
- From the Seven Stories Exercise:
  - being <u>part of a research group</u>;
  - enjoy <u>Third-World countries</u> (takes two columns);
- Goals from the Forty-Year Vision: <u>head up not-for-profit organization</u>;
- Education: <u>Master's in Public Policy</u>;
- Work Experience: <u>seven years' marketing experience</u>.

This takes a total of eleven columns across the top.

2. **Down the side of the page, list possible jobs, fields, or functions** that rely on one or more of these elements. For example, combine marketing

---

*You must have long-range goals to keep you from being frustrated
by short-range failures.*
Charles C. Noble, Major general

with environment, or computers with research and Third-World countries.

At this point, do not eliminate anything. Write down whatever ideas occur to you. Ask your friends and family. Do library research and talk to lots of people. Open your eyes and your mind when you read or walk down the street. Be observant and generate lots of ideas. Write down whatever anyone suggests. A particular suggestion may not be exactly right for you, but may help you think of other things that *are* right.

3. **Analyze each job possibility**. Check off across the page the elements that apply to the first job. For example, if the job fits your basic personality, put a checkmark in that column. If it uses your education or relies on your work experience, put checkmarks in those columns. If it fits in with your long-range goals, put a checkmark there.

Do the same for every job listed in the left column.

4. **Add up the checkmarks for each job, and write the total in the right-hand column**. Any job that relies on only one or two elements is probably not appropriate for you. Pay attention to ones with the most checkmarks. Certain elements are more important to you than others, so you must weight those more heavily. In fact, there are probably some elements that *must* be present so you will be satisfied, such as a job that meshes with your values.

Those jobs which seem to satisfy your most important elements are the ones you will list as some of the targets to explore on the Preliminary Target Investigation worksheet (two pages ahead). Also list positions that would be logical next steps for you in light of your background.

CASE STUDY: AGNES
Broadening Her Targets

Agnes has been a marketing/merchandising/promotion executive in the fashion, retail, and

banking industries. Her only love was retail, and her dream job was working for one specific, famous fashion house. Perhaps she could actually get a job with that fashion house, but what kind of job could she go for after that? The retail and fashion industries were both retrenching at the time of her search, although she could probably get a job in one of them. She needed more targets, and preferably some targets in growing industries so she would have a more reasonable career path.

In addition to the retail and fashion industries, what other industries could Agnes consider? In the banking industry, where she had been for only three years, some of the products she promoted had been computerized. In combining "computers" with "retail" we came up with "computerized shopping," a new field that was threatening the retail industry. Computerized shopping and related areas were good fields for Agnes to investigate. What about something having to do with debit cards and credit cards or Prodigy—all computer-based systems aimed at retail? Or what about selling herself to banks that were handling the bankrupt retail companies that she was so familiar with? We came up with twenty areas to explore. Agnes's next step is to conduct a Preliminary Target Investigation (which you will read about soon) to determine which fields may be worth pursuing in that they hold some interest for her and there is some possibility of finding a job in them. At this point she has an exciting search lined up—one with lots of fields to explore and one that offers her a future instead of just a job.

The Five O'Clock Club®

Brainstorming Possible Jobs Worksheet

Assessment Results →																			Total check-marks across
Possible Jobs																			

The
Five
O'Clock
Club®

Chiron:
Finding a Future

*Growing up means eliminating
what doesn't work for you.*
Jan Halper, Ph.D., *Quiet Desperation—
The Truth about Successful Men*

Chiron is worn out. He is forty-five years old, and has had lots of different jobs in his life. Getting jobs has never been a problem. He has just gotten another one, and is afraid that it too will go nowhere. His wife is in her early thirties, and they would like to have children, but feel they cannot afford them on Chiron's income, which is approximately $60,000 a year.

In addition to his day job, where he works thirty hours a week, Chiron still has the small business he started on the side—keeping the books for a small company—just in case. He earns very little at this business, which is why he answered the ad for the job he just landed: director of development for a small not-for-profit in the medical field.

My Role As a Counselor

Chiron came to see me because his career path had caused him so much stress. He couldn't take the instability. My job was to help him uncover the central things that may be holding him back in his career—the things that may cause him not to live up to his abilities.

To save him money and time in the career-counseling session, I asked Chiron to complete the exercises in this book before we met. I told him that if he could not complete all of them, he should at least complete the Seven Stories.

Chiron was very serious when he came for his session. He hoped he could turn his life around. I will give you some highlights from our sessions.

Every client is different, and every counselor is different. But most counselors have similar goals. The purpose of the exercises is to get a sense of the person's career-related issues in an organized, methodical way. The exercises simply help a person talk about those issues. In addition, I try to teach the client the process we are going through so that he or she can think more deeply about the issues and do more self-analysis when I am not around.

Our Initial Session

We reviewed Chiron's Seven Stories Exercise. I will show you how the discussion went. First, I asked him to rank his seven stories so that we could work first on the one he ranked number-one.

The First Story

Kate: "Chiron, tell me your first accomplishment."

Chiron: "I planned and organized a free folk concert."

Kate: "When did this happen, or how old were you?"

Chiron: "It happened in 1972. I was twenty-three or twenty-four."

Kate: "Tell me about it."

Chiron: "I came up with the idea and organized the event. This was back when people were still upset about the war in Vietnam, and there had been a lot of protests. I wanted to turn that discontent into something good."

Kate: "So exactly what did you do? What was involved?"

Chiron: "I coordinated with various government offices to get permission for the concert. The government folks liked the idea because it was peaceful. It wasn't a political protest. Everything was donated, and everyone performed for free."

Kate: "How successful was it? For example, how many people attended?"

Chiron: "Twenty to thirty thousand people attended."

Kate: "Good grief! That's a lot of people! What prompted you to do this event? What led up to it?"

Chiron: "I wanted to make a difference. I wanted to do the community a favor."

Kate: "This was your number-one accomplishment. What about it made it number-one for you?"

Chiron: "I picked this experience as number-one because I was doing good and also having fun."

Kate: "What kind of time frame was involved? How long did the whole project take?"

Chiron: "Two months from start to finish."

Kate: "Even if you've already told me, what about it was most enjoyable for you? What was the most fun?"

Chiron: "Coordinating the folk groups and the other performers and all of the government offices. I also loved working with the press."

Kate: "What about it gave you a sense of accomplishment?"

Chiron: "Creating something out of nothing and having it be a success."

The Second Story

Kate: "That was great. Let's look at your next accomplishment. What was it?"

Chiron: "I taught myself journalism and got hired as a reporter."

Kate: "When did this happen and how old were you?"

Chiron: "Around 1978. I was twenty-nine."

Kate: "So tell me about it."

Chiron: "I went after a job creatively. I targeted one newspaper where I knew there was a job opening. The other people going after the job were all journalism majors. But I figured out how to write a story by studying books on my own. Then I covered some news events as if I were actually writing for the newspaper. I sent the editor the stories and said, 'This is how I would have covered the story if I had been writing for you.' I did this with a few stories, and actually had a lot of fun doing it. After each one, I would call him. I got the job and beat out all those people who had better qualifications."

Kate: "That's a great accomplishment. What led up to your doing it?"

Chiron: "I had spent two sessions working with the Connecticut legislature, and that's what got me interested in being a journalist."

Kate: "You mentioned as your success the fact that you got hired; what about the job itself? You didn't mention that as a success."

Chiron: "I loved the job."

Kate: "What about it did you love?"

Chiron: "I covered a diverse range of subjects: kids and skateboards; arson. Each time, I had to teach myself the subject area."

Kate: "What did you enjoy the most?"

Chiron: "Teaching myself and getting hired and covering a wide range of subjects. I enjoyed doing the research required."

Kate: "Is there anything else you'd like to tell me about this experience?"

Chiron: "Yes. I loved meeting new people."

Kate: "How long did you have this job?"

Chiron: "Only two months. My wife got transferred to a new job in another city. We weighed it and decided to move."

Analysis of the First Two Stories

After I have heard two stories, I give the client some feedback so he or she will see the process I use. Later, the client should be able to do a better job analyzing the stories than I could. After all, he or she was there; I wasn't.

In this case, I gave Chiron my initial impressions, based solely on what he had told me:

"Chiron, it may be that your other stories show things very differently from these first two, but I'll tell you what I've noticed so far, for what it's worth.

"Both of these happened a long time ago— fifteen to twenty years ago. Part of our quest in going through the assessment process is to come up with goals for you so that your *next* experience has a better chance of winding up as one of your top seven stories.

"A second thing I noticed is that they were both of short duration. In addition, a lot of the jobs on your résumé were also of relatively short duration.

"This is not necessarily bad. A person can choose to work on short-term things forever, such as people who get involved in fads—like the 'pet rocks' people. They don't expect these fads to last. They expect them to be short-lived. Then they move on to the next thing. Planning fads is their focus, and they become expert at it.

"Other examples are people who run events, or head up special projects. Some people can be very successful working on short-term projects—but they tend to have a specific area of expertise and they tend to *intend* to have project-oriented work.

"On the other hand, a person can decide to hunker down and remain in something more long-term so that he or she can become somewhat expert at it. That's another way to go.

The traditional admonition of one generation to the next,
"Get a job," has been replaced with the more complex and bewildering mandate,
"Go out and create a job for yourself."
George Gendron, editor, *Inc.*

"So, a person can choose to have a short-term project orientation, or a longer-term orientation. One is not better than the other. The important point is *planning*. An opportunistic approach of doing whatever happens to present itself rarely works. It's gets very tiring to constantly learn new things and not to build on your previous experiences.

"Other threads that appear in both stories are:

"You came up with an idea and did it. You had to be convincing. There was a lot of creativity and coordination. You showed initiative in both stories.

"I'm struggling to find a subject matter that appears in both. This may have no significance at all, but politics appears in both. In one story, you had to deal with the government, and in the other, you watched the state legislature for two sessions.

"Another possible thread having to do with subject matter is 'the press.' In the first story, you dealt with the press. In the second story, you *were* the press."

As I showed Chiron my thought patterns, he could decide whether or not what I was saying had any significance. He could think more about his own experiences. Then he could decide what's important about them and come up with conclusions of his own.

The Third Story
Kate: "Tell me your third accomplishment."
Chiron: "Last year, I started my own bookkeeping business for a grocery store."
Kate: "Tell me about this one."
Chiron: "I needed something to do. I had lost my job. Friends and I brainstormed ideas. I liked the idea of performing a service that people would appreciate. I also like food, and I have an M.B.A., so doing bookkeeping for a food business seemed logical."
Kate: "What for you was the real accomplishment?"
Chiron: "I started the business from nothing. I built it myself. And now it's successful. When I collect the money every week, it tells me that I made this thing work."
Kate: "Even if you've already told me, what about this did you enjoy the most?"
Chiron: "It was 'my thing,' and I made money from it."

Other Accomplishments
Chiron then went on to tell four additional stories. For example, the fourth was when he ran a successful political campaign for someone who was running for city council. At this time, Chiron was only about twenty-six years old.

After we reviewed all seven stories, I told Chiron that I noticed that three had the government or politics or power in them. They all showed his ability to convince, required creativity, organization, and initiative.

In the bookkeeping business, he did *not* mention any interaction with the people—the people he did the bookkeeping for or even the bookkeepers he had hired to help him. In all of the other stories, he had mentioned enjoying the people: meeting new people through journalism, working with the legislature and the folk groups, or recruiting and organizing volunteers in the political campaign. This "people orientation" was an important element missing in the bookkeeping business. My impression was that he did not like the business. What he liked was the idea that he had started it and made it work well enough.

Other strong threads appeared to be:
*   running a campaign
*   being a natural leader
*   being a major influencer
*   developing strategies
*   doing his own thing.

What did Chiron have to say about this? He was solemn and intense: "Yes. I see myself as the General. In the army, there's a platoon leader who deals with day-to-day tactics. I'm the General who sees the overall picture. I'm making only $60,000 a year, but I really feel that I should be making double this."

I replied, "Based on what you've told me, I too see you as the General. You seem to be the type of person who *has* to lead, to develop strategies, to influence people. It may be that the subject matter doesn't matter much—as long as you feel you're contributing to the public good—providing a service."

That's it for his Seven Stories Exercise. The other assessment results were also important, although I won't go into them here. I did find it significant that he has an M.B.A.

As I review the results, I look to make sure all of the results are in agreement. For example, if a person says he or she does not value money, but imagines living in a palatial house, I would want to know how he or she planned to afford such a place. Most often, people's results are in sync. That is, there is usually some correlation between the various exercises.

Unresolved conflicts can hold a person back. In Chiron's case, there were a number of conflicts. The most important showed up in his Values exercise. Chiron places a very high value on his lifestyle. In fact, he and his wife go away just about every weekend to the cabin they have in the woods. They are able to do this because it doesn't cost much, and Chiron essentially works only 36 hours a week in both of his jobs combined. He leaves work early every Friday so they can go to the country. In addition, he takes French horn lessons and goes to the gym once a week. Traveling is another interest of his. At present, his lifestyle is important, and he is not willing to give it up. Yet he also wants to make $120,000 a year.

That's a lot of money. People who make that much—even far less than that—work very hard and tend to work long hours. Chiron would have to resolve this conflict of wanting to maintain his lifestyle, work a 36-hour week, and yet make a large amount of money. This rarely happens unless a person develops some highly valued expertise.

It Is Not Easy to Find Out
What Is Holding a Person Back

Chiron's conflict may seem obvious to you: How could he not see the problem? You can see Chiron's problem because I'm spelling it out for you. However, I may be wrong. It may be that the real problem is not apparent to me. Chiron is the only one who can know for sure why he is not reaching the level to which he aspires.

Perhaps you too have something that is holding you back. It may not be obvious to you or to anyone else. Our conflicts and beliefs are subtle and often rigid. Most people do not recognize their own conflicts. Even when a conflict is pointed out to them, it is difficult to take the steps necessary to correct it. People usually continue to do what they have been doing. Changing one's beliefs takes a great deal of insight and courage.

It would take some time for Chiron to resolve this conflict in his values. So we moved on to the next part of the process. We worked on Chiron's Forty-Year Vision. He came up with a number of possibilities. It's best if you too come up with a number of scenarios for yourself. Then you can match them against your requirements. To be thorough, Chiron also filled out the "Brainstorming Possible Jobs Worksheet." Across the top of the worksheet, I noted his assessment results: his Seven Stories, his interests, values, education, and so on. That worksheet is shown on the next page.

Down the left-hand side of the worksheet, Chiron brainstormed possible jobs, and also asked his friends to think of job possibilities for him. Those suggestions helped him to think of still others. Then he put check marks wherever a job possibility fit in with a characteristic. This helped him to get rid of possibilities that would not fit most of his requirements.

The Three Scenarios

After all of this, Chiron came up with three possibilities that he thought he would find satisfying. He also thought that all three of these could happen within the next five years—when he would be fifty years old. The three possibilities were:

- be president of my own company
- be political director of a large national organization
- be COO of the medical not-for-profit for which he now worked.

We examined each of these so he could realistically see what would be involved—at least at the start. Then he could research each further, and think more about the direction he really wanted his life to take.

Brainstorming Possible Jobs Worksheet

Possible Jobs	Driving force: idealism	Service-orientation	Artistic	Enterprising	Writer/journalist	Sales/influencing	Leader/the "General"	Strategist	Meet with leaders	"Business owner"	Advisor	Politics/government	Food/health	Non-bureaucratic	M.B.A.	Earn $100,000/yr.	Make large impact	Complex problems			Total check-marks across
Lobbyist	✔				✔	✔		✔	✔		✔	✔									7
Bookkeeping business		✔		✔						✔	✔										4
Political campaign mgr.	✔	✔		✔	✔	✔		✔	✔		✔	✔									9
Executive, present co.	✔	✔	✔	✔	✔	✔	✔	✔	✔	✔	✔	✔			✔	?	✔	✔			15
Development director	✔	✔		✔	✔	✔		✔	✔		✔							✔			9
Journalist	✔				✔	✔		✔	✔		✔										6
Political activist	✔	✔			✔	✔	✔	✔	✔		✔	✔									9
Union organizer	✔	✔			✔	✔	✔	✔	✔		✔	✔									9
Arts organization	✔	✔	✔		✔	✔	✔	✔	✔		✔	✔									10
Fund-raiser: music	✔	✔			✔	✔		✔	✔		✔	✔									9
Pres. of my own co.	✔	✔		✔	✔	✔	✔	✔	✔	✔			✔	✔	✔	?	✔				14
State senator	✔	✔				✔	✔	✔	✔		✔	✔									9
Pol. director, large org.	✔	✔		✔	✔	✔	✔	✔	✔		✔	✔				?	✔				11
. . . and so on																					

> *Not everything that is faced can be changed;*
> *But nothing can be changed until it is faced.*
> James Baldwin

Analyzing the Possibilities

Let's take a look at each possibility. Chiron and I had a preliminary discussion so he could get a feel for how long it would take for him to move to the level he described in each of the three scenarios. In real life, a person has to do a "Preliminary Target Investigation " by talking to people in those fields and assessing the likelihood of being able to make such a transition.

Scenario 1: "Be president of my own company"

I asked Chiron what kind of company he could see himself heading up. He thought a publishing company sounded good. What size staff would he have? He thought ten to twenty people. What kind of publishing company? He thought a magazine, such as in the health, cooking, or travel area. He imagined it as being a few monthly publications, subscription only (as opposed to street sales).

It takes most people about two years from the time they decide to start their own small business until the time they actually start it. They have a lot of research and planning to do: Who else is in that market? How are they doing? What are they doing? How much will it cost? Where will I get the money? Even if a person works 15 hours a week on the new business while working full-time doing something else, it still takes two years.

Therefore, by the time Chiron is forty-seven, he will be able to start the business—probably on the side while continuing to work at his day job. He could run it for a few years part-time until it is far enough along that he could tackle it full-time. Then he would be forty-nine or so. It is unlikely that he would have a staff of ten to twenty at that time. It is more likely that it would be five or so employees— if he is lucky.

Even if Chiron opted to raise the money instead of trying to finance the enterprise himself, that still takes lots of time.

The question is whether Chiron has the discipline to investigate this idea objectively, plan it, and carry it out. If not, he should not go impulsively into this business just because it sounds like a fine idea to him. He will only repeat past mistakes where he tackled something without being properly prepared.

Scenario 2: "Be political director of a large national organization"

Chiron imagined himself in an organization that has a corporate staff of 12 or so. He would be the chief lobbyist with a staff of four to six. I asked him to pick an organization—any organization— just to make this example more real. He selected the National Association of Manufacturers, which is headquartered in Washington, D.C. Let's brainstorm this scenario.

Of course, Chiron would have to be willing to live in Washington, D.C., at some point. After resolving that barrier in his own mind, one scenario for moving ahead with this vision would be to get a job as a junior lobbyist *in an area that would eventually be of interest to the organization he targeted*. It would not be good enough to get lobbying experience, for example, in the utilities or tobacco field. He would need relevant experience because his future employers would want to capitalize on the contacts he had made. Then he could become a more powerful lobbyist, and he would be desirable to organizations such as the one he mentioned.

Chiron would have no trouble getting his first lobbying job. After all, it would not be that high-level, and Chiron is very convincing in interviews. But since it would require a geographic move, that step could take a year. Then he would have to do extremely well in that field so he would have a few things to brag about. That would take two or three years, for sure. Then he would have to get into the right organization, and move up within it. That would be a few more years. I guessed that Chiron would be in his ideal job, making the kind of money he wanted in nine years, at age fifty-four.

I think it's do-able, and he has plenty of time, since most of us are living longer. The question, again, is one of commitment.

The third scenario will take the same length of time to achieve and require the same commitment. Life takes time. Making good money takes most people a lot of time and commitment. Chiron needed to decide what his priorities were. That also would take time.

Chiron had always prided himself on his ability to learn things quickly. However, at a certain age, those areas that were our greatest strengths can become our greatest weaknesses if we don't watch out. Chiron tends to not learn any area in depth, keeping him stuck at $60,000 or so a year.

There is no end to this story yet. We will all have to wait and see what Chiron decides to do with his life.

Chiron's Options

Lucky Chiron has many options. Many people would envy the life he and his wife have created for themselves. Chiron and his wife do not work long hours, earn decent money, go to the country every weekend, and have time to pursue other interests. Sometimes people are unhappy with their lives until they complete the assessment and discover they don't have it so bad after all. In Chiron's case, he and his wife can keep their lives—and their income—essentially as is. To gain the career stability Chiron wants, all he needs to do is stick with something long enough to become expert. Then he will have the kind of life many Americans want.

On the other hand, he could join the rat race with the rest of us. He may choose to do that because, for example, he thinks he needs the money to have and raise children (although people do raise children on what Chiron makes, and most wives work today).

If he wants to make a good deal more than he does now, he will have to work a good deal harder. Those who have spent years becoming expert in a marketable area can work less hard. But Chiron still has to develop marketable skills to command more money. Within that, he has many choices.

He has energy and brains and talent. He needs direction and hard work. That's not so bad.

For each of the three scenarios he targeted, he could develop a plan similar to the one Deborah did in "Developing a Detailed Plan," a few chapters back. That would help him to chart a course that he could then stick to if he is committed enough. The sooner he makes a commitment to a clear direction, the more likely he is to achieve that direction. If he keeps on hedging, his energies will continue to be dispersed. In his present job, he could develop a skill that he feels sure would also help him later.

If the direction he selects later proves to be wrong, Chiron will still be better off for having chosen something and for developing a marketable skill. Then he can build on his new marketable experience.

As far as the bookkeeping business is concerned, I think Chiron should keep at it until he has made a commitment to a new path. Otherwise, he may continue his pattern of jumping from one thing to another without properly researching it. Although the bookkeeping business is not the right career path for him, the more important lesson he needs to learn is commitment. Then the future will look bright for Chiron.

You too have many options. And you too have plenty of time in which to achieve them. But you too must investigate them, and make a commitment. And give yourself a break. Remember that life takes time.

You do not sing because you are happy;
you are happy because you sing.
William James

In a fight between you and the world,
bet on the world.
Franz Kafka

Some luck lies in not getting what you thought you
wanted but in getting what you have, which once you
have got it you may be smart enough to see is what
you would have wanted had you known.
Garrison Keillor

I arise in the morning torn between
the desire to improve the world and
a desire to enjoy the world.
This makes it hard to plan the day.
E. B. White

Having a Balanced Life

*Let our advance worrying become advance
thinking and planning.*
Winston Churchill

---

*The more time we spend planning a project, the less
total time is required for it. Don't let today's busy-
work crowd planning time out of your schedule.*
Edwin C. Bliss, *Getting Things Done*

---

*BIFF: And suddenly I stopped, you hear me? And in
the middle of that office building, do you hear this? I
stopped in the middle of that building and I saw—the
sky. I saw the things that I love in this world. The
work and the food and time to sit and smoke. And I
looked at the pen and said to myself, what the hell am I
grabbing this for? Why am I trying to become what I
don't want to be? What am I doing in an office,
making a contemptuous, begging fool of myself, when
all I want is out there, waiting for me the minute I say
I know who I am!*
Arthur Miller, *Death of a Salesman*

---

*The most difficult thing—but an essential one
—is to love Life,
to love it even while one suffers,
because Life is all. Life is God,
and to love Life means to love God.*
Leo Tolstoy, *War and Peace*

---

*It is often said that accomplishment makes [dying]
easier, that those who have achieved what they set out
to do in life die more contentedly
than those who have not.*
Judith Viorst, *Necessary Losses*

It is very easy to have a life that is out of balance.
Some people intentionally have an "out-of-balance" life so they may achieve in a specific area. Or a person's life may become out of balance in one area for a certain length of time so that he or she may "catch up" in that area. However you decide to live your life, it is still good to know what you are missing.

> ## Pay attention to all areas.
> ### For a balanced life, *grow* in all areas:
>
> - **Spiritual**   • **Recreation**
> - **Financial**   • **Family**
> - **Career**   • **Social**
>   • **Health & Fitness**

People need to pay attention to their careers to meet their basic obligations. But be sure you have a "career" and not just "work." **Career** has a concept of personal development. **Work** has a concept of "I need money to do something else with."

To grow in every area:
1. Have goals in every category.
2. Set priorities.
3. Develop a plan.
4. Live.
5. Review. (Go back to step 1.)

It's a good idea to review annually what you did last year and what you plan for next year. Keep your plans in a folder and review them over the years. Look for growth in each area. Or do it twice a year. You can pick a theme for the year—something that needs extra focus. Some people do a five- or ten-year plan.

Set goals for yourself. The goals you set must be measurable: you must be able to tell when you've accomplished a particular goal.

Set goals that make you stretch. All successful people have failed. It's how you deal with it that's key. If you've never failed, you've never reached.

Life planning is a lot like business planning. A common approach is this one:

1. Get a dream/vision. Formulate a purpose.

2. Write it down.
3. Create long-term, measurable goals.
4. Create a series of strategies and action steps to get there.
5. Evaluate these goals and strategies: make sure they represent a "stretch" yet are reasonable.
6. Share these goals with someone.
7. Get some good counsel and advice. (Be prayerful about it.)
8. Act on it.

Criteria for SUCCESS
Someone found this on a plane and passed it on to me:
S - Sense of Purpose —written goals.
E - Excellence — commitment to be the best at whatever you do.
C - Contribution.
R - Responsibility for your actions — You don't work for a company; you work for yourself.
E - Effort.
T - Time Management.
S - Stay with it.

Write down your goals for each area, and your steps for reaching your goals in each area. Some people review their lives once or twice a year. Some families develop a plan together every year. Pay attention to all areas. Feel free to add extra areas that have specific importance to you. For a balanced life, *grow* in all areas:

Area to Plan/Grow	Goals for Each Area	Steps for Getting There
• Spiritual		
• Financial		
• Career		
• Health & Fitness		
• Recreation		
• Family		
• Social		
• Other		

What You Can Do in Your Present Situation

What has changed most fundamentally is the greater responsibility being given to workers to take charge of ensuring higher quality and to take a proactive role in organizing their own work—responsibilities that in the past management jealously kept for itself.
Hedrick Smith, *Rethinking America*

Language reflects social reality, and the reality of the pre-nineteenth-century world was that people did not "have" jobs in the fixed and unitary sense; they "did" jobs in the form of a constantly changing string of tasks.
William Bridges, *JobShift: How to Prosper in a Workplace Without Jobs*

Now you have a vision of your future, and a plan of what you should do to achieve that vision. You will need new skills and new relationships. To advance, you may feel as though you must get out of the job you are in right now. However, you may be able to add skills, experience and a knowledge base without leaving your current position. Look at the following list of ideas. You may want to add some of these to your Career Plan.

- Talk to colleagues about needs in your present company. Make plans to fill those needs.
- Expand the network of people with whom you interact internally and externally.
- Join an association that fits in with your long-term goals; get on a committee.
- Find out what people in your function do outside of your present company (or the function you are interested in long-term).
- Learn a new technical skill.
- Manage a project.
- Volunteer for a task force.
- Train staff on new software.
- Select/determine software or equipment.
- Write a proposal to fill a need.
- Make a presentation.
- Take some classroom training.
- Substitute for your manager in a meeting.
- Run a meeting.
- Assist with the budgeting process.
- Organize a community activity or do volunteer work to gain a new marketable skill.
- Train a new person.
- Research and write a report.
- Write and implement a "what if" suggestion.
- Observe the demeanor of someone in a high-level position (even if only via video).
- Continue to develop your plan.
- Think of what may stop you from reaching your goals, and overcome those barriers.

The first five items are generally considered to be the most important. These are action steps that will usually help you to do better in your career—no matter what your career goals are. Consider adding them to your list if they are not already on it.

Life Takes Time

Great ideas come into the world as gently as doves.
Perhaps then, if we listen attentively, we shall hear,
amid the uproar of empires and nations,
a faint flutter of wings,
the gentle stirrings of life and hope.
Albert Camus

To sum up, here is the process:
Step 1: Understand yourself: your values, interests, skills, and so on. The better you understand yourself, and the more honest you are about it, the better you will be able to assess the opportunities that will come your way.

Step 2: Figure out what you want. What on this earth would you be best served doing? What should your future be like?

Step 3: Figure out how to get there. Later on, we will show you how to develop a Career Plan for yourself.

Step 4: Figure out what within yourself might stand in your way. Chiron had a conflict in values, and also a tendency to lack commitment to a specific path. If he can resolve these issues, nothing can stand in his way.

Internal Issues

Here are some common examples of internal issues that hold people back:
- a conflict in values. "I want to earn $300,000 a year as an exporter in Montana (where there are few export jobs), work a two-day week, and spend three years with someone like Mother Teresa."
- a lack of self-esteem. People rise to their level of self-esteem. If you have low self-esteem, stop thinking about yourself, and instead think of what you were put on this planet to do. Do what you were meant to do. God did not mean for you to bury your talents, but to use them and make them multiply.
- an inability to imagine a more fulfilling future; depression. Get some help with your Forty-Year Vision. Start writing. Think about meeting with a Five O'Clock Club career counselor.

- a lack of focus. Some people see too many possibilities and cannot decide what to do. They flit from one thing to another and do not become an expert at anything.
- a lack of possibilities. Other people imagine doing the same thing for thirty years. They need to explore more and see what's out there.
- Too many skills; master of none.
- Too few skills; need to be a 21st century person.
- Too tense; don't have enough fun.
- Too much fun; don't buckle under and work.

Add your own thoughts to this list. There are plenty of things that hold people back.

"External" Issues

In addition, most job hunters have something that they think will keep them from getting their next job. It could be that they feel they are too young or too old, have too little education or too much, are of the wrong race, creed, nationality, gender, sexual orientation, weight, height, or are very aware that they have a physical disability.

While it is true that there is prejudice out there, job hunters who are too self-conscious about their perceived handicaps will hold themselves back. In addition, they may inadvertently draw attention to their "problem" during the interview. Your attitude must be: "What problem? There is no problem. Let me tell you about the things I've done."

Now let's move on to look at some of the things *you've* done.

A competitive world has two possibilities for you.
You can lose. Or, if you want to win, you can change.
Lester C. Thurow, Dean,
Sloan School of Management, M.I.T.

Monitor how you're thinking and behaving, and try to stop negative thoughts and behaviors in their tracks. Ask yourself: Why am I thinking or behaving this way? What's the positive alternative? What might make it easier for me—now and in the future—to think or act positively in this type of situation?
Jack Maguire, *Care and Feeding of the Brain*

How to Decide What You Want to Offer

*The fastest way to succeed is to
look as if you're playing by other people's rules,
while quietly playing by your own.*
Michael Korda

Your motivated skills and your dreams help you set your long-term direction. In order to go somewhere, you must know where you are right now. In this chapter, you will look down and see where your feet are. You will become more pragmatic. What have you done so far in your life? What do you have to offer the world?

What Do You Have to Offer?

In deciding what you *want* to offer, first list all you *have* to offer—a menu to choose from. When you go after a certain kind of position, emphasize those parts that support your case. If you decide, for example, to continue your career in the same direction, you will probably focus on your most recent position and others that support that direction.

If most of your satisfaction as an adult has occurred outside your job, you may want to change something about your work life. If you decide to change careers, activities outside your regular job may help you make that change.

Many years ago, when I was interested in changing from computers to advertising, I offered as proof of my ability the three years I had spent at night promoting nonprofit organizations, and my portfolio of press coverage for those organizations. Later, when I wanted to work as a career counselor, my proof was my many years' experience in running The Five O'Clock Club at night, the seminars I had given on job hunting and career development, and so on. When I wanted to continue working in business management, I simply offered my on-the-job experience in making companies profitable.

If you have available the entire list of what you have to offer, you can be more flexible about the direction in which you want to go.

How to State Your Accomplishments

Present what you have to offer in terms of accomplishments. Tell your "story" in a way that will provoke interest in you and let the "reader" know what you are really like. Accomplishment statements are short, measurable, and results-oriented. We each handle the situations in our work lives in different ways. What problems have you faced at work? How did you handle them? What was the effect on the organization?

Some of us are project-oriented and others are process-oriented. If you are project-oriented, you will tend to take whatever is assigned to you, break it into "projects" in your mind, and then get those projects done. You like to solve problems, and you get bored when there are none. Your accomplishments will state the problems you faced, how you solved them, and the impact you had on the organization.

On the other hand, if you are process-oriented, you like to run the day-to-day shop. You can be trusted to keep an existing situation running smoothly, and your accomplishments will reflect that. You like stable situations and systems that work. You will state that you ran a department of so many people for so many years.

Work on this exercise now. Start with any of your Seven Stories that are work-related. Note the way you wrote about each accomplishment when you were telling your "story." Chances are, it was a more exciting way to describe that accomplishment than the way you would normally write about it on a résumé or talk about it in an interview. Use those stories as your starting point, and be sure to include details so the reader will be able to see what you actually did. After all, they were important enough for you to include in your Seven Stories. Don't ignore them now.

Next, write down your current or most recent position. State your title, your organization name, and list your accomplishments in that position.

Do not worry right now if you do not like your job title, or don't even like your job. In our résumé book we will change your title to make it reflect what you were actually doing, and we can emphasize or deemphasize jobs and responsibilities as you see fit. Right now, get down on paper all of your accomplishments. Then we will have something to work with.

A project-oriented accomplishment could look like this:

• Designed and directed a comprehensive and cost-effective advertising and sales promotion program that established the company as a major competitor in the market.

A process-oriented accomplishment could look like this:

• Reviewed ongoing market performance of investor-owned utility securities. Used multiple equity valuation techniques. Recommended redirection of portfolio mix to more profitable and higher-quality securities.

After you have completed your accomplishment statements for your present or most recent position, examine the job before that one. State your title, your organization name, and list your accomplishments.

Work on as many accomplishments as make sense to you. Some people cover in depth the past ten years. If you can, cover your entire career, because you never know what may occur to you, and you never know what may help you later. In doing this exercise, you may remember jobs you had completely forgotten about—and pleasant and satisfying accomplishments. Ask yourself what it was about that job that was so satisfying. Perhaps it is another clue about what you might do in the future.

Do not wish to go back to your youth. What was challenging then will probably not satisfy you today. Look for the *elements* of those early jobs that satisfied you. These elements should be compared with your list of motivated skills to determine lifelong interests.

You will feel better after you have completed this exercise. You will see on paper all that you have to offer. And your accomplishments will be stated in a way that will make you proud.

Discipline yourself to do this exercise now, and you will not have to do it again.

After you have listed your work experiences, list accomplishments outside work. These, too, should be short, measurable, and results-oriented. These outside experiences can help you move into a new field. In fact, that's how I and many others have made career transitions. By volunteering to do advertising and public relations work at night, I developed a list of accomplishments that helped me move from computers to advertising. In those days, my outside experience went like this:

• Walnut Street Theatre Gallery
Planned, organized, and promoted month-long holography exhibition. Attendance increased from less than one hundred visitors per month to over three thousand visitors during the month of this exhibition.

• YMCA
Handled all publicity for fund-raising campaign. Consulted with fund-raising committee on best techniques for them to use. Received plaque in recognition.

• United Way
Received four United Way awards for editorial work in 1979; two awards the prior year. Spoke at the United Way's Editors' Conference.

• Network for Women in Computer Technology
Chair of the Program Committee.

Later, career counseling became my volunteer work, and that eventually helped me move into the field I am now in. In the early days, my outside experience was stated like this:

• Organized and ran The Five O'Clock Club. Conducted weekly groups as well as individual counseling. Trained people in career decisions,

Where I was born and where and how I have lived is unimportant.
It is what I have done with where I have been that should be of interest.
Georgia O'Keefe

marketing techniques, and practice interviewing. Brought in outside lecturers.

I also listed the organizations for which I had done job-hunting seminars, and stated my relevant work experience—such as when I was a training manager.

List all of your accomplishment statements. Depending on the positions you are going after, these accomplishments may be included or not. They may, for example, be unimportant for ten years, and later on become important again, depending on your job target.

Your volunteer work may be important, just as mine was. Summer jobs can count, too.

To get better at stating your accomplishments—no matter what your level or experience—read The Five O'Clock Club's book on résumés.

This is *your* chance to brag—everyone else does. You will rework the wording of your accomplishment statements, and make them sound great, as long as they are truthful. When you have done this, you will feel terrific because you will be represented well on paper.

For now, think about what you've really done. For most people, the problem is not that they stretch the truth on their résumés; the problem is that they don't say what they've *really* done.

Figuring out what you've really done is much more difficult than simply reciting your job description. That's the importance of doing the Seven Stories exercise. It helps you step back from a résumé frame of mind so you can concentrate on the most important accomplishments of your life (in terms of what you really enjoyed doing and know you also did well). Then the exercise helps you think about each accomplishment in terms of what you *really* did: what led up to the accomplishment, what your role was, what gave you satisfaction, what your motivation was, and so on.

If You Think You Haven't Done a Thing With Your Life

Many people are intimidated when they see other people's accomplishments. They think they have none of their own. Chances are, you aren't thinking hard enough about what you have done. If you think you haven't done much, think again. If you are reading this book, we already know that you are competent, ambitious, and intelligent. Even people in the lowest-level jobs have accomplishments they are proud of. At all levels in an organization, people can be presented with problems and figure out how to handle them.

Don't compare yourself with others, and don't worry about what your boss or peers thought of what you have done: maybe they did not appreciate your talents. Brag about what you have done anyway—even though your boss may have taken credit for the work, and even though you may have accomplished it with the help of others. Think of problems you have faced in your organization. What did you do to handle them? What was the result for your organization? Think of an accomplishment. Write it down. Then pare it down until you can show the reader what you handled and the impact it made.

Finally, don't say anything negative about yourself. Don't lie, but don't hurt yourself either.

In this chapter, you were to write down everything you've done so that it will serve as a menu you can draw on, depending on the kinds of jobs you are going after. In our résumé book, you will see how people struggle to develop well-written accomplishment statements. In the next chapter, we will become more focused: your goal during your search process is to start out thinking broadly, and then focus.

The next thing most like living one's life over again
seems to be a recollection of that life,
and to make that recollection as durable as
possible by putting it down in writing.
Benjamin Franklin

How to Target the Job You Want

I always wanted to be somebody,
but I should have been more specific.
Lily Tomlin

You are on your way to finding your place in the world. Using the Seven Stories and other exercises, you made a list of your motivated skills and what you want in a job, and then you brainstormed a number of possible job targets that might fit in with your enjoyable accomplishments and/or your vision of your future. Some of these targets may be very long-term. Then you thought about what you would be willing to offer. (You took it an extra step by stating these as accomplishments.)

Now we will work on firming up your job targets. You will do some preliminary research on each target through the internet and by talking to people to see if these areas still interest you and are practical. Then you will *focus* by selecting two, three, or four areas on which to concentrate, based on what appeals to you and what you think you have that is marketable. Then you will conduct a thorough campaign aimed at each area. Because each campaign takes a lot of work, it is best if we spend some time refining your targets.

Selecting Job Targets
—Your Key to Job-Hunting Success

Selecting a job target means choosing: a specific geographic area, a specific industry or organization size, and a specific position within that industry. A job target must have all three.

Select your targets. Using our book, *Getting Interviews*, conduct a campaign aimed at each. Concentrate your energies, and you increase your chances for success.

Approach each target with an open mind. Commit to a target, but only as long as it makes sense. You can change your mind after you find out more about it. It makes no sense to strive to be a ballerina after you find you have absolutely no ability as a dancer. Commitment to a target lets you discover your real possibilities and increases your

chances of landing a job of your choice. The unsuccessful ballet student may have something else of great value to offer the world of dance—such as the ability to raise funds or run a ballet company.

The Results of Commitment

Commitment increases the chance that you will come across clearly and enthusiastically about the industry and the position you seek; it will help you do a thorough job of networking in the chosen area, of investigating and being knowledgeable about the area, of conducting a thorough search, and of being successful in that search.

If the result of your initial commitment is that you realize a job target is not what you thought it would be, you have resolved the issue and can move on.

Jim, a marketing manager, had targeted four industries: environmental, noise abatement, shipping, and corporate America, a backup target in case the other three did not work. He conducted an excellent search aimed at the environmental target, an area he had always wanted to explore. It was only after a brief but committed job search that he found the environmental area was not for him: the people in it were different from what he had expected. He would not be able to do the things he had imagined he would do there. That target no longer interested him. The noise abatement and shipping industries, however, were very exciting to him, and he found a good match for himself. Later, his exploration of the environmental area paid off. He was employed by a shipping company in the containment of oil spills.

Commitment to a target means you'll give that target your best shot —and results in a better job hunt than if you had no target at all.

Target a Geographic Area

Targeting a geographic area is usually the easiest part of the targeting process. Some people decide that they want to work near their present homes, while others decide that they would be willing to move where the jobs are. Are you willing to move anywhere? Are a small town and a big city the same to you? Would you move to the coast? To

Arizona? Would you rather be near your family? If you want to stay where you are now, target that area as your first selection—and you'll have a better chance of getting offers there. If you really care about where you live, *target it.*

Think about where you stand on this. You will be assigning yourself an impossible task if, for example, you want to be an export manager but want to work only in a geographic area where there are no export-management positions. If you must live in a particular area, be realistic about the kinds of jobs open to you there.

Resolve this issue. Then you will know if you'd be willing to change your target industry so you can live where you want, or change your geographic area so you can work in the industry or function that interests you.

Target an Industry and a Function in That Industry

Many people say they don't care what industry they work in. When pressed, they usually have stronger opinions than they thought.

If you think *any* industry would be okay for you, let's find out. Would you work in the not-for-profit sector? If so, where? In education? A hospital? How about government? A community organization? Does it matter to you?

Would you work for a magazine? A chemical company? The garment industry? How about a company that makes cardboard boxes? Or cheese? Does it matter to you?

Does it matter if the organization has forty employees? What about forty thousand? Four hundred thousand? Does it matter to you?

You've Selected a Target If . . .

. . . you can clearly state the industry or organization size in which you'd be interested, your position within each industry, and some guidelines regarding geographic location.

For example, if you're a junior accountant, you may already know that you want to advance in the accounting field. You may know that you want to

work for a small service organization as an assistant controller in the geographic area where you are now living.

If you have clearly selected your targets, then you can get on with finding interviews in your target area. To do that, you would conduct a campaign in your target area. (Job-hunting campaigns are covered in our book, *Getting Interviews*.)

Here is one person's target list:

By geographic area:
- Washington, D.C.
- New York City

By industry:
- Book publishing
- Magazine publishing
- Advertising
- College administration (weak interest)
- Administration of professional firms (weak interest)
- Nonprofit associations
- Direct-marketing organizations.

By function:
- Business manager/General manager-publishing
- International controller
- Corporate-level financial planning analysis
- General V.P. finance/General manager—nonprofit organizations.

Other Issues You May Want to Consider Even If You Have a Target

Does the style of the organization matter to you? Would you rather be in a fast-paced, dynamic organization with lots of headaches or one that's more stable, slow paced, with routine work as the norm? Which would you prefer?

What kind of people do you want to work with? Friendly people? Sharp, challenging people? People interested in making a fast buck? People who want to make the world a better place? Think about it. You may have said before that you just

about it. You may have said before that you just want a job—any job—but is anything still okay with you?

If you want to be in sales, for example, would it matter if you were selling lingerie or used cars or computers or large office building space? What if you were selling cats? Rugs? Butter? Saying you want to be in "sales" is not enough.

Let's take it a step further. If what appeals to you about being a salesman is that you like to convince people, why not be a politician? Or a clergyman? Or a doctor? Or if what appeals to you is money, why not become a trader? Or a partner in a law firm? Remind yourself where your heart lies.

CASE STUDY: WILLIAM
Finally—An Organized Search

William wanted a job—just about any job he saw in the want ads. He spent months answering those ads. He thought he was job hunting, but he wasn't. He was simply answering ads for positions for which he was unqualified. William didn't stand a chance.

After a long time, William gave up and agreed to follow The Five O'Clock Club system. At first he resisted because, like so many job hunters, he did not want to "restrict" himself. William thought that focusing on only two or three job targets would limit his opportunities and lengthen his search. He wanted to be open to whatever job came his way.

Many job hunters, like William, simply want a job. But William needed to put himself in the position of the hiring manager: Why would he want to hire William? In his cover letters, William took the "trust me" approach. He did nothing to prove his interest in the industry, the organization, or even the position for which he was applying. His credentials matched the ad requirements only by the greatest stretch of the imagination.

A shotgun approach like William's may lead to a job offer, but it may also lead your career in a direction that is not what you would have preferred. Later, you may find yourself back in the same boat again—wondering what to do with your

life, wanting to do almost anything but what you are doing, hoping your next job will miraculously be in a field that will satisfy you.

William's basic problem was not that he wanted to change careers, but that he didn't know what he wanted to do. He was willing to do anything—anything except focus on a specific area and go after it.

William eventually narrowed himself to two targets in which he was truly interested. Then he worked to find out his chances for getting jobs in those fields. William did the exercises in this book, and came up with this list to focus his search:

What I want in a job:

- A challenge in meeting new situations/variety.
- A complex situation I can structure.
- Something I believe in.
- A chance to express my creativity through my communication skills.
- A highly visible position.
- An opportunity to develop my leadership and motivational skills.
- Sole responsibility for something.

What I have to offer (that I also want to offer):

- Enthusiasm for the organization's basic mission/purpose.
- Penetrating analysis that finds the "answer."
- The ability to synthesize diverse parts into a unified whole.
- An ability and desire to be in new/untested situations.
- Effective in dealing with many kinds of people.
- Strong oral and written communication skills.

Goal: A small- or medium-sized organization where I can feel my impact:

- Service
- Health care
- Human care
- Science
- Academia and learning
- Human understanding

Let not my thinking become confused by listening to too many opinions, but let me consider each one individually, to see if it can be of help to me.

To make good choices, I must develop a mature and prudent understanding of myself that will reveal to me my real motives and intentions.
Paraphrased from Thomas Merton, *No Man Is An Island*

Description of targeted areas:

- Targeted geographic areas:
  - Major East Coast cities or locales:
    - New York
    - Philadelphia
    - Boston
    - Baltimore
    - Washington

- Targeted industries:
  - First priority is health care:
    - Pharmaceuticals companies
    - Biotechnology companies
    - Hospitals
    - Maybe research labs
  - Second priority is not-for-profit community organizations.

- Targeted positions:
  - marketing/competitive analysis
  - organizational positioning
  - operations planning

William's first campaign was aimed at pharmaceuticals companies. He discovered what they looked for in new hires, and how he could get a position. In addition, he pursued his second objective: not-for-profit community organizations.

The result: As usual, a career transition takes time. William discovered he could make a transition into the pharmaceuticals industry, but decided not to take the backward step that would require. He learned of a job being created in a not-for-profit organization. Although he was not qualified for this position, he knew he could handle it, and it matched the list of what he wanted.

William went through the steps described in the chapter "How to Change Careers," to convince his prospective employer he could indeed handle the job and was eager to have the chance to do it. This was difficult because the other candidates were better qualified than William—they had been in this kind of job before. For William, it was a career change.

William decided to write a number of proposals. To write them, he first needed to do research, which would not be easy. After some library research, he called the heads of development at six major not-for-profits. He told them he was hoping to get a position at a certain organization, and wanted some ideas of how he could write a proposal of what he would do if he were hired.

Amazingly, his sincerity won the day. All six gave him information over the phone. Because he had done library research, William was able to ask intelligent questions. He wrote a proposal, stating in his cover letter that he had spoken with the heads of development at major not-for-profits, and asked for another interview. It would be nice if that were all it took: William got another interview, but was rejected a *number* of times. Yet he continued to do research, and eventually showed enough fortitude and learned enough that he was hired.

The position was just what he wanted: a brand-new marketing research position at a major not-for-profit organization. He would head his career in a different direction and satisfy his motivated skills. His career was back on track, under his own control. And he's still with the organization today.

Select *Your* Targets

The only difference between caprice and a lifelong passion is that the caprice lasts a little longer.
Oscar Wilde

List your targets in the order in which you will conduct your search. List first the one you will focus on in your first campaign. If you are currently employed and have time to explore, you may want to select as your first target the most unlikely one. (Job hunters sometimes want to target areas they had only dreamed about before.) Concentrate on it and find out for sure whether you are truly interested and what your prospects are. If it doesn't work, you can become more realistic.

On the other hand, if you must find a job quickly, concentrate first on the area where you stand the best chance of getting a job—perhaps the

Our doubts are traitors,
And make us lose the good we oft might win
By fearing to attempt.
William Shakespeare, *Measure for Measure*

new job, you can develop yourself in the area that interests you in the long run. Remember, it's okay to take something less than your ideal job; just keep working toward your dreams.

Someone who made this work is Nat, who wanted to work for a Japanese company. He thought the Japanese culture suited his temperament. Yet Nat was forced to take a job at another organization because the Japanese process was slow (approval had to come from Tokyo). Still, Nat kept pursuing the position with the Japanese firm.

Eventually, his dream job came through—at much more money than he had been making. The Japanese company realized that Nat's personal style, uncommon in America, meshed with Japanese management methods. His maturity—he was fifty-five years old—was also a plus. Nat, his new job, and his new employer were a good fit. Despite many obstacles, Nat pursued his dream and got it. And it was worth it in job satisfaction and in having some say over what happened in his own life.

If you are targeting a geographic area different from where you are now, be sure to conduct a serious, complete campaign aimed at that target. For example, you will want to contact search firms in that area, do library research, perhaps conduct a direct-mail campaign, and network. For in-depth information on all of these topics, please consult our book *Getting Interviews*. Use the work sheets on the following pages to plan your targets.

Measuring Your Targets

You've selected one to five targets on which to focus. Will they be enough to get you an appropriate job?

Let's say, for example, that your first target aims at a small industry (ten organizations) having only a few positions that would be appropriate for you. Chances are, those jobs are filled right now. In fact, chances are there may be no opening for a year or two. The numbers are working against you. But if you have targeted *twenty* small industries, each of which has ten organizations with a few positions appropriate for you, the numbers are more in your favor. On the other hand, if one of your targets is

large and has a lot of positions that may be right for you, the numbers are again on your side.

A Rule of Thumb

A target list of two hundred positions results in seven interviews which result in one job offer. Therefore, if there are less than two hundred potential positions in your targets, develop additional targets or expand the ones you already have. Remember that when aiming at a target of less than two hundred, concentrated effort will be required.

However, sometimes one organization by itself may be enough. What if a very qualified secretary wanted to work for a regional telephone company? What are the chances she would find a job there? A regional telephone company may have *thousands* of secretaries, and a qualified person would certainly be able to find a job there within a reasonable time frame.

In a tight job market, however, you will probably need to *expand your job-hunting targets*. If you are searching only in Chicago, or only in the immediate area where you live, think of other geographic areas. If you are looking only in large public corporations, consider small or private companies, or the not-for-profit area. If you are looking for a certain kind of position, what other kinds of work can you do? Think of additional targets for your search, and focus on each target in depth.

In *Getting Interviews*, you will learn how to position yourself for each of these targets. That way, when you go after a target, you will have a better chance of looking appropriate to the people in each target area.

Live all you can; it's a mistake not to.
It doesn't so much matter what you do in particular,
so long as you have had your life.
If you haven't had that, what have you had?
What one loses one loses; make no mistake about that.
Henry James, *The Ambassadors*

Target Selection

After you have done some preliminary research, select the targets that you think deserve a full campaign. List first the one you will focus on in your first campaign. If you are currently employed and have time to explore, you may want to select as your first target the most unlikely one, but the one that is the job of your dreams. Then you can concentrate on it and find out for sure whether you are still interested and what your prospects are.

On the other hand, if you must find a job quickly, you will first want to concentrate on the area where you stand the best chance of getting a job—probably the area where you are now working. After you get that job, you can explore your other targets. (To expand your targets quickly, consider broadening your search geographically.)

If you are targeting a geographic area different from where you are now, be sure to conduct a serious, complete campaign aimed at that target. For example, you will want to contact search firms in that area, do Internet or library research, perhaps conduct a direct-mail campaign, and network.

Target 1:

Industry or organization size: _____

Position/Function: _____

Geographic area: _____

Target 2:

Industry or organization size: _____

Position/Function: _____

Geographic area: _____

Target 3:

Industry or organization size: _____

Position/Function: _____

Geographic area: _____

Target 4:

Industry or organization size: _____

Position/Function: _____

Geographic area: _____

Target 5:

Industry or organization size: _____

Position/Function: _____

Geographic area: _____

The Five O'Clock Club®

Measuring Your Targets

You've selected one to five (or more) targets on which to focus. Will this be enough to get you an appropriate job?

Let's say, for example, that your first target aims at a small industry (ten organizations) having only a few positions that would be appropriate for you.

Chances are, those jobs are filled right now. In fact, chances are there may be no opening for a year or two. The numbers are working against you. Now, if you have targeted twenty small industries, each of which has ten organizations with a few positions appropriate for you, the numbers are more in your favor.

On the other hand, if one of your targets is large and has a lot of positions that may be right for you, the numbers are again on your side.

Let's analyze your search and see whether the numbers are working for you or against you.

Fill out the following on your own target markets. You will probably have to make an educated guess about the number. A ball-park figure is all you need to get a feel for where you stand.

For Target 1:
Industry or organization size: _____
Position/Function: _____
Geographic area: _____

How big is the market for your "product" in this target?
  A. Number of organizations in this target market: _____
  B. Number of probable positions suitable for me in the average organization in this target: _____
  A x B = Total number of probable positions appropriate for me in this target market: _____

For Target 2:
Industry or organization size: _____
Position/Function: _____
Geographic area: _____

How big is the market for your "product" in this target?
  A. Number of organizations in this target market: _____
  B. Number of probable positions suitable for me in the average organization in this target: _____
  A x B = Total number of probable positions appropriate for me in this target market: _____

For Target 3:
Industry or organization size: _____
Position/Function: _____
Geographic area: _____

How big is the market for your "product" in this target?
  A. Number of organizations in this target market: _____
  B. Number of probable positions suitable for me in the average organization in this target: _____
  A x B = Total number of probable positions appropriate for me in this target market: _____

Rule of thumb:

A target list of 200 positions in a healthy market results in seven interviews that result in one job offer. Therefore, if there are fewer than 200 potential positions in your targets, develop additional targets or expand the ones you already have. Remember that when aiming at a target of less than 200, a more concentrated effort will be required.

Preliminary Target Investigation:
Jobs/Industries Worth Exploring

Until you know that life is interesting—and find it so—you haven't found your soul.
Geoffrey Fisher, Archbishop of Canterbury

Life is God's novel. Let him write it.
Isaac Bashevis Singer

A study was made of alumni ten years out of Harvard to find out how many were achieving their goals. An astounding 83 percent had no goals at all. Fourteen percent had specific goals, but they were not written down. Their average earnings were three times what those in the 83 percent group were earning. However, the 3 percent who had written goals were earning ten times that of the 83 percent group.

Forrest H. Patton, *Force of Persuasion,*as quoted by Ronald W. Miller, *Planning for Success*

Counterbalance sources of stress in your life with sources of harmony. Develop closer ties to the people you love. Set up dependable routines in your schedule to which you can look forward during times of stress: a few moments each evening in a hot bath, regular nights to eat out, one day per month in bed, seasonal vacations. Create environments around you that are physically and emotionally restorative: a peaceful workspace, a blossom-filled window box you can see from where you eat, a permanent exercise nook. Regularly perform simple tasks that you can be certain will give you a sense of accomplishment.
Jack Maguire, *Care and Feeding of the Brain*

Although it takes up only a few paragraphs in this book, Preliminary Target Investigation is essential.

Your Preliminary Target Investigation could take only a few weeks if you are high in energy and can devote full time to it. You have to test your ideas for targets in the marketplace to see which ones are worth pursuing. As you research at the library, on the Web and by meeting with people in your fields of choice, you will refine those targets and perhaps develop others. Then you will know where to focus your job search, and the search will be completed much more quickly than if you had skipped this important step.

People who conduct a Preliminary Target Investigation while employed sometimes take a year to explore various fields while they continue in their old jobs. If you are not at all familiar with some of the job targets you have selected, do some Preliminary Target Investigation *now* through the Web, library research (be sure to read "Researching Your Job Targets" in Part IV.) and networking. You will find that some targets are not right for you. Eliminate them and conduct a full campaign in those areas that seem right for you and which offer some reasonable hope of success.

Whether you are employed or between jobs, Preliminary Target Investigation is well worth your time and a lot of fun. It is the difference between blindly continuing in your old career path because it is the only thing you know, and finding out what is really happening in the world so you can latch on to a field that may carry you forward for many, many years. This is a wonderful time to explore—to find out what the world offers. Most job hunters narrow their targets down too quickly, and wind up later with not much to go after. It is better for you emotionally as well as practically to develop more targets *now* than you need so you will have them when you are actively campaigning. If, on the other hand, you do not have the inclination or time to explore, you can move on. *Just remember, you can come back to this point if your search dries up and you need more targets.*

Most job hunters target only one job type or industry, take a very long time to find out that this

*Dream. Dream <u>big</u> dreams! Others may deprive you of your material wealth
and cheat you in a thousand ways, but no man can deprive you of the control and use of your imagination.
Men may deal with you unfairly, as men often do; they may deprive you of your liberty; but they cannot take
from you the privelege of using your imagination. In your imagination, you always win!*

Jesse Jackson

target is not working, get depressed, try to think of other things they can do with their lives, pick themselves up, and start on one more target.

Instead, **brainstorm as many targets as possible** *before* **you begin your real job search**. Then you can overlap your campaigns, going after a number of targets at once. If some targets do not seem to be working as well for you as others, you can drop the targets in which you are no longer interested. And when things don't seem to be going well, you will have other targets to fall back on.

1) **List below all of the jobs/industries that interest you at this point.**

2) If you are not at all familiar with some of the targets you have selected, do some Preliminary Target Investigation *now* through library research or networking. Eliminate the targets that are not right for you, and conduct a full campaign in those

areas which *do* seem right for you and seem to offer you some reasonable hope of success.

As you find out what is happening in the world, new fields will open up for you. Things are changing so fast that if you conduct a serious search without some exploration, you are probably missing the most exciting developments in an area.

Spend some time exploring. Don't narrow your targets down too quickly; you will wind up later with not much to go after. It is better for you emotionally, as well as practically, to develop *now* more targets than you need so you will have them when you are actively campaigning. If, on the other hand, you do not have the time or inclination to explore, you can move on to the next step. **Just remember: you can come back to this point if your search dries up and you need more targets.**

JOBS/INDUSTRIES THAT INTEREST ME AT THIS POINT:
(Conduct a Preliminary Target Investigation to determine what is really going on in each of them.)

_____

_____

_____

_____

_____

_____

_____

_____

_____

_____

_____

_____

_____

_____

Targeting: The Start of an Organized Search

To organize your targeting:

1) Brainstorm as many job targets as possible. You will not conduct a campaign aimed at all of them, but will have backup targets in case certain ones do not work out.

2) Identify a number of targets worthy of preliminary research. (If they are large targets and represent a lot of job possibilities for you, you will need fewer targets.)

3) Research each one enough—through the Internet, the library and a few networking meetings—to determine whether it is worth a full job-search campaign. This is your Preliminary Target Investigation.

4) If your research shows that a target now seems inappropriate, cross it off your list, and concentrate on the remaining targets. **As you continue to network and research, keep open to other possibilities that may be targets for you. Add those to your list of targets to research**.

As you add new targets, reprioritize your list so you are concentrating first on the targets that should be explored first. Do *not* haphazardly go after everything that comes your way.

5) If you decide the target is worth pursuing, conduct a full campaign to get interviews in that area:

- Develop your pitch.
- Develop your résumé.
- Develop a list of all the companies in the target area and the name of the person you want to contact in each company.

6) Then contact each organization through networking, direct contact, ads, or search firms.

Serendipitous Leads

Make a methodical approach the basis of your search, but also keep yourself open to those serendipitous "lucky leads" outside of your target areas that may come your way. In general, it is a waste of your energy to go after single serendipitous leads. It is better to ask yourself if this lead warrants a new target. If it does, then decide where it should be ranked in your list of targets, and research it as you would any serious target.

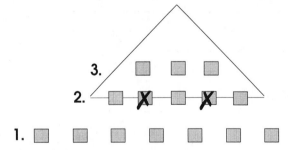

The boxes above represent different job targets. The triangle represents your job search. As you investigate targets, you will eliminate certain ones and spend more time on the remaining targets. You may research your targets by reading or by talking to people. The more you find out, the clearer your direction will become.

During Targeting Phase 1, you brainstormed lots of possible job targets, not caring whether or not they made sense.

During Targeting Phase 2, you conducted preliminary research to determine whether or not you should mount a full campaign aimed at these targets.

During Targeting Phase 3, you will focus on the targets that warrant a full campaign. This means you will do full research on each target, and consider using all of the techniques for getting interviews: networking, direct contact, search firms, and ads.

*Out of every crisis comes the
chance to be reborn . . .*
Nena O'Neill

---

*This is the true joy in life, the being used for a purpose
recognized by yourself as a mighty one, the being
thoroughly worn out before you are thrown on the
scrap heap; the being a force of nature instead of a
feverish selfish little clod of ailments and grievances
complaining that the world will not devote itself to
making you happy.*
George Bernard Shaw

---

*True commitment transforms you. You really know
where you stand. You have a base on which to build your
life. You're not in shifting sand anymore.*
Christopher Reeve, former star of *Superman*,
in an interview with Barbara Walters.
Reeve became a quadriplegic
after a horseback-riding accident.

---

*We will make the best possible life out of this life that we
now have and there's no question that he will continue to
be a leader and continue to be a strong person and a
funny person and a lively person.*
Mrs. Christopher Reeve (Dana),
in that same interview

---

*We must not be afraid of the future. We must not be
afraid of man. It is no accident that we are here. Each and
every human person has been created in the "image and
likeness" of the One who is the origin of all that is.
We have within us the capacities for wisdom and virtue.
With these gifts, and with the help of God's grace, we can
build in the next century and the next millennium a
civilization worthy of the human person, a true
culture of freedom. We can and must see that the tears
of this century have prepared the ground for a new
springtime of the human spirit.*
Pope John Paul II, speech to the United Nations
General Assembly, October 5, 1995

By selecting and ranking your targets, you have completed a very important task. If your targets are wrong, the campaigns you aim at those targets are wrong. Maintain an exploratory mindset—assessing the targets you are pursuing, and being open to others.

Next you will start to develop your Personal Marketing Plan, essential when you are really ready to search (and you'll use our book, *Getting Interviews*). Chances are, you can't fill in your Plan until you do some research, which is covered next in this book.

Make an organized search the basis for your campaign. Some lucky job hunters know lots of important people and just happen on to their next jobs. Sometimes those jobs are even satisfying. If that has happened to you in the past, count your blessings, but do not rely on that approach to work for you in the future. The world has changed, and organizations are more serious about whom they hire.

In our book, *Getting Interviews*, you will begin an intensive campaign to get lots of interviews in each of the targets you have selected. The campaigns will overlap so you will be able to compare the performance of each and gain perspective. You can begin your campaign right now, by reading the next few chapters—about conducting research.

**Do not think that
you have to complete your research
before you start reading *Getting Interviews*.
The job-search process *is* largely a
research process.
You will continually refer to
the research portions of this book
throughout your campaign.**

PART FOUR

QUICK AND EFFECTIVE RESEARCH

HOW TO GET ON THE RIGHT TRACK

Researching Your Job Targets

Looking for a place to start your research?
Read these chapters and then study the bibliography at the back of this book. It is the most comprehensive annotated job-search bibliography on the market.

This section focuses on basic, traditional research. It works, but it can be time-consuming unless it is coupled with computer-based research.

Read *all* of the chapters on research. Then study the bibliography at the back of this book—being sure to look at the sections on the internet, as well as library research using paper, CD-ROM and On-Line Databases.

Why Is Research Important?

Research can help you decide which field to go into and is a solid way to develop a list of your target organizations. Then you will decide how to contact them and you'll measure your progress against this list. Research will improve your networking and interviewing skills and increase your confidence during interviews. You will create a good impression, and look like an insider rather than like someone who is trying to break in. Research will give you an edge over your competition and help you decide which organization to join.

Library Research

Find a university or big-city library that's conveniently located and has an extensive business collection. You will not be completely on your own: librarians are often expert at helping job hunters, so plan to spend some time with the business reference librarian. Be specific. Tell the librarian what you want to accomplish. I always say, "The librarian is your friend." I personally love libraries (although I research on the Internet). I was a librarian in both high school and college. Get comfortable with the environment. Spend time using the reference books. Photocopy articles you can read at home.

Be prepared for the probability that the library will not look as it used to: many card catalogues have been replaced by computer terminals. If electronic information is a new technology for you, do not be intimidated. Ask for assistance. Computer-aided research will make your work immeasurably faster, easier, and more accurate. Let it work for you.

Basic Research

For most job hunts, you will need to **set aside at**

least two full days strictly for library research. If you are not sure of the industry you want to pursue, you may spend two days just researching industries (or professions). One of my favorite sources is the *Encyclopedia of Business Information Sources*. It lists topics, such as "oil" or "clubs" or "finance" or "real estate." Under each topic, it lists the most important sources of information on that topic: periodicals, books, and associations. Using this tool, you can quickly research any field in depth. You also may want to read the U.S. Department of Labor's reports on various industries or professions.

Once you have selected tentative industries, network to find out the buzzwords, and to refine your pitch. In addition, networking at this point may uncover other tentative targets, which you may simply add to your list of targets, or you may research them at this time.

While networking, you may find someone who will give you a list of people in that field—perhaps an association membership list. Or perhaps someone will invite you to an association meeting and you can get a list there. Otherwise, you could buy the subscriber list from a trade magazine. Or you may need to spend time in the library to gather the list of organizations. You may use an industry directory or the local business publication which provides listings of organizations.

I have had a lot of success using directories on CD-ROM databases. They cut my library time in half. By the way, don't let the term "database" intimidate or confuse you. Any collection of information with an organized arrangement can be called a database. Even your phone book could be considered a database, for that matter.

Taking Notes

If you are researching via computer, in most cases you can simply print out the lists of organizations you have selected along with relevant information. If you are not using a computer, use standard letter-size sheets to copy down the organization name, address, phone number, size (number of employees and sales), and other relevant information (such as business type if

you are not familiar with the organization). Then list the names and titles of all the people you think you may want to contact.

Make note of three to five people in larger organizations who are two levels higher than you are, and perhaps the names of one or two in smaller organizations. *Many* people in one organization may be in a position to hire or recommend you. In larger organizations, often the manager of one group has no idea that another manager may consider developing a new position or replacing someone.

If you are uncomfortable writing to all three to five people at once, write to one or two, wait for rejection letters, and then write to a few more. People listed in general directories have a lot of people writing to them because their names are so readily available. Therefore, you may use a targeted mailing, which takes more research per organization but increases the number of meetings you are likely to get.

In a smaller organization, such as one of two hundred people or less, the head is likely to know of all potential openings. Who is in charge of the job openings? The president? Perhaps the general manager? Note both names so you can write to both at once, or one first and the other later. Although names in smaller organizations are tougher to come by, these people don't get as many letters as people in larger organizations.

If you think you can work in many industries, get a sense of those that are growing and also fit your needs. Make a long list of the organizations that interest you. Call each one for an annual report or other literature (you can easily call thirty organizations in half an hour or so). Then find articles on each industry or organization.

Your effort is only as good as your list. (One job hunter had a list of sixty organizations. But most were out of state and he had no intention of relocating. Only eight were within his geographic target.)

Make sure your list contains organizations you are at least somewhat interested in. Then you'll know you are contacting eight good names—not sixty that aren't worth your time. If you know the real size of your target—and it is small—you

*Don't overlook the importance of worldwide thinking. A company that
keeps its eye on every Tom, Dick and Harry is going to miss
Pierre, Hans and Yoshio.*
Al Ries and Jack Trout, *Positioning: The Battle for Your Mind*

may decide to contact them with a different technique, such as a targeted mailing with a follow-up phone call.

What To Do With Your Lists

Armed with your list of organizations, you have lots of choices. If your target market is large, you may conduct a direct-mail campaign. Or you may divide up your list, do a direct mailing to sixty organizations, a targeted mailing to twenty (with follow-up phone calls), and network into a few. Or you could network around and ask for specific advice about the organizations on your list: which are the good ones, which ones seem right for me, could you recommend others, do you know the names of the people I should contact at these organizations, and may I use your name?

You can also get the names of organizations through magazine articles that cover certain industries, or through networking interviews with people who know that industry. You can "research" by going to meetings where the speaker or the attendees are people who should know people in your targeted area.

However you get the names of the people or organizations, try using a computer to access a few CD-ROM databases to obtain some more in-depth information. This will make your letters and/or networking meetings much more compelling. Which databases you use depends on the information you are seeking. In the next chapter you will find information on the most well-known—as well as on many obscure—automated, electronic tomes.

Where Else Can You Find Information?

• Personal observations. When you go for an interview, observe everything around you. What are the people like? What are they wearing? How well do they seem to get along?

Ask people: How do you like it here? How long have you worked here? Get there early. Ask everyone you see--the receptionist, people in the bathroom, the person who gets you coffee. This will give you a real feel for what it's like to work there, and will also let you know what the turnover rate is. If everyone says they've been there three or four months, you can be sure *you'll* be there only three or four months. Don't depend on the interviewer as your sole source of information.

• Associations. Associations are an important source of information. If you don't know anything at all about an industry or field, associations are often the place to start. They tend to be very helpful, and will assist you in getting the jargon down so you can use the language of the trade. *The Encyclopedia of Associations* lists a group for whatever you are interested in. If you are interested in the rug business, there's a related association.

Call them. If they have lots of local chapters, chances are there's one near you, and it will be a great place to network. Call the headquarters, and ask them to send you information and tell you the name of the person to contact in your area. Then call that person, and say you are interested in the association and would like to attend its next meeting. If there is no local chapter in your area, associations can still send you information.

Associations usually have membership directories, which they will sell you. They often publish trade magazines and newspapers that can update you on the business, for instance by noting the important issues facing the industry and telling who's been hired and who's moving. (Perhaps you should try to talk to the people you read about). They may even have a library or research department, or a PR person you can talk to. Often they sell books related to the field.

An association's annual convention is a very quick way to become educated in a field. These conventions are not cheap (they run from hundreds to thousands), but you will hear speakers on the urgent topics in the field, pick up literature, and meet lots of people.

Join an organization related to the field that interests you. Networking is expected. When you meet someone you think may help you, ask if you can meet on a more formal basis for about half an hour.

You can write to members, or network at meetings. If you want to contact them all, you can either continue to network or conduct a direct-mail campaign.

Associations are such an important source of information—especially about the jobs of the future—that they are covered in even greater detail in the next chapter.

• <u>The press</u>. Read newspapers with your target in mind, and you will see all kinds of things you would not otherwise have seen. Contact the author of an article in a trade magazine. Tell him or her how much you enjoyed the article and what you are trying to do, and ask to get together just to chat. I've made many friends this way.

• <u>Mailing lists</u> are not that expensive. You will pay perhaps $100 for several thousand names—selected by certain criteria, such as job title, level, industry, size of organization, and so on. You can rent lists from direct-mail houses or magazines. For example, one job hunter contacted a computer magazine and got the names and addresses by selected zip codes of organizations that owned a specific kind of computer. It was then easy for him to contact all of the organizations in his geographic area that could possibly use his skills.

• <u>Chambers of Commerce</u>. If you are doing an out-of-town job search, call them for a list of organizations in their area.

• <u>Universities</u> have libraries or research centers on fields of interest. A professor may be an expert in a field you are interested in. Contact him or her.

• <u>Networking</u> is a great research tool. At the beginning of your search, network with peers to find out about a field or industry. When you are really ready to get a job, network with people two levels higher than you are.

• <u>The Yellow Pages</u> is a useful source of organizations in your local area.

• <u>Databases</u>. A CD-ROM database is an organized arrangement of data that is contained on a compact disk. This is important because:

1. One disk can hold several volumes worth of printed material. For example, the *Encyclopedia of Associations* is comprised of thirteen volumes. That would fill a couple of bookshelves. However, all thirteen of these volumes are contained on *one* CD!

2. Information can be updated much more frequently on a CD. Publishers can and do release current information on a quarterly basis that is simply "down-loaded" onto a disk. Contrast this with print volumes that have to be reprinted and republished, which can take years. By the time that happens, the new information is often already out of date.

3. You can access and retrieve desired information in a fraction of a second when using CD technology. You simply type into the computer terminal the "key-word" you want to look up. Any information that contains that key-word is presented to you almost instantly. On the other hand, when you use printed works, the job of searching for specific pieces of related information can be very time-consuming.

• <u>The Internet</u> has become one of the most important research tools for a job search. It's use is covered in depth in *Getting Interviews*.

Get Sophisticated About Using Reference Materials

Research will result in your Personal Marketing Plan, which follows this chapter and which will guide you through your search. But you'll need more research to construct it. Wendy Alfus Rothman, a top career counselor, provides an in-depth examination of how to use specific research resources in all phases of your job search. Her actual case studies show how creative use of the dazzling array of reference works available today has helped real people make great career moves.

Personal Marketing Plan
Joe Doakes

Target Functions: **Vice President/Director/Manager**
- Management Information Services
- Applications Development
- Information Systems
- Information Systems Technology
- Systems Development
- Business Re-Engineering

Responsibilities:
- Identification of new information systems technologies and how they could affect the profitability of a company.
- Management of projects for the implementation of information systems or new technologies.
- Providing for and managing a business partner relationship between the information systems department and the internal company departments that utilize its services.
- Implementing and managing a business partner relationship between the company and its primary vendors and its customers utilizing systems technologies, such as EDI (Electronic Data Interchange).

Target Companies:

Attributes	Location
• People-oriented	• Primary - Northern New Jersey or Westchester/ Orange/Rockland Counties in New York
• Growth-minded through increased sales, acquisitions, or new products	• Secondary - New York City, Central New Jersey, Southern Connecticut, Eastern Pennsylvania
• Committed to quality customer service	• Other - Anywhere along the Eastern Seaboard
• Receptive to new ideas on how to do business or how to utilize new technologies	

Target Industries:

Consumer Products:	Pharmaceuticals:	Food/Beverage:	Chemicals:	Other:
Unilever	Merck	Pepsico	Castrol	Medco
Kimberly Clark	Schering-Plough	T.J. Lipton	Witco	Toys-R-Us
Avon	Warner-Lambert	Kraft/General Foods	Allied Chemical	Computer Associates
Carter Wallace	American Home Products	Nabisco	Olin Corp.	Becton Dickinson
Sony	Bristol-Myers Squibb	Hartz Mountain	Union Carbide	Dialogic
Minolta	Pfizer	Continental Baking	Air Products	Siemans
Boyle Midway	Jannsen Pharmaceutica	Nestle's	General Chemical	Automatic Data Proc.
Revlon	Hoffmann-LaRoche	Haagen-Dazs	Englehard Corp.	Vital Signs
L&F Products	Ciba-Geigy	Tuscan Dairies	BASF Corp.	Benjamin Moore
Houbigant	Sandoz	Dannon Co.	Degussa Corp.	
Mem	A.L. Laboratories	BSN Foods	GAF Corp.	
Chanel	Smith Kline Beecham	Campbell Soup	Lonza Inc.	
Airwick	American Cyanamid	Cadbury Beverages	Sun Chemical	
Church & Dwight	Boeringer Ingelheim	Labatt		
Johnson & Johnson	Roberts Pharmaceuticals	Arnold Foods		
Reckitt & Colman	Winthrop Pharmaceuticals	S.B. Thomas		
Philip Morris	Glaxo	Sunshine Biscuits		
Clairol	Block Drug			
Estee Lauder	Hoechst Celanese			
Cosmair	Ethicon			

Sample Personal Marketing Plan

Personal Marketing Plan
Jane Doe

Target Functions: **Vice President/Director/Manager**

• Marketing   • Strategic Planning   • New Business Development

Target Industry: #1 Carriers/Telecom	**Target Industry**: #2 Internet	**Target Industry**: #3 Online Finance	**Target Industry**: #4 Content/Media	**Target Industry**: #5 Information. etc.
Reasoning: Have industry experience. Growth likely, esp. wireless. Concern: That I get a pure marketing job.	**Reasoning:** To learn fast, if equity situation. Or be high up in a larger co. Overlap with other industries.	**Reasoning:** Related to my exp. Concern: There may be a separate area for the Net at larger cos.	**Reasoning:** I'm interested. Concerns: Nature of large cos. in it; the opportunity startups will have.	**Reasoning:** List of random affinities that can't be classfied elsewhere.
Sub-Targets: 1. Wireless/line carriers 2. Cable companies 3. Satellite cos.	**Sub-Targets:** 1. Content providers 2. Net-related startups 3. Convergence players 4. E-business	**Sub-Targets:** 1. Venture capital for addtl. contacts 2. Companies doing e-commerce	**Sub-Targets:** 1. Publishing 2. Data 3. E-commerce 4. Related cos.	**Sub-Targets:** 1. New product incubators 2. Information providers 3. Advertising
Company Names: Omnipoint ATT CellularSprint BT/MCI Cablevision Comcast Qwest Tel-Save Telligent RAM Mobile Data Metromedia Periphonics Brite Lucent AT&T Road Runner Iridium Globalstar Consat Community Tele. Geotek NTL PanAmSat Cellular Vision	**Company Names:** N2K Airmedia WebGenesis Gist Mercury 7 Multex e-Share GoAmerica Razorfish Juno Relevant Knowledge I-Pro PC Meter Nielsen Physicians Online IDT ICon BroadVision Firefly DoubleClick Burst! Commonwealth Net	**Company Names:** 1. Flatiron Partners Kleiner, Perkins, Caulfield D.E. Shaw Hambrecht & Quist 2. DLJ Bloomberg S&P Bridge Information ILX_Thomson SmithBarney Merrill 3. Other online financial companies	**Company Names:** ABC, NBC, CBS AOL Prodigy Dow Jones Reuters News Corp. Time Warner Cendant Find/SVP Advance Publ. Bertelsman CPC Ziff Davis Dow Jones EMI Forbes Harcourt General Hearst McGraw-Hill Polygram Primedia Readers Digest Reed Elsevier SONY Viacom Disney Washington Post	**Company Names:** 1. Idealab 2. Gartner Group Yankee Group Jupiter Comm/ Find/SVP Forrester research Giga Meta D&B McGraw Hill DM-related firms PC Meter/NPD 3. Yoyodyne Poppe Tyson Modem Media CKS Group Cortex I-traffic Margenotes SiteSpecific

The Start of Your "Internet Marketing Plan"—Target Industries

Want an Internet-related job? Research is your key. Use the chart below to kick-start your research. First select the industries you are interested in. Some may not appear on the chart, but remember that "the Internet" itself is not an industry because it's too broad. So choosing the Internet or even a general category such as interactive marketing, electronic commerce, or web-graphics would result in no direction that could result in research. We want Five O'Clock Clubbers to define their sub-targets and then specific companies or projects within companies that have an interactive basis.

Then **develop your own chart**—with your own sub-targets and lots of companies—in your targeted geographic areas—that you have never even heard of before. That's the nature of research.

Take a look at the "Positions" on the next page and see where you might fit in. Finally, calculate the total number of positions you are chasing. Aim for 200.

Industry	Website Development	Financial	Online Retail	Other Industry Specialties		New Media	
Company Names or Categories	• outside shops 51% - VSI - Tenagra - The Online Ad Agency - CyberSight - Webvertising - Doubleclick • internal web development at large orgs. - 25% • Adv. Agencies - 24% - see below	• Brokerage Firms, such as Schwab • Other financial service providers • real-time trades, such as Chicago Board of Trade • etrade.com • Motley Fool • Edgar • others	• books: -Amazon.com • retailers: - Netmarket • travel: - BizTravel - Preview • computers: - onsale.com - dell.com • autos: autobytel.com • real estate: - Owners.com • clothing • music	• Healthcare: - Physicians Online - Medscape • "Channels" at AOL • sports e.g., Sportsline • Online fax • Stock photos • Foreign Bus. • Bus. to Bus. • Population Segments: - Thirdage.com - Children's products	• Telephone Directories - Switchboard - Four11.com • Job Search - Monster • probably whatever industry you are in	• Networks (CBS, NBC, ABC, Fox) • Cable (HBO, MS-NBC, CNN, etc.) • Print Magazines Newspapers • Viacom Interactive Media • Fortune.com • Newscorp/ MCI On-line Ventures	• Bolt, Beranek & Newman • Avalanche Systems • Modem Media • Neographic • Tom Nicholson Co. • Entertainment e.g., Disney, Universal Studios • others
Industry	Browsers/ Search Engines	Advertising Agencies	Credit Card	Consulting	Telecommuni- cations	Technology	Information Service Providers
Company Names or Categories	• Alta-Vista • Yahoo! • Excite • Netscape • Lycos • InfoSeek • Hot Bot • others	• Bronner Schossberg • Poppe Tyson • Chiat/Day • Saatchi & Saatchi • Deutsch • Grey Interactive • Ogilvy One • others	• Amex • Mastercard • VISA • others	• AT&T Solutions • Mercer Mgmt. • ISS Corp. • The Diamond Group • Advanced Tech American Mgmt.Systems • Hubbell Center for Advanced Mgmt Tech	• AT&T • Viacom • MCI • Web to phones • I-Phone • others	• IBM • Apple • Sun Micro-systems • Cambridge Technology • others	• Standard & Poors • Dun & Bradstreet • Dow Jones • First Data Corp. • Bloomberg • others
Industry	Intranets	Research	Internet Effectiveness	Venture Capital	Legal	Internet Service Providers	
Company Names or Categories	• IBM • PointCast • Internal Intranets at large compa-nies, hospi-tals, etc.	• KPMG • ActivMedia • Nielsen • Vanguard • Forrester • Gartner • Jupiter	• Relevant Knowledge • I-Pro • PC Meter	• General Atlantec • Summit • Hummer Winblad • Keystone • Flatiron	• Morrison & Foerster • others	• AOL • Prodigy • Microsoft Network • others	

Over the past ten years, about 1 million factory jobs have disappeared from the manufacturing sector. But at the same time, Wall Street, the movie business, and the computer software and services industry have created about 1 million new jobs. The momentum of the economy is creating an intense demand for educated and creative individuals who can contribute to the growth of the economy.
Michael Mandel, The High-Risk Society

More on Seeking an Internet-Related Job ...

Targeted Geographic Areas and Positions

A target consists of an industry, position and geographic area. Patricia Raufer wrote, "There are many opportunities, especially for smart job searchers willing to do two things: Follow the Five O'Clock Club methodology and research the Information Highway in depth." None of the Five O'Clock Clubbers in this article had any interactive or Internet job experience before they landed their jobs. "These people got jobs—not because they knew the industry inside-out after working in it for five years—but because they did what the Five O'Clock Club always tells career changers to do: Read. Network. Join organizations and attend meetings. Show how your skills can be transferred."

Geographic area: Until now, most of the new media job growth has been in San Francisco, New York, Seattle, Austin and Boston, with Los Angeles joining in.

However, as companies start to see interactivity as part of their everyday business processes, more jobs—especially intranet efforts—will be found in firms in all parts of the country.

Positions: The positions or functions you can perform in Internet-related industries depend on your background, what you want to do, and the industry you are targeting. (Technical positions are described on the next page.) Positions include:

Standard corporate functions: such as chief financial officer, accounting, administration, human resources, training, legal, strategic planning, operations management, public relations, MIS, and so on.

Marketing-oriented functions—because companies want to make money. At Website development companies, account representatives handle relationships with major corporate clients. At companies that sell banners or other advertising, ad sales is an important function. Other marketing-related positions could include marketing strategy, promotion, packaging, interactive database marketing, fulfillment, customer service (can be very large), customer lifecycle profitability marketing, and . . . you name it.

Creative and content development includes content experts (for an industry you happen to know about, such as financial services or healthcare), project managers, producers (just like film production, except Internet production), traffic, graphic designers, copywriters, editors, journalists, researchers, and audio and video technicians.

Intranets: Don't forget the large and growing target of Intranets—companies using the interactive media internally. They need corporate trainers and writers as well as systems people.

The deeper you probe, the richer an industry becomes. Just as computers now affect virtually every person in every industry, so too will interactive technology. You can see how vast its impact will be. Therefore, the key to your search is research and a deeper understanding of what is happening.

Total up the number of positions you are targeting in all of your targeted industries.
The Five O'Clock Club formula is that your search should target 200 positions.

Some of the industries in which wages have grown the fastest in recent years are the ones that are successful in the global market, such as entertainment and software. In manufacturing, a factory engaged in making products for export pays its workers 7 to 11 percent more, on average, than a similar factory producing for domestic consumption only.

Michael Mandel, *The High-Risk Society*

Five O'Clock Clubber Anne Dewey's model for the
Three Main Types of Technical Jobs
increasing in complexity and technical requirements

<u>Box 1</u> — **These are the "html-type" jobs** related to everything the user actually sees on the computer screen: graphics, design, copywriting, editing functions, etc. Working at this level requires fewer technical skills, but some utility with software programs. This is the creative end of interactive and Anne notes that fine arts majors, designers, artists and writers are often most appropriate for these kinds of jobs.

<u>Box 2</u> — **This is the "middle-ware" ground**, where the pathways, interrelationships and connections within the Website and contacts to other sites are designed, constructed, supported and maintained. These jobs may require more experience and some training, but much of it can still be "on the job" and Anne believes that middle-ware is where the bulk of interactive opportunities are today.

<u>Box 3</u> — **This is the back-end, complex and technical side** of interactive systems, really the realm of Cobol and other highly skilled levels of programmers. It is also here that large "legacy systems" reside. These are a company's major databases, such as customer profiles, marketing data, employee records, even airline flight schedules. Often information in these databases originated in 25-to-30-year-old mainframe computers. That data must now be converted or adapted through complex programming to be accessible to and meaningful with today's systems. Companies invest significant sums in quality maintenance of their legacy systems because this is where their most valuable data reside. For obvious reasons, credit card companies have perfected the use and maintenance of their legacy systems.

Where to start your investigation of the Interactive Marketplace

<u>Publications to read:</u>
- Internet and online services publications:
  - Wilsonweb.com for marketing
  - www.wwac.org for artists
  - www.siliconalley.com for industry gossip
- *Wired, Silicon Valley Reporter, Online, Fast Company, New Media Magazine, AlleyCat News, Web Magazine; Inter@ctive Week;* and the Monday *New York Times* Business section.

<u>Books to read:</u>
- *The 500-Year Delta* by J. Taylor/W. Wacker
- *The Internet Unleashed* by Jill Ellsworth

<u>Groups to join:</u>
- NY New Media Assoc. (NYNMA.org)
- New media associations in other cities
- The technical committee of your industry organization

<u>Events to attend:</u>
(research to find out what is going on in your geographic area)
- New York New Media's Cybersuds
- MIT Enterprise Forum
- Trade shows

Always remember—as you go out to seek your fortune, your fame, your fulfillment
—always remember that it's not who you know in this world that counts, it's whom.
Osborn Elliott, Dean emeritus of Columbia's Journalism School

Position Yourself Better on Your Résumé

To break into the Internet, highlight what you *do* know about the Internet. Play up the freelance or volunteer work you have done and the Internet courses you have taken, rather than focusing on your most recent job—unless it was Internet-related. Do not present yourself as an outsider trying to get in. It takes so little to become an insider! Here are modified excerpts from one Five O'Clock Clubber's "before" and "after" summary statements.

Profile

Creative Executive specializing in the publishing and new media industries. Expertise in bringing ideas and talent together to create commercially successful, high quality products. Developed and managed a wide variety of projects that consistently came in on time and within budget.

Career History

> **3-line "Before" Summary**

International Media, Inc. 1996-present
Creative Consultant
Responsible for creating and designing characters and concepts to be used for television programming and Internet service.

Plutonium Entertainment Company
Editor-in-Chief,

and so on.

> **"After" Summary**

Creative Executive
specializing in the new media and entertainment industries
with more than 20 years' experience in:

- Product Development   • Project Management   • Content Development

- **Content Provider**: For **Internet** company providing commercial video search engine service, developed characters and concepts for corporate branding.

- **WebSite Developer**: For **on-line community/retail Website**, creating content, a marketing strategy and interactive game.

- **Brand Director**: As **Editor-in-Chief of Pluto Group**, Plutonium Entertainment, oversaw the **#1 best-selling comic-book character** in the country, producing **annual revenues of $46 million**.

- **Product Innovator**: As Creative Director, Porter and Sklark, initiated and developed new product category, producing wholesale grosses of **$90 million** over 5-year period.

Team leader and troubleshooter with proven ability to bring together ideas and talent
to create imaginative, commercially successful, high-quality products.

The Five O'Clock Club®

Research Resources for an Effective Job Search

by Wendy Alfus Rothman

Wisdom is the principal thing; therefore get wisdom: and with all thy getting get understanding. Exalt her, and she shall promote thee: she shall bring thee to honour, when thou dost embrace her.
Proverbs 4: 7-8

If you are like most job hunters, you may have gotten stuck in one or more parts of your job search. You are probably wishing for some magic potion to get you moving again, and in a more productive way.

Research can be the answer. Try to set aside the common notion that research sounds tedious and boring. This is why most people skip it. But they are missing out. You will be at a great advantage if you learn to use this most valuable tool.

Maybe you need help in targeting the right field or industry: you already know what you do well, but you can't turn that information into targets.

Or maybe you need help setting up informational meetings: you just don't know what to say to people that doesn't sound like "job begging." (You know what job begging is: it's when you call your contacts intending to sound intelligent, low-key, and professional, and you end up saying, "So do you know of *any* job openings that might be good for me?")

Or perhaps you wish you were better prepared for a meeting so that you could feel confident in your ability to differentiate yourself and rise above your competition. Perhaps you are not sure how to follow up after an interview in order to keep the process moving along.

Whatever phase of the search cycle you are in (phase 1: defining targets and organizations within those targets; phase 2: interviewing; or phase 3: negotiating and closing), it's highly likely that you wish you had fresh questions to ask others, and fresh answers to the same old questions others ask you.

That is exactly what research is all about. It is the fastest way to turn a mediocre job search into a powerful, proactive campaign. It gives you the information that drives your search to its destination. It will magnify the results of each step of the job-search process. It is the way to get unstuck from a stalled or stagnating search. (And research can help you keep your job once you have it!)

There are two kinds of research: primary and secondary. Primary research basically means

The will to persevere is often the
difference between failure and success.
David Sarnoff, *Wisdom of Sarnoff and the World of RCA*

talking to people. Secondary research means reading materials in print, wherever those materials happen to be—in the library for example, or on the Internet. You need to do both kinds. It is usually wise to do some secondary research before you start talking to people so that your questions are more intelligent and focused.

If you take the time to do this, you will feel more confident and empowered, and people will respond better. If you are a person who prefers book work to people work, be careful that you do not spend all your time reading. And be careful of the time you spend surfing the Internet, as we point out in the chapter that follows this one. While the Internet is a fast, robust, and basically extraordinary resource, it can also be seductively distracting. In the next chapter, we give you guidelines that will keep you focused during your Internet research sessions. Use the Internet wisely!

Regardless of where the information comes from, use it in your conversations with people who can move you closer to your goal of obtaining the job that is right for you.

The biggest problem in doing secondary research is that there is so much information available. And there are a multitude of ways to access the information, from the traditional to the futuristic. So if you are not yet technically able … do not panic and do not use that as an excuse for not doing research. People did research long before an Internet was around, let alone frequently used. There are plenty of places for you to get information that you need. So go get it and go get online as well!

There are reference books, directories and guides, trade journals and newspapers, CD-ROM databases, online databases and electronic information transfer. The task can seem overwhelming. In fact, the real challenge lies not in finding data but in mining through it all to find what is relevant and knowing how to use it.

But it doesn't have to be so daunting. You can systematically move through the process, beginning with obtaining big-picture industry information, then moving on to organization information, then on to job and salary information.

Start by identifying what you want to know. Each stage of the job-search process has its own set of questions, and therefore its own corresponding research tools. Let's begin at the beginning.

PHASE 1:
Identifying Targets

In Phase 1 of a job search, you are trying to identify industry targets. First, you do a skills assessment to analyze what you do well and what you like to do.

Then the idea is to turn that knowledge into something that is useful to your search campaign.

Many people get stuck here for a time. Hoping and praying (a popular technique) won't get you unstuck. What *will* get you unstuck is gathering relevant information to help you make a systematic decision.

Here is the information you should be looking for when selecting industry targets:

1) trends and future prospects in a particular industry;

2) areas of growth and decline in that industry;

3) the kinds of challenges the industry faces that could utilize your skills;

4) the "culture" of the industry;

5) the major- medium- and minor- league organizations in the industry.

In the bibliography at the back of this book, you will find many sources for answering these questions. One or more of them will work for you.

After you get the information, you can begin to determine whether or not you are in sync with a particular industry and whether or not there is a place for you there. It does not require an enormous amount of time and data to begin to address these questions. You really only need a little bit of information, but it has to be the *right* little bit.

One of the first things I suggest to my clients, who are not online capable, is that they go to the library (almost any library will do for this), and look through **The Encyclopedia of Associations**, published by Gale Research in Detroit, Michigan. This encyclopedia lists a staggering total of

22,000 associations that represent trade and industry groups.

Every industry and almost every niche within that industry are represented here. Thus it is an incredible way to brainstorm possible industry targets. You really begin to get a sense of what you don't know, and what you could find out.

In addition to stimulating fresh ideas, the encyclopedia also provides names of contacts and chief officers, addresses of headquarters, phone numbers, the number of members and chapters, special committees and departments, a description of membership, and the aims and activities of the group.

The people who are listed here are people who normally welcome your inquiries—otherwise they wouldn't have their names in the encyclopedia! They are often more than helpful if you phone and ask them to share some information about their industry.

Also listed in the encyclopedia are publications that are a terrific source of information. They can introduce you to industry jargon, issues of importance, authors of significance in the field, and organizations that are making news. They also usually have their own section of classified ads that do not typically appear in newspapers.

Another thing that is valuable from this resource is that most associations publish a four-year convention schedule that you can call and request. These schedules include an explanation of panel-discussion groups and conference workshops. They give a sense of what topics have been important in an industry over the past few years.

You can also take note of who led the discussions and workshops, thereby discovering who plays or played a role in shaping the industry. **This resource should not be overlooked!**

If you are Internet ready, I suggest going to any of the industry-related links listed in the attached bibliography. Remember that the Internet resources change constantly, so if these links are not always available do not despair. They will guide you to others. And right now, my most favorite site for industry information and company information is Vault.Com. So I'll share a bit of information about them before I continue with real life examples of research savvy job seekers.

Vault.Com

I met with one of the founders, Mark Oldman. His passion for providing the inside scoop about work and work life is clear. Vault.Com is a career information company that is dedicated to letting job seekers know what life is like at the nation's big-name employers. VaultReports produces Employer Profiles, which are insider guides on more than 1500 companies and over 60 industries. In addition, they publish a Vault Report Industry Guides book series including guides to High Tech, Management Consulting, Investment Banking, Top Law Firms, Media and Entertainment and dozens more. They are listed in the appropriate sections of the attached bibliography in this book. The Website supports this vision, but the firm is truly content-driven, and the integrity and sincerity of their data is what makes them so valuable. A full third of the staff at Vault.Com is dedicated to editorial content. After all, the information you read only matters if it is accurate and properly researched. And in the case of Vault, it is. The content of their volumes is downloadable from their Website, and their online ordering is also easy to use.

Another innovation from Mark and his partners, H.S. and brother Samer Hamadeh, is the electronic message board appropriately called the Electronic Water Cooler. There are over 1000 company- and industry-specific message boards that allow employees to share information about what it's like to work in a company or industry, and allows people to pose questions as well. Within its launch in 1999, they gathered more than 10,000 messages in a matter of months.

Two more services include: Vault Job Board, which is a free online job listing service, and VaultMatch, which is a proprietary online recruitment service that collects customized profiles of job seekers and matches them with job openings at leading companies.

Additionally, Vault has created partnerships with other career resources through links—all of which provide services to help round out research for job seekers. These include links to career experts, to other research sources like Hoovers, and to other book offerings related to job search to name but a few.

Mark and his partners will continue to develop new products and offerings, because they listen to their constituency and they truly care about providing career information that is pointed, accurate, and really helpful to the job seeker at all levels.

There are many other ways to obtain big-picture information as well. In the following section, we'll take a look at some examples of real-life situations. The people we have highlighted happened *not* to use Internet resources. It doesn't matter—the process is exactly the same. Learn from what they learned, and learn *how* to learn a facile job-search process. It's a great time to be in the job market—the world belongs to Talent!

CASE STUDY: THOMAS
Turning an Assessment into a Target

Many people don't even know what they don't know. After seventeen years as a very successful human-resources executive in government administration, Thomas thought he wanted to target the health-care industry, but he didn't really know much about it. He just knew that it was an important growth industry of the nineties. He figured that hospitals were large bureaucracies, similar to government agencies. Therefore he thought he would at least fit into the culture.

After doing an assessment, he realized that, ironically, one of the reasons he wanted to leave his job in the first place was that he actually didn't like working for a large bureaucracy. Now he really didn't know what to do. Rather than helping him, he felt that his assessment had limited his options.

He had learned that he was happiest when he was helping and directing people. He had also discovered that he wanted to work for a smaller organization, but he had absolutely no idea what to do with this insight.

He decided to do some research. He went to a reference book called **The Encyclopedia of Medical Organizations and Agencies.** This directory lists more than 12,200 organizations and agencies and has 69 subject chapters.

Glancing through the Table of Contents, Thomas realized that health care didn't mean just big hospitals. It could also mean HMO administration, biotechnology, environmental medicine, reproductive medicine, elder care, substance abuse and corporate employee-assistance programs, sports medicine, or many other areas.

By realizing what he hadn't known, he was able to begin to more clearly define his target. And this was just from reading a Table of Contents!

Next, Thomas discovered CD-ROM (Compact Disk Read-Only-Memory) databases. These disks contain highly topical and specialized information that one can access in a fraction of the time it would take to access the same material in its printed form.

The one Thomas chose was **CD Plus/Health.** It is an index to the nonclinical aspects of health-care delivery. These include administration and planning of health-care facilities, health insurance, personnel, HMOs, and related topics. Data are supplied from the National Library of Medicine, the American Hospital Association, and the printed Hospital Literature Index.

As Thomas learned more about the industry, he realized that Employee Assistance Programs (EAPs) are often set up as a business service to corporations through insurance companies. They operate as small business units, while being part of a larger organization—exactly the environment he had been looking for.

Thomas' human-resources and administrative skills would be transferable to these programs, and EAPs would definitely allow him to make a difference in people's lives.

The crisis consists precisely in the fact that the old is dying and the new cannot be born. In this interregnum, a great variety of morbid symptoms appear.
Antonio Gramsci

Thomas had found a viable industry target that had both appeal and promise for his personality and background.

CASE STUDY: JOAN
Clarifying Her Career Direction

Joan was six years into her career as an attorney, fulfilling her parents' dream and what she had once thought was her dream as well. However, the twelve-hour days and six- to seven-day work weeks were taking their toll. She decided she wanted a change. Like many people, all Joan knew was what she *didn't* want to do. She did some research to alleviate her confusion.

First she browsed through the **U.S. Industrial Outlook.** This is a U.S. Department of Commerce publication that analyzes recent trends and forecasts for over 350 manufacturing and service industries. It is available in both printed and CD-ROM form.

It offers concise industry overviews, assesses international competitiveness, ranks the ten fastest- and ten slowest-growing manufacturing industries, lists trends in selected service industries, and projects the growth rates for 156 manufacturing industries and groups.

Joan also browsed through **Standard and Poor's Industry Surveys.** This reference book is updated quarterly. It consists of two volumes of up-to-date data for all major domestic industries. Prospects for a particular industry are followed by a historical presentation of trends and problems for that industry. Tables and charts accompany the text. Sales, earnings, and market data for the leading companies in an industry are provided.

As Joan researched, she read more and more about the high-technology industry. She began to see how much she had already known about this industry but had always taken for granted. And she realized how much she liked it. She had used many computer systems throughout her education, and continued to use them for her legal research and preparation of briefs.

She continued her secondary research, using the **ICP Software Directory** on CD-ROM. It is a directory with descriptions of more than 15,000 publicly available business-applications software from over 5,000 vendors for microcomputers, minicomputers, and mainframes. It also includes proprietary software products and vendor-contact information.

It became clear to Joan that the software industry was consolidating, with a great deal of acquisition activity. Her legal experience had been in the area of corporate acquisitions.

Research had helped Joan see a great opportunity to use this legal background as a launching pad to enter the arena of high-technology.

Expanding Your Targets and Identifying Organizations

Once you select an industry, you need to make sure that there are enough organizations within that industry to warrant the efforts of an entire campaign. For example, if you find that there are only five small organizations in your area, you will know before you begin that the odds are not in favor of your success.

Too many people get frustrated during their job search, thinking that they are doing something wrong, when the simple fact is that they do not have enough organizations in their target.

If you see that your target is limited, you can make sure that your expectations are realistic. Instead of being depressed that your campaign isn't producing results, expand your target.

Expanding your target usually means identifying more than just the big organizations that everyone else is targeting. It means identifying the mid-size and smaller ones—in fact, they are the ones that usually do most of the hiring.

This does more than expand your search; it also helps you understand each organization's competitive position. Often this is actually more than the people working in the organizations know. Sometimes they are so busy doing their jobs that they don't have time to stay current in their own industries!

After doing this kind of research, you become

a person with valuable information to share, rather than just another person looking for a job (remember job begging?). Here are some questions appropriate at this point in your research with regard to each organization on your list:

1) How large is this organization?
2) Who owns it?
3) How long has it been in business?
4) What are its major products or services?
5) How many employees work there?
6) What are the revenues of the organization?
7) How many branches does it have, and where are they located?
8) How many divisions are there, and which are the most profitable?
9) What are the names of the people that would be in a position to hire me?

Once you can answer these questions, you can prioritize the organizations in your target as: most likely, possible, or long shots.

You can begin to strategize how to approach them for interviews: some through networking, some through direct contact and letter campaigns, some through search firms and headhunters, maybe some by answering ads.

You can see that without an extensive list of organizations in your target industry, it would be extremely difficult to have six to ten things in the works. With the list, your problem may well be which six to ten things to pick first.

CASE STUDY: SARAH
Better Networking Through Research

Sarah worked for a major cosmetics firm. She loved her job and the industry, but due to some internal politics, she decided she needed to change companies. She knew lots of people to call for networking.

When she called them, she would ask them if they knew of any job openings. They invariably told her no. Sarah grew more and more uncomfortable at the prospect of picking up the phone.

Instead, she went to **Ward's Business Directory of U.S. Private and Public Companies**. It profiles 100,000 companies and details their vital statistics. A special feature of Ward's Directory is

that it includes companies with relatively small sales volumes.

The directory has information on private as well as public companies. It offers a ranking of companies, small to large, by sales volume within an industry.

All this gave Sarah a quick way to find a company's competitive place among its peers, and to target even further.

As she researched, Sarah realized how little she knew about other firms in her own industry—especially smaller ones. Using Ward's Directory, she was able to construct a list of ten mid-size cosmetics and health/beauty product firms that she felt were poised for growth.

Now when she called her network contacts, she asked their opinions about the viability of those firms. In addition to being impressed that she had done her homework, her friends knew something about the companies she had identified. They had opinions about which ones would fly and which ones would not. These friends were even able to introduce her to some people in several of the companies she had highlighted.

She learned what she needed to know. She never once had to ask about a specific job opening. Thus she eliminated the embarrassment that she used to feel in her networking.

Research was an empowering experience for Sarah. It enabled her to jump-start a stalled campaign.

PHASE 2:
Preparing for the Interview

One of the biggest errors job seekers make is not properly preparing for the interview. They read the books that give you "answers to difficult interview questions." But the problem is that everyone else has read those same books—including the people interviewing you!

It's pretty simple—the more you know about an organization's issues and objectives prior to interviewing with them, the better prepared you will be and the better able to answer any question.

Most job seekers are busy worrying about

The ability to learn faster than your competitors may be the only sustainable competitive advantage.
Arie P. de Geus, *Harvard Business Review*, March/April, 1988

their own issues and objectives. Be smart: focus on the problems of this particular organization. After all, the reason a manager hires someone is that he or she believes that that person can help the firm in some specific way.

The manager is only interested in your issues if they provide evidence of your ability to solve organization problems. This is true whether you are a receptionist or a CEO.

CASE STUDY: GARY
Becoming an Insider

Gary was interviewing at a major consumer-products company for a position as an organizational psychologist in the staffing area. This company was embarking on an enormous project to set up assessment centers to identify high-potential employees for succession planning.

Gary knew next to nothing about assessment centers, but he knew he had better change that situation fast. So off he went to the library.

He used a CD-ROM database called **ABI/Inform**. Updated monthly, it indexes and abstracts 800 business and management journals appearing world-wide. These publications cover a wide variety of topics, including management, accounting, finance, economics, advertising, labor relations, and real estate.

Gary keyed in assessment centers. Up came a synopsis of all the articles that have been written about the subject for the past three years. Within thirty minutes, Gary became something of an expert on the history of assessment centers.

He learned about who first used them, their strengths and weaknesses, the "gurus" of the field, and what directions assessment centers will move in over the next few years. He learned the lingo, the history, and the players.

When Gary went back for his third interview, he ended up interviewing with *seventeen* people in that one day. Someone even followed him into the bathroom to keep the interview going! He won them all over with his expertise in the matter of assessment centers. The decision to

offer him a job was unanimous.

PHASE 3:
Negotiating and Closing Deals

CASE STUDY: JENNIFER
Finding Out What She's Worth

Jennifer had been a marketing manager for a tobacco company for a few years. When the company restructured, she lost her job. She had spent a lot of personal time doing volunteer work as a lobbyist for an association. This led her to decide that she wanted to become a lobbyist for a corporation as her next career move.

Initially she had no idea how to find out about these positions. She did not even know that corporations call lobbyists "government-relations representatives." She learned it by reading through **The American Lobbyists Directory**. It lists 57,000 lobbyists and 25,000 organizations, complete with contact information and phone numbers.

Through this resource, Jennifer was able to identify companies in her target, and generate interviews with many of them. These interviews went well and her follow-up was great. In fact, she was about to get three offers. However, one major topic had not yet been addressed: salary.

Jennifer had deliberately avoided this issue, waiting until the companies knew they wanted her. Now she was at the point where she couldn't stall them any longer. Her problem was that she had absolutely no idea what market rates were for these positions, and she knew she couldn't negotiate without this critical knowledge.

Immediately Jennifer went to the library and got a copy of the **American Salaries and Wages Survey.** It answers salary questions for more than 4,500 occupational classifications at different experience levels, as well as for different areas of the country. She was able to find out salary ranges for her industry, her position, and her geographic location.

Jennifer wanted still more. She went to the

Encyclopedia of Associations and got the names of four different associations that deal with government-relations people and lobbyists. She called them and explained what information she was seeking.

The associations were able either to tell her salary standards or put her in touch with people in their local chapters who could.

When Jennifer went in for her salary-negotiation interviews, she knew the market rates, the highs and lows, and what she could reasonably request. With this information, she was able to negotiate the most attractive package.

Using Research Throughout the Campaign Process

Your research techniques may change as your campaign evolves. It is possible that you will only need to do a little bit of investigative work before you land a new position. On the other hand, you may find yourself returning again and again to resources that enrich all the stages of your job search.

CASE STUDY: SHELLEY
Uncovering Options for a Career Change

Shelley had spent eight years as a financial analyst in a major brokerage firm on Wall Street. He liked financial analysis, but didn't really like the options for career growth within the brokerage industry.

After doing an assessment, he decided that he wanted to position himself for growth within a mid-size corporation, with the goal of becoming CFO. Shelley thought he would try to target something within the environmental area. However, he didn't know very much about it and was pretty sure that he wouldn't have enough qualifications to break in. So he stayed where he was, feeling trapped in his career.

After some counseling, Shelley realized that he needed to do research to learn more about his target industry. He consulted two reference books.

The first was **The U.S. Industrial Outlook,**

also available in a CD-ROM version. It has reports and prospects for over 350 manufacturing and service industries, and is put out by the U.S. Department of Commerce on an annual basis. It analyzes trends and presents forecasts for hundreds of industries. Data are given in both narrative and tabular forms. A list of additional references is included at the end of each chapter.

The second reference book was **The Environmental Industries Marketplace**, also published by Gale Research. It gives detailed information on companies in the industry. Together, these books helped to break down this $100-billion market into its component parts.

Shelley quickly realized that his target was too big. He would have to pick from among the many areas these two books identified. Before, he had thought, "The environment is for me." Now he learned that much of the industry wasn't for him.

For example, he discovered that his skills might not be transferable to areas dealing with controlling abuses, such as air and noise pollution or hazardous waste. He could more clearly see opportunity for himself working with organizations that provide services to the environmental industry, such as consulting, research or financial services. They related to his experience in financial research and analysis from his days on Wall Street.

Now Shelley had identified a target and specific organizations within that target. He knew what he wanted, but he also knew that he would be perceived as an outsider by those in a position to hire him.

Using **The Encyclopedia of Associations,** he was able to contact two industry groups that sent him their newsletters. Reading through these, he learned the jargon, the hot issues and the major trends.

Shelley began to network. As he did, people referred him to organizations that might actually hire him. It was time to prepare for interviews.

He wished he could just wave a magic wand and know everything that had been written about the organizations he was interested in over the past few years. He wished he could just browse through their annual reports, but that would take so long, and his first interview was in just two days . . .

Off to the library! Shelley used **ABI/Inform**, mentioned before, and **Business Periodicals On Disc**. BPOD combines the ABI/Inform database of article references and abstracts of more than 800 business and management periodicals with the ability to view or print the complete text from many of the periodicals. It is updated monthly, and covers from 1987 up to the present.

He also used the **National Newspaper Index**. It offers combined in-depth indexing of five major newspapers: *The New York Times, The Wall Street Journal, The Christian Science Monitor, The Washington Post,* and *The Los Angeles Times.* It covers the most recent four years, and is updated monthly.

After only about thirty minutes, he had practically the next-best thing to that magic wand: a powerful synopsis of the past three years' worth of press about the organizations he would be interviewing with.

As far as the annual report and financial information were concerned, he just had to plug into **Corporate Text**. It provides copies of annual reports for companies traded on the NYSE, AMEX, NASDAQ, and OTC, and is updated monthly.

He also used **LaserDisclosure**. It is a full text database of exact reproductions of original SEC filings, including graphs and photographs, from more than 6,000 companies traded on the NASDAQ, OTC, AMEX, and NYSE. It is updated weekly.

So throughout the job-search phases, Shelley used research tools to keep moving forward. He armed himself with enough information to be sincere, informed, and competitive in the growth industry of his choice.

CASE STUDY: JONATHAN
Searching for the Small Private Company

Jonathan was a human-resources manager who specialized in staffing and succession plan-

ning at a major bank. After twenty years there, he accepted an early-retirement package, but was not yet ready to leave the workforce.

After analyzing his options, he decided he wanted to be in a much smaller company. He investigated the future of human-resources and staffing issues and concluded that temporary services/interim staffing was a good target.

He knew lots of people in the industry—they had been his vendors at the bank! He thought he wouldn't have any problems networking around to find a great job with a small growth firm.

After five or six calls, he realized that he wasn't getting anywhere talking to the people he knew. Without realizing it, he sounded arrogant and inappropriate. He would ask, "Don't you think I would be a great addition to your industry, with all my connections and knowledge?" Although he didn't know why, he did notice that his contacts were not particularly impressed.

Jonathan needed to do some research. First he went to **The Encyclopedia of Business Information Sources**. It is a bibliographic guide to more than 21,000 citations, covering over 1,000 subjects of interest to business personnel.

This resource includes: abstracting and indexing services, almanacs and yearbooks, bibliographies, biographical sources, directories, encyclopedias and dictionaries, financial ratios, handbooks and manuals, online databases, periodicals and newsletters, price sources, research centers and institutes, statistics sources, trade associations and professional societies. It too is published by Gale Research, Inc.

In it, Jonathan found that a firm called Kennedy Publications in New Hampshire publishes a list of temporary-service companies and their areas of specialization. He sent away for it.

He became knowledgeable about the differences between international, national, regional, and independent firms. He also learned the differences between managed services, outsourcing, payrolling, and employee leasing.

He decided that a regional service would probably be the most likely to need someone at his level. He only found five in that category, and that was not enough.

To see if he could expand his target, he went through **Dun & Bradstreet's Million Dollar Directory.** It has information on some 160,000 U.S. businesses that have indicated net worths of more than $500,000.

Still, he was only able to get another five names. He thought perhaps the companies he was interested in were too small and/or private and therefore not in these reference materials. So he tried the **MacMillan Directory of Leading Private Companies.** It has information on over 12,500 companies and wholly owned subsidiaries with sales of $10,000,000.

He also looked through the **Over the Counter 1,000 Yellow Book.** It has the leading growth companies quoted on NASDAQ. It is a comprehensive directory introducing leading, younger growth companies in the U.S.A. It provides the addresses, phone numbers, and titles of 20,000 executives who manage these smaller companies on the cutting edge of innovation.

He also used the **Small Business Sourcebook.** It is a guide to sources of information furnished by associations, consultants, educational programs, government agencies, franchisers, trade shows and venture-capital firms for 100 types of small businesses.

After all that research, he decided that he should include some national firms as well, in order to expand his target. If he included firms that franchised and firms that were international, but not yet operating on American soil, that brought his total number to 55.

Jonathan next used **Gale Globalaccess: Associations.** It provides information on non-profit membership organizations of international, U.S., regional, state, or local interest.

This resource includes professional societies, labor unions, and cultural and religious organizations. From it, Jonathan got the names of four associations and five trade journals. He spoke to people who belonged to NATS (National Association of Temporary Services) and he read appropriate literature.

Now that he understood the issues more clearly, he felt confident enough to try networking once again. Instead of bragging about his connections, he was able to talk about industry problems and how he would tackle them.

He impressed his contacts with his preparation and insight. It even appeared that he knew plenty of competitive information and trends that these same people wanted to hear about.

Because of the relationships that he developed at this stage of his job search, he eventually was introduced to the company he would end up working for.

CASE STUDY: MARRISSA
Researching the International Market

Marrissa had just returned from overseas, where she had been living and working as a personal assistant to the U.S. ambassador in an Eastern European country. She came back to the States for personal reasons, and needed to find a job. She was fluent in several languages and knowledgeable about diverse cultures.

She wanted to remain a personal assistant to a high-level executive. However, she didn't know where to start investigating corporate opportunities that would value her cross-cultural background without requiring a tremendous amount of travel.

Marrissa began with the **Directory of Foreign Manufacturers in the United States, Fourth Edition,** published by Georgia State University Business Press, 1990. It lists approximately 6,000 foreign-owned manufacturers with operations in the United States. There is indexing by state location, parent company location, and by product.

Next she went to the **Worldwide Branch Locations of Multinational Companies.** Arranged by country, this volume lists contact and descriptive information for about 500 parent companies and their key branch locations. She also used the **European Consultants Directory.** It contains more than 5,000 European consultants and their fields of endeavor.

In this high-risk society, each person's main asset will be his or her willingness and ability to take intelligent risks. Those people best able to cope with uncertainty—whether by temperament, by talent, or by initial endowment of wealth—will fare better in the long run than those who cling to security.
Michael Mandel, *The High-Risk Society*

She went on to consult a reference book called **Principal International Businesses**, published by Dun's Marketing Services. It provides annual information on approximately 55,000 leading companies in 140 countries throughout the world.

Last, she used the **International Directory of Corporate Affiliations**, published by the National Register Publishing Company. It is an annual directory of information for over 1,600 foreign parent companies with listings of their divisions, subsidiaries, and affiliates. Also included are 1,500 U.S. companies with foreign holdings.

Marrissa obtained so much information that she designed an entire direct-contact campaign, demonstrating her ability to create executive correspondence. She was able to interview with several firms, turning down several offers before she secured an appropriate position.

You Can't Always Get What You Want, But If You Work At It, You'll Get What You Need

You've now read several case studies demonstrating the power of research. Sometimes it's difficult to see how these techniques will help you personally. Often the information you get doesn't look as you had hoped. You need to be creative.

Let me say something about being "creative." People frequently give that advice, without explaining.

Doing research does not mean simply collecting data. What you do with the information is critical to your success. Being creative means recognizing the relevance of seemingly irrelevant information. That is what will differentiate you from others.

For example, two clients of mine sold communications equipment in the high-technology industry. Both clients were interviewing at the same company. Both used the same research tools and both were able to learn the same two things: that the company in question had recently been denied FCC approval of a new product and

that their third-quarter earnings were significantly lower than anticipated.

My first client, Peter, had been hoping to find specific sales figures, information about the company's top customers, and about their primary competitors. He was greatly disappointed in his meager findings.

Alvin was my second client. Like Peter, he had been hoping for similar sales-oriented information. However, instead of being disappointed, he was creative.

During his interview, he referred to the FCC problem to ask pertinent and thoughtful questions. He asked how one product could so greatly affect the firm's profit picture. He asked about the positioning of *other* products, about the R&D cycle, about how government regulations affect the overall marketing strategy of the firm. In other words, he used the same limited research information to demonstrate his awareness of the company's problems and his concern with something bigger than his own job: the viability of the corporation and its longer-term goals.

Alvin was perceived as an experienced salesperson, able to produce quickly, with an understanding of how sales are linked to the company mission. Peter was perceived as a salesman. Period. Who do *you* think got the offer?

There are many stories like this one. If you find yourself doing research and wondering, "How on earth will this help me?" remember Peter and Alvin. Turn your bewilderment into the question: "How does *this* piece of information impact my particular area of expertise?"

If the answers were easy, everyone would have them. Taking the time and effort to go that extra mile is what makes you stand apart from your competition.

The information is out there. An extensive bibliography is at the back of this workbook to serve as your guide.

CASE STUDY: BEVERLY
Putting It All Together

Beverly had been moving through her career

successfully as a computer programmer and systems analyst for the last 12 years. She worked for a financial services firm with a large MIS department. Her company was going through a restructuring, and she found herself faced with a small buy-out opportunity. Surprising herself, she realized she was interested in "taking the money and running." Running to *what*, she didn't know.

She completed the Seven Stories and other Assessment exercises and realized that while she certainly liked technology, she was missing a sense of connection and fulfillment in her work. She didn't like working exclusively with data and by far preferred more intensive people interaction.

Armed with this information, Bev set off to conquer her job search. But where to begin? She listed some possible ideas based on her assessment: She could stay in financial services and look for a different job title in a different department (but what?); she could explore technology companies; or she could consider human resources—surely that was "people-oriented."

Bev already knew that financial services was consolidating—she had lived through it. Perhaps there were growth opportunities in other kinds of finance firms, and so she would research them. But she really wanted something different from financial services. She didn't know much about human resources and didn't feel like starting from scratch. So, by default, she began with technology firms.

Now Bev was ready to begin her Big Picture industry research and here is what she wanted to learn: *What problems are facing the technology industry that I could help solve?* This was her mission. Step one: Find out what was happening in the industry.

Bev spoke to an ex-colleague of hers (primary research)—the MIS manager at the bank—and asked what trade journals she had that were dedicated to the technology industry. Bev was told about a journal and a newsletter (both of which she already had at home, lying in a stack of unread papers). Her contact also told her the name of the sales rep from the vendor that the bank used. That person might be a good contact for understanding trends in technology firms as well. You will recognize this interaction as networking. It is networking with a purpose, and it was made possible through a tiny bit of research!

Bev read through the journals that evening (secondary research) and in two out of four articles saw the name of a technical research firm that was providing many of the statistics for growth and decline in the industry. As she read, she realized that this industry was also consolidating; that the growth trends were primarily around software; that many of the challenges were in integration of existing systems with new technologies. She didn't know yet how that translated into problems she could solve, so she kept on digging. (Research count so far: two journals, one person.)

She called the research firm that had been quoted in the papers (primary research) and explained that she was researching growth areas in technology and the challenges they brought. No one at the company was willing to talk to her, but they did send her some articles that they had

Strategies for Workers in the High-Risk Society

High-Risk, High-Return Strategies	Low-Risk, Low-Return Strategies
• Take a job exposed to the global marketplace	• Take a job insulated from foreign competition
• Take a job in a high-tech industry	• Take a job in a low-tech industry
• Earn an advanced degree	• Stop with a college education
• Work as a consultant or subcontractor	• Find salaried employment
• Work for a reengineered company	• Work for a stable company

Michael Mandel, *The High-Risk Society*

published recently on the subject matter. Bev went to the movies and read some science fiction while she waited for the mail to arrive.

When it did, she read through the information (secondary research), and one of the articles caught her interest. It discussed the migration of technology from MIS departments to boardrooms and executive suites. As technology was becoming more and more accessible, usage was shifting from "techie types" right to the end users. Executives and managers were traveling with laptops, working from home and on the road, doing their own spreadsheets and word processing, even their own presentations. *Bev thought about her own experience.* This is really important in utilizing research. *You have to take what you read and apply it to your own experience for interpretation.*

"It's true," Bev thought. "I know a lot of execs from the bank who had to begin to use their own systems. But they really struggled," she remembered. The problem? They didn't have anyone to teach them how to use the machines and the software, and they were often embarrassed by their lack of knowledge. So they never learned the software, and often their careers suffered.

"Now there's a problem I can solve," she thought. "I could teach executives, managers and professionals how to use technology." That would certainly address her technical expertise and her interpersonal skills. She had hit upon a workable idea: technical training. Research count: 1 networking meeting (primary research), 2 periodicals (secondary research), 1 research phone call (primary), 3 articles (secondary), 1 movie and 2 science fiction books!

Armed with her hypothesis (that she might find a niche in technical training), she began to explore that opportunity. Off she went to the library again to use a directory (secondary research) for some quantitative analysis: how many technical training firms were located in her geographic area? She used both Dun & Bradstreet and Ward's Directory, both on CD-ROM. There were hundreds of companies! Some teeny tiny and some Fortune 1000. She also used the National Directory of Associations to identify training organizations to get qualitative information about the business.

Some of the training organizations were schools, and she went to visit them (primary research). She spoke to some of the instructors who encouraged Bev to get hands-on experience before looking for work. As part of her research, she took a few classes at the school and observed for herself what made a good trainer and what didn't. The school wouldn't hire her without experience, and so she went back to her friends at the bank. She called a colleague in the sales department and offered to teach him how to use his laptop . . . for free! Word quickly spread and Bev was getting phone calls from several other managers in the sales department. *They* were willing to pay for her expertise. It turned out that she was a good one-on-one trainer. Now, how much to charge?

Bev called one of the associations she had identified through the Directory (primary research) and asked if anyone there could help her price her services. They did, and they also gave her the names of a few services that placed technical trainers on a per-project basis.

Bev ended up spending a full year as an independent contractor, teaching individuals and small groups how to harness the power of their technologies. She could have continued with her business longer, but one of her clients made her an offer to join his company on a permanent basis as a Training Director in the International Department of a consumer products firm. Before people went overseas, they went to Bev's department to get a full two weeks worth of individual technical training. Bev now hires people, trains people, travels, and manages the entire department with full P&L responsibility. Total research count: *It's an ongoing process.*

The
Five
O'Clock
Club®

Getting the Most Out of the Internet:
Research Pointers from Wendy Alfus Rothman

by David Madison, Ph.D.

One of the nation's leading authorities on job-search research, Wendy is the author of the annotated job-search bibliography at the back of this book. She also conducted an Internet Research workshop for the Five O'Clock Club Career Counselors Guild; the following article is based on that workshop.

Research: to those of us who grew up in the pre-Internet world, the word brings to mind scientists and scholars, libraries and drudgery. Research—for whatever purpose—is not a turn-on for most people. And it is probably the least popular component of that least popular of pursuits, looking for a job. Hence job-hunters will often confess that they're stuck, without being able to articulate the reason. They can't bring themselves to admit that skimpy research is probably the reason that they're stuck. We hear, "I know I don't have enough going…" or "I seem to have lost momentum…"—but people usually fail to end these sentences as they should, "…because I haven't done enough homework." Research is the key to strengthening every phase of the job-search process.

The Internet is an incredibly handy tool to help the job-hunter get *unstuck*.

Before we get down to specific tips to help you find exactly the information you need, a word of caution is in order. Remember what the Internet is not. If you assume that it will make your résumé accessible to thousands of hiring managers who will rush to set up interviews, you will be disappointed. It can certainly help you broadcast your paperwork. But remember that broadcasting résumés is not a proven technique for getting quality interviews—no matter what the venue. The Internet is not an instant solution to anything: it not a magic wand.

Skimpy research is often the reason job hunters get stuck. And the Internet is an incredibly handy tool for getting unstuck.

Making Hard Work (Almost) Easy
The Internet allows you to carry out, with ease, speed and amazing depth, the necessary hard work of a sophisticated job search. Research that could have taken hours in the library can now be done in a matter of minutes in your own home or office. If you want to use the Internet to give your job-search a boost, or help propel your career to new heights, remember this mantra: *The Internet is a research tool and research is my key.*

You Won't Find Your Job in Tahiti
Another word of caution. One of the great thieves of time is television: the number of TV hours logged every week by Americans is staggering. The Internet possesses the same seductive powers; shortly after logging on to investigate professional associations you could find yourself, having clicked on only a few "interesting" links, in the Web site of the Tahiti Tourist Bureau!

After an hour or two on line—totally fascinated by all the "stuff" that the Internet puts at your fingertips—you can fail to get the information you need. It's very easy to get distracted and to spend time simply playing (and fooling yourself that you're "doing research."). If you're new to the Internet, there's no harm in allotting a few hours to just exploring and snooping, surfing the Net, finding out how it works. But don't kid yourself that this is research.

If you want to use the Internet as an effective tool to advance your job search, it is vital to have a goal and remain focused: "I'm going on line for 45 minutes, and this is what I need to know when I get off."

To help maintain this focus, keep basic Five O'Clock Club methodology in mind. We stress the importance of an organized job search— organized by phases and targets. Follow the same principles in your use of the Internet.

First: Learning About Industries
For example, in-depth industry research is one of the keystones of a solid job search. Indus-

*And no grown-up will ever understand that this is a
matter of so much importance!*
Antoine de Saint-Exupéry, *The Little Prince*

try research is vital for those who are considering career change; even before setting out to get informational interviews in a new industry, the job-hunter wants to sound as much like as an insider as possible. But even a 20-year veteran of an industry who just wants to get ahead can benefit from a "refresher course" about his/her own industry. No matter what your industry target, a few hours of Internet research will yield abundant information.

**Keep basic Five O'Clock Club
methodology in mind. We stress the
importance of an organized job search—
organized by phases and targets.
Follow the same principles in
your use of the Internet.**

The home pages of the major servers offer easy entry to basic industry research, and in the paragraphs that follow, you'll find only a sampling of possible approaches.

One of the channels on AOL, for example, is called "Research and Learn." Click there and you'll find, among many other tabs, "Careers." Enter there and you can scroll through a list of about twenty industries, from "Accommodations & Food" to "Retail." Pick one and hit "Go," and you face a multitude of subcategories (under Accommodation & Food, for example, you'll find e.g., Catering, Event Planning, Hotels & Motels, Nutrition and Health). Also listed are associations, directories of trade shows and conferences, seminars, even message boards and chat rooms. In just a few clicks and a few minutes you are at the heart of solid industry information.

Another way in is through AltaVista. **The Directory on the AltaVista home page** offers over a dozen categories, one of which is "Business & Finance." Clicking there will lead to "Business Professions," which in turn brings up a list ranging from "Architecture & Planning" to "Science & Technology." This list also includes "Business & Finance." Click on that and you will

find many subcategories, including : Accounting, Banking, Corporate Finance, Insurance & Risk, Investing and Real Estate. To cite but one example, click on Banking and you will find a huge menu of banking industry web sites, including Thomson Financial Bankwatch, whose home page directory includes Recent Research. This yields four months of articles about the banking industry, including the name and phone number of the researcher.

You can also dig for industry information through **Expert Marketplace**. You're required to "join," but it's free and sign-up is on-the_spot. The Home Page offers many options, but for starters click on "Business Improvement Centers," which will present about a dozen fields to choose from. Clicking on any of them, you will find the following: **Free Business Case Study Alert Service Click Here**. If you sign-up to get the case studies, Expert Market Place e-mails you articles on the industry you've selected.

JobDirect.com also requires you to sign up, and it's geared toward college kids, hence the way into industry information is called "Wet Feet"! But the information is not dumbed-down and is useful to any researcher. You can, in fact, skip JobDirect.com and go directly to **Wetfeet.com**. Clicking here will pull up a list of about 25 industries. Choose any of these and you'll be prompted, among many other things, to "Industry Overview." Under many of the industry categories there are links to information about specific companies. Under each industry there's also a tab called, "What's great and what's to hate." For anyone contemplating career change, there may be good "reality therapy" in these essays.

A suggestion: take a few minutes to examine carefully such home pages as ExpertMarketplace.com and Wetfeet.com. There are lots of options that can lead in many helpful directions. Although we rejoice that Internet research can be a speedy affair, take time to carefully check out what's offered on such powerful sites.

Research is to see what everybody
has seen and to think what nobody else has thought.
Albert Szent-Gyorgyi,
American biochemist

Do You Really Want to Work for That Company?

Industry research has been a fundamental first step, especially if you're in the assessment stage, trying to get your bearings. Industry research has helped you define targets, and within each target you may identify 2, 12, 20 or more appropriate companies. Moving ahead to perform in-depth research on each company will enable you to interview smartly, of course. But research can help you get the interview. A generic cover letter ("Dear Sir, Enclosed for your review is my résumé…) is useless, but a cover letter can advance your cause if it reflects solid knowledge of the company and states the reason for your interest in that company. An opening paragraph that grabs the reader will heighten interest in you and your résumé: "Dear Sir, Since your company has recently introduced five new products in the European market…." You can grab the reader with that kind of sentence if you've done your homework.

**Performing in-depth research
on each company will enable you
to interview smartly,
of course. But research can
help you get the interview.**

A good place to start is **Hoovers.com**. A search by company from the home page will yield plenty of information and a multitude of links; some links are coded with a small yellow star to indicate that there is a fee, but there is a lot that you don't have to pay for. After you have pulled up the company you're researching, you can click on "Current Stories Mentioning X" and "Archived Stories Mentioning X" to see press coverage and start harvesting data to create a "grabber" intro for your cover letters and enhance your understanding of the company. One of the links on Hoovers.com will help deepen your industry understanding as well; you'll find helpful essays on industries by clicking on "Industry Snapshots."

Prnewswire.com also allows you to source news stories; from the home page, click on "company news," and search for companies by name. Another good source for finding articles about companies with just a few clicks is the **Personal Finance Channel on AOL**. This is designed to help investors (you can create and monitor a phantom portfolio), but job-hunters can make use of the company information. One section on the Personal Finance page is called "Quotes, Charts, News & Research." It allows you to search for the ticker symbol of the company; after you've entered the symbol, click "Get Quote." A page of information for the company you've requested emerges, which includes, "News Headlines for…", and this gives you full texts of recent articles about the company. A click as well on "Research Reports" is likely to yield more articles and tables. Again, pay attention to the links that you see on these pages: helpful information is likely to be readily at hand to build your understanding of companies you've targeted.

Quicken.com also allows you to rapidly access articles about companies. By entering the ticker symbol (which it also helps you to find), you will bring up a full page of data about a company, with links to "Recent Headlines" and "Older Stories." Clicking on "Analyst Research" will pull up reports—some free of charge and others available for purchase.

Jobvault.com is probably one of the most robust of all the sites. It provides information on more than 1,200 companies, whose extensive profiles are accessed according to industry or by search. Clicking on "Fashion," for example, will bring up links to articles about the industry and its leading personalities. 40-50 fashion companies are listed (everything from Calvin Klein to Sears); click on the company and you're into a virtual library of data (including job listings), "the inside scoop," as the creators of Jobvault.com like to claim. The information is relevant, easy to read and thorough.

Businessweek.com can also be helpful in job-search research. Many articles are available at no

Research is the process of going up alleys
to see if they are blind.
Marston Bates
American Zoologist

cost, but there is a membership charge for probing its full archive of articles back to the early 1990s. However, if you click on Careers from the home page, you will find a link entitled, "Who's Hiring: Looking for a Company?" Clicking there will bring up a huge list of companies alphabetically, with their job postings and a link to the company Web site.

Speaking of which, don't overlook the obvious, but be somewhat wary: company Web sites are propaganda pieces, so you can't believe everything you read. But you can still get a lot of information, e.g., company history, names of officers, products, geographic reach, job listings, etc. And you can get a feel for the corporate culture. If all the top company officers come out of Harvard and Yale, you won't be surprised if they haven't adopted have casual Fridays; it may or may not be the kind of place you'd like to work.

Don't forget that the Internet changes daily, indeed hourly. Home pages are updated, links change, but you can be sure that information you're seeking hasn't gone away.

Nothing Remains the Same

Don't forget that the Internet changes daily, indeed hourly. Home pages are updated, links change, but you can be sure that information you're seeking hasn't gone away. Be persistent if the way into information isn't the same now as it was a month ago, or if it's not the way we've described it here. And don't assume that you will be able to find an interesting article again ("I'll look at it later")—some articles are posted on the Internet only for a few weeks or months, and the links you thought you would remember, you don't. Copy an article when you see it. It's also a good idea to copy/paste it to your word processor, save it as a file, and keep a disk of Internet articles. Build a personal archive of literature relevant to your profession and career.

Remember to keep your eye on the time: there

are the interesting links that landed you in Tahiti, but there are also the chat rooms. An hour or two in a chat room will usually yield rumor and scuttlebutt as opposed to hard information—chat rooms are commonly used for griping—but chatting is not researching. When you log onto the Internet, keep your goal in mind.

Copy an article when you see it. Build a personal archive of literature relevant to your profession and career.

Pressing the Flesh...Instead of the Enter Key

Ironically, we have always found that research, which most people approach with reluctance, becomes a favorite "hiding place" for jobhunters (along with "my résumé isn't quite ready yet"). It's a safer place than interviewing. And because so much is available on the Internet there might be a temptation to keep digging, keep learning, keep tapping away at the keyboard, amassing data.

But the purpose of research is to move you forward, to prepare you to meet people at the right levels at the right companies who will say, "We need you." So enjoy your time on the Internet, savor the fact that it has taken much of the pain out of research, find the information that you need, then get out the door.

Silence has many dimensions. It can be a regression and an escape, a loss of self, or it can be a presence, awareness, unification, self-discovery . . . Positive silence pulls us together and makes us realize who we are, who we might be, and the distance between these two. Hence, positive silence implies a disciplined choice and what Paul Tillich called the "courage to be." In the long run, the discipline of creative silence demands a certain kind of faith. For when we come face to face with ourselves in the lonely ground of our own being, we confront many questions about the value of our existence, the reality of our commitments, the authenticity of our everyday lives.
Thomas Merton, *Love and Living*

PART FIVE

HOW TO
MANAGE YOUR FUTURE

The Five O'Clock Club®

New Shapes in Careers: How to Repackage the Work You Want To Do

by Betsy Jaffe, Ph.D.

Who can forget that line inspired by the movie *Jaws*?. . . "Just when you thought it was safe to go back in the water . . . ?" Just when you'd figured out how to survive in the workplace, the rules change . . . again. There's no escaping that sense of impending change, the uncertainty of what's next in these global business waters we find ourselves in. Nothing about managing a career seems the same.

That classic, up-the-ladder career with a place for everything and everything in its place is gone. Rarely, now, are there clearly defined, structured positions to move into. The organization person who built a solid career one block at a time has disappeared. Now, there's no sense of security about the route you can take or the connections you need to make, and there's no sense of being set for life.

Technological, global and economic trends have played havoc with the best of five-year plans. Because of these and other changes, five new career shapes have emerged, each requiring a new look at how work is done, how income is earned and what's required to succeed. There are new opportunities in each shape, new ways to package what you do. Think of these shapes in terms of your own career.

The New Classic Career

First, the New Classic Career in large organizations incorporates a much flatter ladder (if there still is one!). The steps take longer and are tougher to climb, and there are fewer rungs. New hollow, virtual or boundaryless organizational structures are continually evolving, so that they are now more psychological than hierarchical. In this information age, the company's "assets" reside mostly in the minds of employees and walk out the door every night.

Horizontal networks, cross-functional teams and strategic alliances call for new strategies. Surviving feels more like swinging on a trapeze, from opportunity to opportunity, role to role, project to project, so skills must be portable across functions. And there's no certainty of who's in charge anymore.

Instead of looking to fill a box on an organizational chart, you're looking for a situation where you can build your knowledge, skills and experience. And you have to make it happen. If you wait to be told what to do, you'll be out on the street asking "What happened?"

> **Surviving feels more like swinging on a trapeze, from opportunity to opportunity, role to role, project to project.**

At a financial services company in Dallas, a vice president of new product development pulls together teams from top management, former competitors and functional specialists, as needed, to launch new pension products. He researches customer needs, talks to professionals in his field, then makes a presentation to sell his ideas . . . without having a staff! He has to make it happen, and he has a lot of freedom to do so. It's risky, but without the red tape of old structures, he and his company are introducing more new services faster.

Career survival in large organizations now depends on your having flexibility, adaptability, the ability to scale steep learning curves and to play on ever-changing teams. You may need to form key alliances with former rivals, break through Chinese Walls at your company, and you must be able to demonstrate the value you bring to a project. It's not the way you operated five years ago. It's a different mentality—not "the way we've always done it."

The opportunities are tremendous as regulations change, underdeveloped countries take off and technology continually evolves, but you've got to sell yourself differently to make the cut. You've got to be a problem solver in operations

> *The man without purpose is like a ship without a rudder—a waif, a nothing, a no man. Have a purpose in life, and, having it, throw such strength of mind and muscle into your work as God has given you.*
> Thomas Carlyle

as well as in finance, in marketing as well as manufacturing. You've got to be more nimble in switching hats across those former functional lines. Those who can are more quickly reemployed. Companies are skimming off the cream, even as they cut.

Over 7 million people hold down more than one job.

On the other hand, what if you've had it with large organizations and crave more autonomy, multiple streams of income, and a more flexible lifestyle? Over the last decade, professionals have quietly reshaped their lives and careers. New patterns and themes have emerged as people have moved between sectors of the economy, formed their own businesses and achieved the balance they want between their career and life priorities.

With 27 million self-employed, part-time and temporary workers, it's no wonder that Classic Careers are becoming the exception rather than the rule! You are less likely to find an employment situation just like the last one you had.

Besides the New Classic Career, there are four other new shapes—Concentric, Concurrent, Combination and Contingency. They align on a change continuum between structured, organized careers characterized by moderate changes at one end, and careers that are more tumultuous and uncertain at the other.

Concentric Careers

Concentric Careers look like bulls-eyes. They build on a core, like with a business or product line. Your main product or area of expertise is in the center. As you expand in products or skills, concentric circles are added beyond the core. Organized people are particularly good at structuring Concentric Careers, and many managers and executives move to such careers when they

form their own consulting firms, becoming manufacturers' reps or building a line of products or services.

A former IBMer in Michigan began with a line of home security items that she marketed through catalogs. As the business grew, she added guard services, home security audits and consultations to businesses about security issues. She expanded on her core of products and services, weeding out losers and adding potential cash cows.

You, too, can take stock, add to your core of expertise or delete those less promising lines of endeavor. If you're a profit center in a larger organization, you can use this strategy, too.

Concurrent Careers

People with Concurrent Careers have two or more parallel, major activities in tandem. These careers may balance each other, bring in added income or be a rehearsal for a career change. People who like variety and the stimulation of multiple activities create such arrangements. The engineer studying for a master's degree in social work, the lighting consultant serving on his co-op board before moving on to building management and the new working parent all come to mind. (Indeed, parenting often feels like a second career!)

There are 27 million self-employed, part-time and temporary workers.

You need a lot of energy, support systems and drive to handle it all, but over 7 million people hold down more than one job. I know of one couple who worked five jobs between them to make ends meet! Another balances seasonal businesses, alternating efforts, between construction and winter sports events management.

A journey of a thousand miles must begin with a single step.
Lao-tzu

Combination Careers

These include a mix of unrelated activities and may make little sense to others. They resemble a pizza—a little of this and a little of that. People who want to escape routine, who crave autonomy and like a variety of short-term challenges have careers like these. Their résumés look like career patchwork quilts!

One part-time editor for an Atlanta-based corporate newsletter moved to New York, Houston and back to Atlanta, all while raising two kids, studying for a degree in psychology and volunteering with the homeless, not to mention being a corporate spouse. Pre-retirees find this a good model for the mix of travel, hobbies, part-time work and volunteering they want in their lives. Though not synergistic, each activity adds to their overall satisfaction.

The new career shapes are: new classic, concentric, concurrent, combination and contingency.

To pull off a combination career, you, of course, need financial resources in the form of multiple streams of income, pensions, and health coverage. It helps to form alliances with others in the same boat, or with those who can provide services that make it all work.

Contingency Careers

The final shape looks like broken lines on a highway. These careers are full of stopgaps and fallbacks to earn money while you hope to get a break doing what you love. Interim management companies and temp agencies provide work for all kinds of professionals: budding entrepreneurs trying to make a go of a new business, consultants between projects and performing artists waiting for that next gig. Artists have worked as receptionists, proofreaders and salespeople for years, while they auditioned for plays, built up portfolios and honed their skills on the side. Now, professionals are doing it.

One voice-over artist installs sound systems as a fallback. A public relations specialist turns her home into a bed and breakfast. Others barter services until things pick up. Skills like writing, consulting and computer and presentation skills are transferable and can help bring in income when times are tough.

**Analytical and organized people seem to lean toward classic, concentric and concurrent careers.
Creative types often have combination and contingency careers.**

So no matter what your preference for security or risk, careers can be and are being fashioned in any of these new shapes. Analytical and organized people seem to lean toward Classic, Concentric and Concurrent Careers as they are more structured and predictable. Creative and more "emotional" types often have Combination and Contingency Careers, which entail more upheaval, risks, ambiguity, insecurity and variation in ways to earn money.

You may have had a mix of several in your career history, or you may opt to in your next move. Knowing that there are new options, even as the ground shifts beneath your feet, can be a lifesaver. Just be sure to make it happen.

Betsy Jaffe, Ph.D., is President of Career Continuum, a New York consulting firm, and author of *Altered Ambitions—What's Next in Your Life?*

This article originally appeared in
The Five O'Clock News.

A Reminder of
Some Basic Career Principles

Here are a few more basic career principles—just to keep you on your toes:

1) Don't let others define you. Set your own standards. Don't measure yourself against others.

2) Know yourself and be yourself.

3) Develop a philosophy of your life as you want it. Be selective about how you spend your time. Make your own choices. Decide what you want to commit to. We each have the same amount of time.

4) Make a plan. If you don't know where you're going, chances are you won't get very far. Make a résumé of yourself five years from now, do your Forty-Year Vision, and develop a Career Plan. Identify what you will need to get there. But keep your options open, and don't stay too long in a job. Keep on developing yourself with an eye on your own future.

5) Be willing to take a risk. Make sure your next position relies on your strengths and your basic skills, and also contains a little "risk"—some new growth area. The jobs or assignments you take should have all three, and they should fit in with your Forty-Year Vision. You need the new growth areas so you will progress and advance.

6) Look for jobs that can provide quantifiable measures of your accomplishments, and look for companies that fit your style.

7) Learn how to manage or change your environment, rather than being a victim of your environment.

8) Get help. Join associations. Meet others in the company. Stay in touch. Don't go through your career alone.

9) Pick a few role models—not just one. Select the characteristics you like from each one. Observe their demeanor, dress, vocabulary, and speech patterns.

10) Don't let your guard down just because you have a new job or assignment. Always have a back-up plan in mind—just in case. Keep yourself marketable, and treat your employer as if you were a consultant. This position is not permanent.

Keep your boss's boss off your boss's back.
First Law of Corporate Survival

Can't do a lot of career planning? That's okay.
Just aim for the second job out.

When you are trying to decide on your next move, think of how that step will position you for the one after that. Even if you can't do a Forty-Year Vision—or a detailed Career Plan—you will still be better off than most people if you think at least two steps ahead.

For example, if one option is to take a position in management consulting as a sales representative, and if you think you may work for another fifteen years, what would be your next step if you lost that job—say, four years from now? If you think you would be marketable in that same kind of position, then you have developed at least a four-year career plan. If you think this job would *not* position you well for the next job, then it may not be a good move.

This kind of thinking is the start of solid career planning.

How to Keep Your Life Course in Mind

I learned three things in Zurich during the war. I wrote them down. Firstly, you're either a revolutionary or you're not, and if you're not you might as well be an artist as anything else. Secondly, if you can't be an artist, you might as well be a revolutionary.
I forget the third.
Tom Stoppard, *Travesties*

Sometimes we forget our important thoughts, or we remember them and they sound strange, or we become afraid of them. Afraid of success. Afraid of failure. Like writing this book. Some days I became nauseated at the thought of working on it. On other days, I simply "forgot" I was writing it, or I became afraid that it all sounded stupid, harsh, boring, trite. Often, I couldn't remember why I was doing it; then I was afraid I would never finish.

Writing a book is a lot like job hunting. Some days you forget why you're doing it—you just know that you must. Or you become sick at the thought of it. You can sometimes become afraid that you sound stupid, or are doing the wrong things, or will embarrass yourself, or you'll never finish.

But somehow—one day at a time—it gets done. A job hunter makes a phone call, writes a proposal, researches an organization. Every day you make a new decision to do your best no matter how you feel about it. You sit down and do what you must do. That is discipline: to continue to job-hunt—or to continue to write—regardless of how you feel. And then you get into it and it flows.

You have to remember where you were trying to head. Job hunting—or writing a book—was supposed to take you somewhere.

When one lives without a clear value structure, it is both difficult to direct life in the long run and difficult to experience a sense of meaningfulness that comes from following a prescribed course.
It is possible to sail a boat, for example, without charts or a compass. However, the absence of a chart prevents the possibility of a journey. One is limited to "day" sailing, so that new destinations and new challenges are out of reach. Eventually the same seascape and circumstances will produce a tedium not unlike the absence of meaning associated with a present-centered existence.
Herbert Rappaport, Ph.D.
Marking Time

It is easy to get caught up in your day-to-day activities. Your life can get off course; you become distracted. You may even discover you have veered from your true path for a number of years. That's okay. Bring yourself back and walk toward your goal. Stay with your own direction—the one that is in your heart. Deep down, you know when things are right and when things are not. Keep walking toward your goal.

Don't be bound by your past. It is important to remember that you are not whatever your jobs have been. We don't exist on a sheet of paper—a résumé. Don't identify too strongly with it. Stay fluid behind those words on the page. They are not you, but simply a sales tool.

The power is in what you are doing now and in your pull toward the future. The power is in the act of living each day to the fullest. It is the direction in which we are each heading that is important. Look to the future. We constantly gain new insights, new visions.

Taking the long view can give you satisfaction. A stonemason working on the Cathedral of St. John the Divine was asked how he could keep on cutting those stones year after year. He said he was not cutting stones—he was building a cathedral.

Interviewing can soften you. It can broaden your horizons and make you realize there is a big world out there with lots of interesting things to do. In talking to people, you can see that it is not all so pat—so clearly spelled out—what a person should "be." There are endless variations, and when you realize how much variety there is, you also realize that, in the end, it is largely up to you to choose what you will be. We each have a place. Find your place. Live your part.

Martin Luther King, Jr., was driven by his dream. *Your* main drives and inclinations also have power. You will come back to them again and again in your life because you are driven to do these things. They will come out. Why not harness that energy and direct it consciously rather than letting it rule you? In the right situations, your drives are a benefit and can add to your success. But in the wrong situations, they will still appear over and over, and they can harm you.

Better to find out clearly what they are, and go where they are valued. Then you will have a happy marriage between you and your environment. Then you will no longer be swimming against the tide, but will let the tide take you to new heights and a new sense of satisfaction.

They say, "Go with the flow." Go with your own flow. Go in the direction you were meant to take. Find out what it is that motivates you, and go with it.

When you find out what you are inside, it will

give you great energy and a happy obsession to realize it. When this happens, people say that their jobs are fun, and not work at all. There is nothing else they would rather be doing.

There is a freedom in fulfilling your function in the world—to know you are in the right place, doing what is right for you. You are fulfilled when you know what you are, know what you are supposed to be doing on this earth, and are doing it. When what you should be doing hits you, and you make it a conscious part of yourself, you won't get easily sidetracked. You will know what's right for you, and you will care.

Accept yourself as you are and be grateful. Then go for it. Be who God made you and do it all the way. Don't hold yourself back, but turn to face the world. Take your dreams and goals seriously, and your life will be simpler and have direction.

If you don't know what your dreams and goals are, then think about yourself. Do the Seven Stories exercise and observe the real you—the you that does certain things no matter what. Ask a friend to help you, and find the threads running through your life.

> *Choose a job you love, and you will never*
> *have to work a day in your life.*
> Confucius

> *Many of us live as though the momentum in our lives*
> *is generated by others. There is often a sense of anguish*
> *when the realization emerges that we have to*
> *generate our own momentum by the images we have*
> *of ourselves and the future.*
> Herbert Rappaport, Ph.D., *Marking Time*

You have plenty of time. How many more years do you have left? Let's say you'll be very active until the age of seventy, eighty, or more. How many years is that? Perhaps I have thirty more active years—maybe forty. A lot can happen in thirty or forty years. Is it too late for me? Is it too late for you? Probably not.

Don't rush toward your dreams, but savor every step and enjoy the present. Reaching your goal is not the point. In fact, it does not matter whether you ever reach your goal. Just live each day.

Live your life, enjoy and make the most of each day. Your goal is simply a guide—not a do-or-die phenomenon. If you can have a goal and enjoy the process of getting there, you have truly lived. It's the process that's important.

> *Why, sometimes I believed as many as*
> *six impossible things before breakfast.*
> Lewis Carroll, *Alice in Wonderland*

It's your life. Play a little. Take chances. You will succeed if you aren't too rigid about succeeding. Test things out. See what works. Don't try to hold on too tightly.

Our dreams recur. Perhaps yours are so deep and so quashed that you don't know what they are. Let them come out, then test them later to see how true they are for you. Dreams are serious things, and you might as well live them. Because, when you are old, you will find great satisfaction in having lived your dreams—in having lived your life. If you don't try to live your dreams, you may later be filled with regret.

> *One of the common themes among depressed adults*
> *who I see in my practice is the deep sense of regret for*
> *not "stretching oneself" at different stages of life.*
> Herbert Rappaport, Ph.D., *Marking Time*

> *There is only one success—to be able to*
> *spend your life in your own way.*
> Christopher Morley

Advance steadily in the direction of your goal, and don't worry about how long it will take you to get there. You will get there as soon as you can anyway. I've seen people advance steadily for many, many years. They somehow wound up doing amazing things that would have seemed impossible and frightening if they had concentrated on them earlier. By taking life one step at a time, and not getting anxious about the future, they moved ahead, taking small steps, but lots of them. The steps that followed seemed smaller still, and not frightening, and they became the persons they were meant to be. They followed their own, not completely defined dreams. As they lived each step, the next step became more clear.

Goals evolve as we test and see what feels right for us. We try a step, and sometimes step back rather than take our lives in a direction that we thought would be right but was not. And then, after a number of years, we look back, amazed at our own progress and surprised that this could happen to us—sure of our direction, still taking the steps one at a time, and testing our direction as we go.

And so our lives unfold. The excitement is in the present—the hope is in the future, and we know we are truly part of the universe as much as each star and each tree. We belong here—doing our part, full of life and living what was once a dream, and unafraid of failure.

> *Ah, but a man's reach should exceed his grasp,*
> *Or what's a heaven for?*
> Robert Browning
> "Andrea del Sarto"

There are some elemental truths about yourself that define the real you. You may have buried them over time, but now stay tuned in and see if you can uncover them. Sometimes these deep dreams of yours may shock your family and friends, and may even shock you. Better that you should know what they are.

I once had a client who had very low self-esteem, and had been doing "safe" work at a major corporation. He would sit hunched, with his head turned up toward where I was sitting, and he would meekly talk about the interviews he was going on. He didn't have a clue about what he should do with his life. There was so much confusion between what he thought he should do and what he had done in the past, it was very difficult for him to find some direction to head toward.

Then one day, as we were discussing all the usual things, this timid, hunched-over person said in a bland tone, "You can't imagine how thrilled I'd be if I could be the leader, running the entire thing and being completely in control."

It seemed impossible that these strong words were coming out of this person's mouth. Looking at him made it seem even more unlikely, yet there was some deep, elemental truth about what he wanted for himself. I wrote down what he said because it was one of those truths that can be so easily lost—so easily dismissed with a "let's be realistic, honey."

I believe that if this person keeps his dream in mind, he will someday be an incredibly dynamic person, "in charge of the whole thing"—whatever that may be. He will learn to hold himself better, to sound more dynamic, and to look the part. And when this dynamic winner emerges, it will be the real him. I believe that the timid, play-it-safe person is not the real him, but some twisted person that emerged when the real him was submerged.

And, if this person remembers his dream, he will surely advance toward it. Ten years from now, he will look back and find it hard to believe that he is the same person. The living comes not in finally reaching his dream—the living comes in becoming the kind of person he truly is deep inside. The living comes in his day-to-day life as he simply lives it.

Those words were the most important he ever said during the many hours I spent with him. It will take him years to be the real him—that's been buried for so long. But what a happy way to spend ten years. I can't think of a better way to live them—concentrating each day on the task before him, but remembering the person he was meant to be—finding his own place in the universe and being proud of it.

I spent a large part of my life being a loser, which I think adds an interesting dimension to my personality.
Michael Caine, *Acting in Film*

As you're the only one you can really change, the only one who can really use all your good advice is yourself.
John-Rogers and Peter McWilliams

Congratulations!

Our deepest fear is not that we are inadequate. Our deepest fear is that we are powerful beyond measure. It is our light, not our darkness, that most frightens us. We ask ourselves, "Who am I to be brilliant, gorgeous, talented and fabulous?"

❧ Actually, who are you not to be? You are a child of God. Your playing small doesn't serve the world. There's nothing enlightened about shrinking so that other people won't feel insecure around you.

❧ We were born to make manifest the glory of God that is within us. It's not just in some of us; it's in everyone. And as we let our own light shine, we unconsciously give other people permission to do the same. As we are liberated from our own fear, our presence automatically liberates others. ❧

Nelson Mandela
1994 Inaugural Speech

Dear Reader:

Congratulations on completing this program. You have just taken an important step toward achieving greater professional satisfaction and success. Because of your efforts, you have increased your understanding of yourself and your goals. This will lead to more effective career decisions.

I know this has been a very intensive process. You are to be congratulated for taking some time out of your busy schedule simply to think about yourself—what's important to you, what you want to achieve, and how you might do that.

Next Steps

What happens next depends on the goals you have set for yourself. You may choose to make improvements in your present position—to make it better suit your long-term goals.

You may want to work with an individual Five O'Clock Club career counselor—to review your results and get a professional's point-of-view.

You may also wish to read the other books in the career-development series provided by The Five O'Clock Club, starting with *Getting Interviews*.

Finally, you may want to join The Five O'Clock Club. Join other ambitious, intelligent people like yourself. Get our monthly newsletter. Attend one of our branches in your geographic area. You will receive guidance and have fun while you are learning how to manage your career.

I hope you will always be a member of The Five O'Clock Club—your Club for improving your career. We are dedicated to giving you the specific information you need to survive and thrive in this changing economy.

Here's to continued success in your career. We wish you growth—in personal satisfaction, inner peace, and financial comfort. We'd like to continue to travel along with you. I hope you feel the same.

Love and cheers!
Kate

PART SIX

CAREER AND JOB-SEARCH BIBLIOGRAPHY

COMPILED AND ANNOTATED BY WENDY ALFUS ROTHMAN

The
Five
O'Clock
Club®

Section One:
Internet Resources

compiled and annotated by Wendy Alfus Rothman

Introduction to the Internet Section

In the last edition of this book – only two years ago – almost everything was in print media.

There was data available on CD-Rom, but it was very expensive and people had very limited access to it. In these two short years, research has simply picked up and moved to the Internet. End of story. If you don't have access to a computer, someone you know does. Find them. Get on the net. There's power in those keystrokes—not just virtual power...tangible power from information that can broad based or fine tuned or anything in between. Learn how to learn on the internet—I'm sure in another two years most of the resources I identify in the bibliography may likely be obsolete. But they will have been replaced by other even better sites that you can find before we publish again. Have fun with your research and empower your job search—oh, the places you'll go...

Organization of the Internet Bibliography

I have organized this bibliography as follows:

- Part 1 contains basic navigational tools, in addition to general search engines.

- Part 2 contains sources of general business references. Understand that with Internet technology, you can link from any of these general sources to more specific company information.

- Part 3 references specific industry related sites, listed alphabetically by industry. I have included some new industries (i.e. e-commerce, new media, multimedia, telecommuting) where there is so much new growth and activity. The sub-sections include the following:

    Aerospace
    Apparel & Textiles
    Art
    Associations
    Broadcasting
    Chemicals
    Construction
    E-Commerce
    Education
    Entertainment
    Environment, Science, Natural Resources
    Event Planning
    Financial Services
    Food & Beverage
    Health
    Hospitality
    Human Resources/Training
    Manufacturing
    Marketing & Advertising
    Multimedia/New Media/Internet
    Not For Profit
    Publishing & Electronic Publishing
    Quality & Benchmarking
    Retail
    Technology
    Venture Capital

- Part 4 contains International Job Search & International News Sources.

- Part 5 contains Job Search engines and sites. The BEST job search engine is your BRAIN and the insight and organization you obtain through The Five O'Clock Club methodology. But you will also want to know about these sites, and so they are they for you to see.

- Part 6 contains references on Start up Businesses/ Franchises/ Family Businesses.

- Be sure to check out The Five O'Clock Club website: **www.FiveOClockClub.com**. You'll find hundreds of articles on career development and job search (taken from back issues of *The Five O'Clock News*), and lots of other information. Their new section for members only contains current issues of *The Five O'Clock News* as well as The Five O'Clock Club's Information Exchange where you can talk to other members and 5OCC counselors.

Part 1: Navigation Tools

Northern Light mines your data and organizes it for ease of use. De-LIGHT-ful!

http://www.northernlight.com
NORTHERN LIGHT
Northern Light's is a fairly new Internet search engine that I particularly like. Not only are the searches powerful, the key differentiator about this site is that it actually organizes the information in to logical and usable folders for you. So instead of giving you 2,000,000 responses to your inquiry, it gives you 5 or 6 folders that house those documents to help narrow your search. The folders are not pre-set—they are created specifically according to your search request. You can also refine your search even further by doing a Power Search, a Business Search, an Investext Search, News Search or a Stock Quote Search.

http://comfind.com
COMFIND BUSINESS SEARCH
A search engine for finding company information on the Web. Claims to be the Internet's largest global company directory. Browse an exhaustive list of product and service categories by the first letter, or search by business category or keyword. You can narrow your initial search by geographic region, which is a nice feature. In each category there's a long list of business topics, products, and services.

Part 2: General Business Reference

http://www.amcity.com
AMERICAN CITY BUSINESS JOURNALS
This is the place to find business news from cities throughout the States. Click on cities from Albany to Wichita to link directly to 35 weekly Business Journals covering each. On the site, you can also search by topic or key word, subscribe to any business journal, find advertising information, read columns by small business experts, and find a selection of feature articles covering regional business topics from across the country.

A great resource that helps you find jobs throughout the U.S. ➜

http://www.compuserve.com
BUSINESS DATABASE PLUS
Business Database Plus is a research service from Information Access Inc. accessible via Compuserve and the AT&T Business Network. The service lets you retrieve full-text articles from two complementary collections of business-oriented articles from regional, national, and international periodicals. The "Integrated Business and Trade Information" database provides access to five years' worth of articles from more than 750 business magazines, trade journals, and regional business newspapers. This database is excellent for identifying business trends, finding regional business news, and discovering information on large companies. The "Industry Newsletters" database provides access to two years' worth of articles from a variety of specialized industry newsletters.

➜ This one is FAB! A personal favorite. And they will e-mail you back topics of interest

http://www.elibrary.com
ELECTRIC LIBRARY
The Electric Library makes research as simple and easy as possible for everyday people. You can pose a question in plain English and the search engine will launch a search of more than 150 newspapers, hundreds of magazines, two international news wires, 2,000 classic books, photographs and maps, as well as well-known works of art. The search result is returned with citations in order of relevancy with document title, author, publication date, size, and even grade reading level. The company does offer 30-day free access. After that, monthly rates are $9.95 and an annual subscription is $59.95. A great value if you need daily access to a news database of this type.

http://www.prnewswire.com
PR NEWSWIRE
PR Newswire provides electronic distribution of full-text news to the business community and the general public. The PR Newswire site is a good source for current news and specific information on an industry or company. You can search by company name or browse an alphabetical index. PR Newswire also offers industry coverage of six major industry groups—automotive, entertainment, energy, financial, health/biotech, and technology.

Facts are friendly. Facts that tend to reinforce what you are doing and give you a warm glow are nice, because they help in terms of psychic reward. Facts that raise alarms are equally friendly, because they give you clues about how to respond, how to change, where to spend the resources.
Irwin Miller, Former CEO, Cummins Engine Co., *The Renewal Factor*

http://www.iquest.com

IQUEST BUSINESS INFOCENTER

A premium menu-based service providing access to databases covering business and industry. IQuest Business offers literally millions of articles, abstracts, and citations from leading business journals and newspapers. Choose from a series of topics to narrow your selection of databases, then search for your topic by entering one or more keywords. If you need to narrow your search, choose Add a Field to enter additional keywords. Be sure to review the pricing information for IQuest on Compuserve prior to entering the resource. It's very easy to quickly run up charges on IQuest if you're not careful.

http://www.compuserve.com

MAGAZINE DATABASE PLUS

Great source of topical info—easy to find and print ➔

Magazine Database Plus is a service that lets you retrieve full-text articles from more than 200 general-interest and niche publications. Do a power search by keyword to article titles related to your research topic, then retrieve/download selected articles to disk. You will be charged for every article you download, so make sure the title seems to be relevant to your project. An excellent resource for general business news and consumer information.

http://www.bigbook.com

BIGBOOK

THE BEST source of general business info in one plaaace ➔

BigBook is one of the most comprehensive directories of American companies available on the Web Begin by performing a *QuickSearch* for a company by company name, state, and/or a specified category. Click on the *Categories* icon to select from an alphabetical index of industry and product categories. Each entry provides contact information for the company and a list of relevant categories for the company's products or services.

http://www.hoovers.com

HOOVER COMPANY PROFILES

A standard; a classic – gets better & better. GOTTA HAVE. Used to be pretty superficial. Now quite hearty and ➔ robust source. The book form of this directory costs several hundred dollars, but the same information is available online through any of the commercial services for only a few cents per minute.

➔

This enormous database provides profiles of major U.S. companies, international corporations, and emerging, growth-oriented firms. The profiles trace the history of each company, review recent developments, describe current products and major competitors, and offer financial data from the company's SEC filings and annual reports. Of special note, the resource identifies major executives, their titles and their compensation. You can also search the Hoover Master List for short profiles and contact information for even larger ranges of companies throughout the United States.

Hoover's Company Profiles is a product of Hoover's Business Resources, which has a long history of publishing directories of America's leading companies. Search for your company of interest and then print or download the extensive company profile. An essential resource for investment or general market research. Hoovers is also available on America Online (keyword: Company Profiles) and Compuserve.

http://www.dnb.com

DUN & BRADSTREET INFORMATION SERVICES

While the Reports typically contain some useful bits of current news on the company, most of the provided information and far more financial data is provided in the Hoover Company Profiles.

This website offers a menu of services provided by Dun and Bradstreet, one of the United States' leading providers of business information. The homepage offers links to separate menus and text articles on a variety of business topics, including management, human resources, and strategic planning. Use the search engine on the Dun and Bradstreet home page to run searches for contact information on more than 10 million U.S. companies at no charge. Or download their Business Background Report on any company for $20. The Report provides information on the company's history, an overview of its operations and descriptions of current management.

Simon: *We can walk right outta here if you want.*
Eric: *And where we gonna go?*
Simon: *Anywhere man. It's a big world.*
Bruce Faulk, *You Still Got to Come Home to That*

A useful resource, but check for the company in → Hoover's Company Profiles (see above) before paying premium prices to use this site.

An essential resource for tracking down → small, specialized firms.

→ The company is somewhat of a icon in the Internet trend analysis business.

http://www.compuserve.com/
DUN'S MARKET IDENTIFIERS
A business directory from Dun and Bradstreet that provides in-depth information for major companies in the United States. Use the site's search engine to search for a company by name or SIC code. Each profile offers contact information and major product and/or service categories for the company. It also offers an extensive corporate history in each record.

http://www.aol.com/
ABI DIRECTORY
Over 10 million firms are indexed by American Business Information in this colossal business directory. This comprehensive mega-directory was compiled from over 5,000 yellow page directories, business white pages, corporate annual reports, SEC 10K reports, chamber of commerce directories, state directories, and other public information sources. Search for a company by name or keyword using the search engine or scan the directory by industry.

http://www.forrester.com/
FORRESTER RESEARCH, INC.
The site of "a recognized leader in market research," Forrester's web page provides an overview of their research services for specific industries, as well as general strategic planning. You can read executive summaries of past research reports or preview upcoming topics for each industry.

www.businessweek.com
BUSINESS WEEK ONLINE
The online version of this respected print magazine offers many free services, including a daily news briefing, searchable archives (you have to pay to read stories), audio updates, a banking center, and a career center. Subscribers get even more, including all domestic and international editions.

www.businesswire.com
BUSINESS WIRE
This site calls itself "the global leader in news distribution," and it's definitely not a site to be ignored. You can get up-to-the-hour information and even look up news on geographical regions, tradeshows, or topics from health to banking. There's also corporate and industry specific information.

www.chamber-of-commerce.com
CLICK CITY
Local business information usually comes from a chamber of commerce. At the Chamber of Commerce International Directory, you can search by state and city for a particular chamber of commerce website. Some hyperlinks contain extensive information while others just include a phone number.

www.marketguide.com
MARKET GUIDE
This so-called "benchmark for quality financial information" offers a timely, comprehensive financial database covering more than 10,000 publicly traded companies. You can search for a specific company, get free real time stock quotes, or enjoy the quick access to price leaders and a market summary.

www.reuters.com
REUTERS
When it comes to "the business of information," it's hard to beat Reuters, which draws on information from 5,000 subscribers and 2,000 journalists. This site is top-notch and its only drawback is that it's almost overwhelmingly jammed full with financial information.

www.wsj.com
WALL STREET JOURNAL INTERACTIVE EDITION
If you're serious about business news, the Wall Street Journal needs no introduction. What you may not know, however, is that a subscription to the online Wall Street Journal also includes SmartMoney Interactive and Barron's Online. You can take a tour, or try it out free for two weeks.

© 2000, The Five O'Clock Club®, Inc.

Every man is born into the world to do something unique and some-thing distinctive and if he or she does not do it, it will never be done.
Benjamin E. Mays, "I Knew Carter G. Woodson,"
Negro History Bulletin, January-March 1981

Part 3: Industry URLs

Aerospace

http://www.nationjob.com/aviation
AVIATION/AEROSPACE JOB OPENINGS
A section of the NationJob Network, here you can search a rich database of job openings and company profiles in aviation and aerospace. The site is updated every week, so check back regularly for new listings.

Apparel & Textiles

http://www.ita.doc.gov/industry/textiles/
OFFICE OF TEXTILES AND APPAREL (OTEXA)
The Office of Textiles and Apparel is a division of the U.S. Department of Commerce. OTEXA offers this website as a method for publicizing its services and providing information regarding the U.S. apparel industry. Click on the *Industry Assessment Division* for current trends in the industry, including access to market research reports, economic analyses, and briefing papers.

http://www.fashion.net
FASHION NET
Fashion Net bills itself as the global meeting point for the world of fashion. In fact, the meeting point is actually broken into two distinct sections. Fashion Net offers one collection of fashion resources for the general public, called Fashion and Style, and a separate collection for the Fashion Industry. Business professionals in the industry will obviously focus on the latter. Access *Fashion Industry* for the *Fashion Yellow Pages,* a directory of apparel companies, and the distinctive Online Presentation/Portfolio service.

Fashion Net provides a *Bulletin Board* for fashion professionals to post announcements and inquiries. The *Bulletin Board* contains a positions offered/positions wanted section, as well as advertisements for freelance services and contract assembly work.

Art

http://artresources.com/
INTERNET ARTRESOURCES
This site is a well-designed collection of artistic resources on the Internet targeted at the visual arts community. Internet ArtResources is actually a compendium of six distinct hotlists related to the visual arts. In sum, the site provides over 4,600 links to art-related sites on the Net. Internet ArtResources provides a brief description of each of its six sections: GalleryWalk, StudioVisit, MuseumStroll, ArtNewsstand, ArtShows, and Artschools. Click on the *Brief Description* hypertext on the homepage for more information on each section. Of obvious value to artists and businesspersons in the arts.

Associations

http://www.asaenet.org/
AMERICAN SOCIETY OF ASSOCIATION EXECUTIVES   (NFP)
The American Society of Association Executives (ASAE) offers this website as a resource to its members and businessperson seeking information on professional associations. With over 100,000 associations in the United States, this is the place to start to find a particular group. In addition, the site offers an extensive set of links to professional associations on the Web under *Gateway to Associations.* Users can explore links to business and industry associations, international societies, and convention centers and bureaus.

Broadcasting

http://compuserve.com/   Keyword: Bpforum
BROADCAST PROFESSIONALS FORUM

→ Great for chatting, networking and participating with other professionals.

This forum on Compuserve is designed for professionals in media broadcasting. It contains an active collection of message boards for an ongoing discussions of issues in the media. You can run a keyword search of the Forum Messages or skim the messages by category. Access discussion groups on such topics as Radio and TV Talent and Women in Broadcasting, or upload your resume onto the *Resumes* section. The Library provides contact lists for the industry, sample contracts, and technical support for audio/visual specialists.

http://www.nab.org/www/userguid/libhome.htm
NATIONAL ASSOCIATION OF BROADCASTERS LIBRARY AND INFORMATION CENTER
NAB is the nation's leading trade association for broadcast professionals. The NAB site provides resources related to the broadcasting industry and professional development. Go to the NAB Library and Information Center for an index of topics contained in the *NAB Library*. There is a collection of *Broadcast Job Listings* that publicize career opportunities in the industry. Great discussions of current regulatory changes affecting the broadcasting industry are available.

http://tvnet.com/tvnet.html
ULTIMATE TV
Ultimate TV combines television industry news with an updated hotlist of TV-related websites. Users can also access press releases from the television networks by clicking on *Press Releases*. The site provides a hearty index of related websites. The index includes sites operated by local television stations, cable channels, the major U.S. networks, and international operators.

Chemicals

http://www.neis.com
THE CHEMICAL INDUSTRY
The Chemical Industry Homepage is an impressive website designed for chemists, chemical engineers, and business professionals in the chemical field. The Chemical Industry Association offers industry news and analysis and links to other chemistry sites on the World Wide Web.

Construction

http://www.biabuild.com
BUILDERS SUCCESS MAGAZINE
Builders Success is an online trade publication of the Building Industry Association, the national professional association of the construction industry. The site offers news from the construction industry and profiles of industry "best practices." The site also publishes *Success Listings*, a directory of contact information for construction companies, subcontractors, and business service firms that support the construction industry.

E-Commerce – NEW INDUSTRY; New Resources

http://www.ecworld.org
ELECTRONIC COMMERCE WORLD INSTITUTE
An advanced site devoted to the study of electronic data interchange (EDI) and electronic commerce. *The Beginner's Corner* provides a glossary of terms related to electronic commerce and an excellent list of FAQs about EDI. It also helps to introduce the available and emerging technologies related to electronic commerce and offers a defense of EDI versus other communications technologies. The site includes a useful Roadmap to ECI for beginners and offers a suggested reading list of periodicals and books for in-depth research.

http://ecrc.ctc.com/
THE NATIONAL ELECTRONIC COMMERCE RESOURCE CENTER
This site is sponsored by the Department of Defense as a resource for promoting awareness and implementation of electronic commerce and related technologies. The site indexes a network of regional electronic commerce centers and offers access to the full-text of *The ECRC*, the Center's quarterly newsletter. A helpful primer on electronic commerce and the Internet.

http://www.commerce.net
COMMERCENET
CommerceNet is a global industry consortium that seeks to promote electronic commerce using the Internet. CommerceNet is composed of over 500 companies and organizations engaged in the information technology field, including telecommunications companies, banks, and Internet and online service providers. The CommerceNet website provides a regularly updated source of intelligence on electronic commerce. The site provides a daily dose of industry news for this field under *EC Daily News*.

If I try to use human influence strategies and tactics of how to get other people to do what I want, to work better, to be more motivated, to like me and each other—while my character is fundamentally flawed, marked by duplicity and insincerity—then, in the long run, I cannot be successful. My duplicity will breed distrust, and everything I do— even using so-called good human relations techniques—will be perceived as manipulative. . . Only basic goodness gives life to technique.
Stephen R. Covey, The Seven Habits of Highly Effective People

Education

http://chronicle.merit.edu/.ads/.links.html
JOB OPENINGS IN ACADEME (Education)
A terrific collection of job opportunities posted in the *Chronicle of Higher Education*. Search the entire list by keyword or limit your search by region or professional category. Start out by retrieving the list of job titles, which include the broad categories: *Faculty and Research Positions, Administration Positions, Executive Positions*, and *Positions Outside Academe*. You can then plug in the region where you desire to find a job—Northeast, South, Midwest, and so on. A list of specialty fields appears. You click on yours and job positions with complete descriptions and contact information appear.

www.academploy.com
ACADEMIC EMPLOYMENT NETWORK
Academic Employment Network's website isn't likely to win any design awards, but it offers content that teachers grade highly. You can search for education positions by state and position. Because teachers often teach a variety of courses, the search engine supports Boolean (AND and OR) searches to help you find the best job for your skills. Once you find the job, useful demographic and cost-of-living information is at your fingertips.

Entertainment

http://www.screenwriters.com
HOLLYWOOD NETWORK
The Hollywood Network is a comprehensive site for the entertainment professional or anyone who is interested in the entertainment industry. Everyone is here—producers, directors, actors, and studio representatives. Online chats, conference information, and all the buzz about who's who and what's what to be in and stay in the industry.

www.showbizjobs.com
ShowBizJobs.Com
Looking for a way to break in to Hollywood? This site by Entertainment Recruiting Network offers everyone a way behind the camera into the positions offered by leading companies, such as Disney and Turner Broadcasting. You won't find "Star" listed in the employment categories, but you'll find everything from Graphic Arts to Theme Park Operations listed. As befits any site that's focused on the entertainment industry, the latest browser versions are a must. If you want to benefit fully from eye candy, beyond all the glitz is a solid resource for established workers and creative aspirants alike.

Environment, Science, Natural Resources

http://www.epa.gov
ENVIRONMENTAL PROTECTION AGENCY
The Environmental Protection Agency offers this website as a source of information about the agency, its regulations, and environmental activism. It is the first place to turn for information on environmental regulations and regulatory compliance.

http://www.enviroindustry.com/opportunities.html
ENVIRONMENTAL INDUSTRY: BUSINESS OPPORTUNITIES
Look here to see a categorized database of job openings and business opportunities in the environmental industries. Categories of "opportunities" include marketing, partnerships, recycling, procurements, and trade leads.

http://www.doe.gov
DEPARTMENT OF ENERGY
The Department of Energy (DOE) is a vast collection of resources related to energy development and natural resources. Everything you would want to know about the Department, or, for that matter, the U.S. energy industry, is found somewhere on this site.

http://www.its.nbs.gov
NATIONAL BIOLOGICAL SERVICE
From this site you can access numerous biological libraries and research centers, see summaries of the bureau's programs and initiatives, and use its search engine to find information pertaining to a particular topic including Ecosystem Management, Libraries, and Government Data.

http://sfbox.vt.edu:10021/Y/yfleung/nrrips.html
NATURAL RESOURCES RESEARCH INFORMATION
A great site for the job seeker interested in the threatened environment and natural resources. Subject categories include Issues, From the Field, News, Taking Action, and Resources. The *Resources* section contains editorials, fact sheets, and report summaries.

Event Planning

http://www.expoguide.com
EXPOGUIDE
EXPOguide is an online resource for securing information on trade shows and conferences. Find links to industry associations, private consulting firms that assist with event planning and trade show organizers.

Financial Services

http://www.corpfinet.com/
CORPORATE FINANCIAL NETWORK
The Corporate Financial Network is a homepage dominated by links to other financial sites on the Web. Click on the *CorpFiNet 500* and scan a list of links in financial categories including Brokerage Firms, Investment Banks, and Venture Capital. The site also offers a set of Finance and Technology Headlines from leading business news services covering Wall Street.

www.insidewallstreet.com
INSIDE WALL STREET
This excellent, informative online magazine features up to the minute information for the financial-world enthusiast. Potential investors can read about the featured company or stock of the week, see the latest market news complete with analysis and commentary by distinguished industry analysts. Get information from the Word on the Street section, and find out about the latest IPO (Initial Public Offerings) on this informative site.

www.euro.net/innovation/Finance_Base/Fin_encyc.html
INTERNATIONAL FINANCIAL ENCYCLOPEDIA
This online resource tool provides definitions for thousands of words and symbols. The international flavor is apparent in the spelling, but the definitions, which span financial, information systems, and technology are informed and well-written.

Food & Beverage

➜ The Blue Directory is probably the most comprehensive collection of food links on the Web.

http://www.pvo.com/pvo
THE BLUE DIRECTORY OF FOOD & BEVERAGE BUSINESS
This site provides a good hotlist of links to the food and beverage industry. The Blue Directory offers a helpful *Allied Services* section for links to vendors who support the food and beverage industry. The *Retailers* section is broken down into *Food* and *Beverage* subcategories, and is further divided by food and beverage types. A separate *Events* icon links you to a list of upcoming food and beverage trade shows.

Health

http://www.social.com/health/nhic/data/index.html
HEALTH ORGANIZATIONS
Here is a U.S. Government database that describes over 1,000 health organizations in the U.S. There is an alphabetical index and a state-by-state listing of all the entries. Each entry provides general contact information and an abstract on the organization, as well as specific publications offered by the group.

http://www.onramp.net/Den-Tel-Net
DEN-TEL-NET (DENTISTRY)
Sponsored by dental specialists throughout North America, this dentistry-related resource contains links to a wide variety of U.S. and Canadian dental sites. Den-Tel-Net offers a guide to sites concerned with periodontics, endodontics, orthodontics, prosthodontics, oral surgery, pedodontics, dental public health, and oral pathology. The site also offers articles on dentistry and dental practices, and is updated every month with new sites and submissions.

Hospitality

http://www.exponet/Hospitality
HOSPITALITY INDUSTRY INVESTMENT PROFILES
The best parts cost money: leads on international hotel and resort development projects in the U.S., Asia, Mexico, the Caribbean, and Central and South America. For your membership fee you get an "inside track on the hospitality industry" in these regions on new and renovated projects, current status of "access to the data." But the site is also pretty terrific for non-members: you can access a series of articles and interviews that provide plenty of industry info. People interviewed include heads of companies involved with tourist-related projects in Pacific Rim countries, including Latin America.

http://www.hospitalitynet.nl/job
HOSPITALITY NET VIRTUAL JOB EXCHANGE
Here you can search for a current job opportunity or register a job opening at your hospitality-related company. Categories include accounting, conference and banqueting, corporate office, food and beverage, marketing and sales, among others. The types of jobs posted include Accounting, Corporate Office, Food and Beverage, Marketing and Sales, Others, and Rooms Division (which refers to valets, guest services, reservations managers, and receptionists). Job postings include contact information, company profile, and description of each position

Human Resources / Training

http://www.tasl.com/tasl/home.html
TRAINING AND SEMINAR LOCATORS
TASL provides an online database of training and seminar providers. You can search the TASL database by event or service, product or provider. You can also search the database for specific scheduled events incorporating a TASL training or seminar. TASL is free to users on the Internet. It contains a wide range of training resources, including public and on-site seminars, short courses and certificate programs.

Manufacturing

http://mfginfo.com/home.htm
MANUFACTURERS INFORMATION NETWORK
The Manufacturers Information Network a complete online resource for all manufacturers and all services related to manufacturing, including Machine Tools, CAD/CAM, and Machinery Builders. The site provides a large hotlist of industry resources on the Net under *Industry Resources*. In addition, the site maintains its own database of manufacturing companies that can be searched using the provided search engine.

Marketing & Advertising

http://www.asiresearch.com
THE MARKET RESEARCH CENTER
Find out about a company's products and services through this site. Additionally, there is a handful of valuable resources like Marketers & Media Online, a comprehensive guide to websites of interest to marketers and media companies. A second resource, called Industry Information, includes information about the market research industry—news, free publications, links, and data concerning jobs and resumes. You will also find a list of the Internet's top 100 advertisers, industry e-mail which lists netizens involved in market research, and an FAQ and definitions lists if you find yourself vague on such terms as *market modeling*, *measuring brand equity*, as well as *market research* itself.

http://www.adage.com
ADVERTISING AGE
The *Advertising Age* home page offers the user a number of options for exploring the magazine. Link to *Daily Deadline* for today's marketing and advertising news. Each story offers a headline and one or two paragraphs' worth of text to keep you current on the advertising. There is special coverage of the world of Interactive Media and Marketing for specialist in online advertising. The Interactive Media and Marketing

section includes articles and opinion pieces, as well as a calendar of upcoming industry events and a great *CyberCritiques* segment that reviews the latest websites.

Advertising Age also sponsors a number of forums on its site for discussions of marketing and media issues. Topics include Digital Media, Ad Campaigns, and Electronic Commerce, and each bulletin board gets a significant amount of traffic. You can also use the website to access archives of past *Advertising Age* stories.

http://www.jup.com
JUPITER COMMUNICATIONS
Jupiter Communications is the leading source of analysis and market intelligence for the consumer online industry. This market research and consulting company focuses on content, advertising, technologies and commercial practices related to targeting consumers via the Internet. The Jupiter website is broken down into four sections—Content, Advertising, Technology, and Commerce—that reflect the company's core competencies. There are lists of upcoming conferences sponsored by Jupiter, a database of press releases, and notices of employment opportunities.

Multimedia/ New Media / Internet – NEW INDUSTRIES! New Resources

→ This is actually a great place to become familiar with the parlance of the Net.

http://www.hotwired.com
HOTWIRED!
HotWired is the Web presence of *Wired* magazine, the leading periodical of the Information Age. HotWired complements *Wired* by provoking a discussion of *Wired* issues and offering new material only available on the website. Coverage of Internet events, industry gossip, and developments in digital commerce. There are also active discussion groups under *Threads* and a 24-hour chat ongoing in *Club Wired.* In particular, the site offers fascinating coverage of the emerging Net culture.

http://techweb.cmp.com/ia/daillies/daily.htm
INTERACTIVE AGE
Interactive Age is the leading periodical covering the growth of multimedia, the Internet, and electronic commerce. *Interactive Age* provides a center for investigating the digital revolution, and hosts several electronic magazines that cover the industry. Through *Interactive Age* Digital one can review the *Computer Age Daily,* an electronic newspaper from the *New York Times* Syndicate, and the *Daily Media* and *Marketing Report.*

http://www.ima.org
INTERACTIVE MULTIMEDIA ASSOCIATION
The IMA is an industry association for corporations and individuals involved in authoring and marketing multimedia products. The IMA website serves as a source of industry news, a technical development tool, and a billboard that announces upcoming industry events. Burning current issues in multimedia are the first concern of the IMA website, and they are addressed under *Hot Topics.* You can also find a glossary of multimedia terms.

→ Fab source for info on the fields of digital media and electronic commerce.

http://www.cgw.com
COMPUTER GAMING WORLD
The ultimate resource for 3-D graphics animation, covering topics such as CAD, animation, visualization, virtual reality, and multimedia for professional media artists. Articles from the print publication are summarized and one or more from each issue are included here in entirety. Topics range from VRML authoring software and AutoCAD/Auto Desk to high-level animation authoring technologies. You'll also find a graphics gallery, bookstore, job directory, a list of schools, and an event calendar.

http://www.mediacentral.com
MEDIA CENTRAL
Media Central is the quintessential place for anyone tracking new media, the internet and broadcasting technologies. Articles are strong on concept and not too technical for the layman reader, originating from an assortment of new media publications including *Media Daily, Direct Newsline,* and *Online Tactics.* The emphasis is on online ventures and new media with daily coverage of the communications industry.

> *I found that values, for each person, were numerous. Therefore, I proposed to write my value names and to annex to each a short precept—which fully expressed the extent I gave to each meaning. I then arranged them in such a way as to facilitate acquisition of these virtues.*
>
> Benjamin Franklin

http://simbanet.com
SIMBA INFORMATION SERVICES
Simba is a consulting and market research firm that specializes in the media industry. The company analyzes the global market for information publishing and distribution and publishes its findings in a variety of formats, including this website. Simba publishes research reports on a variety of sectors within the media industry, including interactive media, television, newspapers, and book publishing. They also offer the *MediaBook*, which provides market summaries for multiple media sectors under a single volume.

Not For Profit

http://fdncenter.org
THE FOUNDATION CENTER (NFP)
The place to explore the not for profit arena. You'll find links to directories of regional, national, and international grant-making corporations and foundations, a complete list of publications related to philanthropy and foundations as well as contact information about the Center's five libraries and 200 cooperating collections spread out across the country.

This megasite is organized into the following categories: About the Center, Libraries and Locations, Training and Seminars, Grantmaker Information, Funding Publications and Analysis, Philanthropy News Digest, The Fundraising Process, and Publications and CD-ROMs. You'll also find not only hotlinks to each company, but a description of what the firm looks for in a grant request.

http://www.cof.org
COUNCIL ON FOUNDATIONS (NFP)
The Council on Foundations is the national association of grant-making organizations, including private foundations, community foundations, and corporations. Its membership represents over 1,500 giving organizations that control more than $139 billion in assets. The Council's website provides information on locating specific foundations in the United States and also offers counsel for grant-makers.

http://www.philanthropy-journal.org
PHILANTHROPY JOURNAL ONLINE (NFP)
Philanthropy Journal Online is published by the *Philanthropy Journal of North Carolina*. The site provides a consistent source of intelligence on the world of philanthropy, with an emphasis on corporate giving and foundations. There are sections of the site dedicated to news covering foundations, corporations and their corporate-giving programs, and voluntarism. An extensive *Meta-Index* provides links to nonprofit organizations throughout the United States, while a set of *Philanthropy Links* provides a direct connection to other websites. There is also a job bank under *Nonprofit Jobs* that describes career opportunities in philanthropy.

Ethics in WHAT?
In Business? ➜
How great is this?

http://www.arq.co.uk/ethicalbusiness
ETHICAL BUSINESS
Click on *Ethical Business Directory* to find a thorough set of hyperlinks to ethics- and environment-related destinations on the Net, divided into those in Europe, in the States, and in the rest of the world. You can review lists of ethical investment funds, organizations involved in ethical and social investment, and ethical trading companies. Ethical Business also includes a bibliography of books and articles on the subject and definitions of concepts to get you started. And you can download the entire text of *The Shareholder Action Online Handbook*. A rich source on this subject.

http://www.igc.apc.org/conflictnet
CONFLICTNET
ConflictNet seeks to offer current information in the field of mediation and dispute management. ConflictNet offers refreshed information regarding conflict resolution, including moderated discussion groups, updates on pending legislation, and continuing education opportunities.

The site also provides a guide to universities offering conflict resolution degrees and individual training and certification program. ConflictNet is a subscription-based online service (BBS) that carries a $12.50 monthly charge plus a $15 sign-up fee. An excellent professional development resource for attorneys, mediators, and other specialists in dispute resolution.

http://camden-www.rutgers.edu/~ccq
CORPORATE CONDUCT QUARTERLY
Corporate Conduct Quarterly is published by the Forum for Policy Research at Rutgers University and deals with issues of corporate ethics and responsibility.

Publishing & Electronic Publishing

http://www.press.umich.edu/jep
JOURNAL OF ELECTRONIC PUBLISHING
This site is home to an archive of copyrighted works covering issues and trends in electronic publishing. It's searchable by subject, author, or title. Subject categories include copyright issues, digital libraries, economics, imaging, policy, and technical issues. If you work in the publishing industry – or want to—you need to add this site you your list of required online reading.

http://www.compinfo.co.uk/tpdtp.htm
COMPINFO-DESKTOP PUBLISHING, ELECTRONIC PUBLISHING, WEB PUBLISHING
The Computer Information Centre provides links to online resources concerning desktop publishing, electronic publishing, and Web publishing. The number of resources logged here is extensive, and includes exhibitions, industry, news, publications, manufacturers, consultants, service providers, and more. Well worth a visit if you work in the publishing industry.

Quality & Benchmarking – NEW INDUSTRY GROUP!

http://www.inforamp.net/~qmi/index.html
QUALITY MANAGEMENT INSTITUTE
QMI offers quality system registration and information in North America. A description of the company's ISO-9000-related seminars is offered, providing a host of information for anyone seeking to learn more about the quality standards business.

http://www.isa.org/
THE INTERNATIONAL SOCIETY FOR MEASUREMENT AND CONTROL
The International Society for Measurement and Control is a non-profit engineering society with nearly 50,000 members world-wide. Its membership includes those involved in all aspects of measurement and control in the manufacturing industries. You'll find news, journals, directories, job lists, links, and more. Services include a large directory of online instrumentation products and manufacturers, a catalog of reference publications, certification programs, and a training institute. In the product directory, you can search by keyword or alphabetically.

Retail

The future of retail— check it out! ➜

http://www.el.com/RF/Rfindex.html
RETAIL FUTURES
Absolutely essential to retail professionals, this site delivers a set of feature articles covering all aspects of the retail business. Published by the Institute for Retail and Merchandising Innovation, the focus of the material is on creative and innovative approaches to retail selling. Categories of articles include Changes in Consumer Behavior, Category Management, On Brands and Brand-Building. The Impact of Electronic Data Interchange (EDI) on Retailing, Regional Marketing, Significant Developments Across a Myriad of Industries, and Breakthrough Design.

Technology

One of the best ➜ sources of articles about the Internet and cyberculture.

http://web.mit.edu/afs/athena/org/t/techreview
TECHNOLOGY REVIEW
MIT's academic journal of technology and public policy. Review the current issue online, search past issues, or scan their online career center.

http://www.techweb.com
TECHWEB
Comprehensive coverage of High Tech Happenings & Jobs. TechWeb synthesizes intelligence from various computing publications, its own staff, and the "word on the street" to provide readable, focused coverage of the

PC industry and related developments in technology. New readers of TechWeb should start with the *Site Index* to get a sense of what the site can offer. TechWeb is organized into four sections that target specific types of readers. *TechWire* provides industry news coverage for an executive audience, *TechInvestor* focuses on the financing of technology, including current stock quotes, coverage of IPOs and venture capital placements, and online portfolio management. *TechHelper* provides support to general computer users, and devotes coverage to broad features and specific questions related to hardware and software. *TechTools* is for the programmer and technical specialist, with detailed coverage of technical questions and troubleshooting tips. There is also a *TechCareers* section for jobseekers and *TechToons* for a midday break from the stress of your high-tech career.

http://www.dataquest.com
DATAQUEST INTERACTIVE
DataQuest is the one of the country's leading market research firms for the computer and information technology industries. On DataQuest Interactive users can discover the latest industry news and preview ongoing research by the firm. The site also offers information regarding DataQuest's market research services and sponsored conferences.

http://www.compuserve.com
COMPUTER DATABASE PLUS
Computer Database Plus provides abstracts and full-text articles from a database of over 200 newspapers and periodicals that cover the computer industry. Computer Database Plus provides industry news, product reviews, and emerging trends in computers, as well as historical information that dates back to 1987.

http://www.aol.com
COMPUTER TERMS DICTIONARY

Great for the tech novice. →

Webster's Dictionary of Computer Terms is organized in a searchable database format to provide the user with a current vocabulary of computer terms. Enter keywords or concepts to search for a specific term or topic. This easy-to-use dictionary offers more than 4,500 terms with origins and full, jargon-free definitions. The Computer Terms Dictionary also features descriptions of important software packages and their related terms.

http://www.aeanet.org
AMERICAN ELECTRONICS ASSOCIATION
Visit the American Electronics Association (AEA) website for the latest news and views from the electronics and electronic component industries. The AEA website offers well-organized information resources for electronics professionals.

http://www.spp.umich.edu/telecom/telecom-info.html
TELECOM INFORMATION RESOURCES

An excellent → **resource for anyone researching the telecommunications industry.**

Telecom Information Resources is an index of telecommunications sites on the World Wide Web. Telecom Information Resources covers all aspects of the telecommunications industry, including economic concerns, public policy issues, and technical questions. The index covers over 20 major topics related to telecommunications, including Technical Information and FAQs, Research Labs, and Network Security.

http://www.yankeegroup.com/
THE YANKEE GROUP

Telecomm Strategy – Sound brilliant in no time! →

Read about the activities of a recognized leader in strategic planning, forecasting, and market research, much of which focuses on the telecommunications industry worldwide. Its briefing sessions, reports, and monthly White Papers are available. Topic areas include the target areas of the company's consulting and research: Client/Server Computing, Management Strategies, Manufacturing Technologies & Practices, Workgroup Strategies, Consumer Communications, Data Communications, among others.

www.dice.com
D.I.C.E.
Ever feel like your search for computer consulting and high-tech jobs is a roll of the dice? The Data processing Independent Consultants Exchange (DICE) understands, and its site gives you a winning edge. You can search the database of available positions and announce your skills and availability to the large base of recruiting firms.

Venture Capital

http://www.herring.com
THE RED HERRING

The Red Herring is the place to visit both for stock market mavens and technology entrepreneurs in search of venture capital, as the magazine's coverage of new media trends and investment is perhaps bar none. Smart and irreverent, the monthly publication tracks emerging trends in technology and entertainment providing a virtual companion to the print publication. It offers company profiles, breaking news, and regular columns from leading industry insiders.

www.nvca.org
NATIONAL VENTURE CAPITAL ASSOCIATION

The National Venture Capital Association (NVCA) represents 260 professional venture capital firms. These firms typically provide the second-stage financing that small companies need to bring a product to the general market or the third-stage financing needed to expand a company. While the website itself doesn't really help small companies that much, they can order the NVCA's annual report and other publications that will help them prepare a search for venture capital.

Part 4 - International Business Resources and International News

EMERGING MARKETS COMPANION

This site is really for foreign investors, but what better way to explore the best international companies and job opportunities? The site reports political and economic news that affects emerging markets around the world. The news sources are organized by news service and region. Users can review business updates from Reuters, Radio Free Europe, Bloomberg Business News, and Credit Lyonnais. The site also provides research reports from NatWest and Fiber, as well as country profiles from the CIA World Factbook. There is even a newsgroup devoted solely to investing in emerging markets available from this site.

A useful primer for staying on top of the rapidly ➜ changing environment for international trade.

http://www.wto.org
WORLD TRADE ORGANIZATION

The World Trade Organization (WTO) site offers a variety of resources for practitioners of international trade, whether a small business or a multinational corporation. The homepage offers a menu of ten choices. Start by accessing *About the WTO* if you're unfamiliar with the organization. The WTO provides a number of publications online related to international trade, trade policy, and trade and the environment.

www.europa.eu.int
EUROPA

Europa is "the Parliament, the Council, the Commission, the Court of Justice, the Court of Auditors, and the European Union's server." Find, in eleven languages, News (press releases from the EU institutions, calendar of events, the Euro rates), the ABCs of the European Union (employment opportunities, official documents, legal texts), Institutions (European Central Bank, and other agencies and bodies), and Policies (legislative activities, loans, statistics).

www.fita.org
THE FEDERATION OF INTERNATIONAL TRADE ASSOCIATIONS

Available for viewing in five languages including English, the Federation of International Trade Associations is a network of 300,000 companies from 300 international trade associations in the United States, Canada and Mexico. This informative site provides a Directory of Member Trade Associations, a searchable database of upcoming events, an index of over 1,000 international trade websites, a hub of trade opportunity leads, and a job bank for people seeking international employment opportunities.

www.glocom.ac.jp
GLOCOM Homepage

GLOCOM is a site developed and maintained by the Center for Global Communications, International University of Japan. Access current news relevant to global communications or view several years' worth of archived

---

news. A section entitled "Views from Japan" is an attempt to make available in a world forum the perspectives of Japanese scholars, business persons, government officials, and social critics.

www.webcom.com/one/world
INTERNATIONAL BUSINESS KIOSK
The International Business Kiosk World Wide Web site says that it is "Your reference page for doing business around the world." In addition to resources and news about international trade, the global business traveler will find a wealth of practical information here.

On Line Int'l
Classified ➡

www.overseasjobs.com
OVERSEAS JOBS EXPRESS
In addition to advertisements for specific jobs, international job hunters will find tips, tools, and services to expedite their search. Overseas Jobs Express (OJE) also publishes a subscription-based print version that contains over 1,500 jobs per issue. International job seekers will also find links to other job sites on the Web, but they may or may not be available to the overseas job hunter whereas all the jobs on the OJE are.

www.afp.com/english
AFP (AGENCE FRANCE-PRESSE) WORLD NEWS ROUNDUP
This French news service offers the latest news, as well as people, finance, and sports categories. AFP claims to have the most far-reaching network of any news service, and also the world's only Arabic sports service.

www.africanews.org
AFRICA NEWS ONLINE
This extensive news service has all the latest information you need regarding Africa. You can search for news by general region or by country. You can also search for news by topic.

www.awo.net
ARAB WORLD ONLINE
If you're looking for news and information about the Middle East, this is your source. Check out this site for the latest in current events, as well as travel and business information. There are also links to several Arab, International, and U.S. organizations.

www.asia-inc.com
ASIA INC. ONLINE
Asia Inc. Online primarily delivers news and information for Asian executives. It has financial slant, but you'll also find features on trends, technology, and lifestyle. Asia Inc. also has a Who's Who of Business in Asia. This is a slick-looking site.

www.asia1com.sg
ASIAONE
AsiaOne is "News about Asia from Asia." This extensive site will give you insight on what's happening in this region. It offers a lot of information about the world of information technology, as well as business. There are many links to other resources here as well.

www.boston.com/news/world
BOSTON GLOBE—LATEST NEWS FROM AROUND THE WORLD
The Boston Globe keeps tabs on all the major events happening around the world. You'll find a lot of stories regarding the international community. You'll also be able to access the rest of the Boston Globe's site from here, which means you can get the latest in national news, as well as sports, business, technology, and health.

www.ft.com/press
THE BROADCAST MONITORING CO.
Operating around the clock, Great Britain's Broadcast Monitoring Co. (BMC) presents news summaries from broadcast and print media within the United Kingdom, across Europe, and worldwide. BMC's News Review obtains featured news briefs from more than 2,000 press and broadcast sources. News briefs, which are listed as hypertext headlines, are updated each day at 7:30 British Standard Time. To see the full text of a news brief, just click its link.

There's a lot of talk about self-esteem these days. It seems pretty basic to me. If you want to feel proud of yourself, you've got to do things you can be proud of. Feelings follow actions.
Oseola McCarty, a washerwoman who gave her life savings of $150,000 to help complete strangers get a college education.

http://cens.com
CHINA ECONOMIC NEWS SERVICE ONLINE
If you are looking for Chinese and Taiwanese financial information, this is a good place to start. You'll find specific information on several regional businesses.

www.csmonitor.com
CHRISTIAN SCIENCE MONITOR: ELECTRONIC EDITION
The 88-year-old international newspaper now has a Web edition, which features all the content of the printed version. You'll also find options unique to the Web, such as hyperlinks to the Mid-Day Edition of Monitor Radio, hourly Monitor Radio newscasts around the clock, Associated Press headlines, and E-mail.

www.iht.com
INTERNATIONAL HERALD TRIBUNE
This news source from Paris dubs itself "The World's Daily Newspaper." Here you'll find the usual top headlines, as well as market reports, fashion, food, music, and travel information.

www.jpost.co.il
JERUSALEM POST INTERNET EDITION
The *Jerusalem Post* is an Israeli news outlet. If you want to read up on what's going on in Jerusalem and Israel, this is your source. In addition to headline news, you can read opinion articles and columns, and catch up on financial news.

www.nytimes.com/yr/mo/day/news/world
THE NEW YORK TIMES-INTERNATIONAL
Access to The New York Times on the Web is free, but you'll need to register before you can check out the day's latest international news stories. This comprehensive news site lists stories by headline. To read a particular article, just point and click. You'll find hyperlinks to related articles and links to other places of related interest.

http://newo.com/news/index.htmml
NEWS RESOURCE
This is a great index of news sources. It begins with a global map. Click on the region of interest, and you'll be taken to a list of relevant news links. This is a very extensive listing of news resources from around the world.

www.newsworld.cbc.ca
NEWSWORLD ONLINE
Newsworld online is an extensive Canadian news service. If you want the latest news affecting Canada, this is a great place to start. In addition to top news events, you can get information on business and the weather. This is a nicely designed site.

www.stack.nl/~haroldkl
WORLD NEWS INDEX
This is an extensive collection of hyperlinks to international news sources. You can check out various regions around the world, or look up international news sources, just by clicking a link.

Part 5-Job Search Engines & Telecommuting

http://www.careercentral.com
CAREER CENTRAL
Career Central is a unique Internet-based recruiting company. It is the first site to effectively use e-mail-based recruiting to connect business and high technology professionals with recruiters and HR professionals.

Unlike a résumé database or searchable job listing site, Career Central employs a targeted and propriety profiling technology—ensuring the best job match for candidates and hiring companies alike. To register with Career Central, candidates are encouraged to fill out a profile at www.careercentral.com.

Once there, candidates can indicate their preference for position, salary, and location as well as provide information on their experience and education. Candidates then receive job descriptions that match their career objectives via Career Central's confidential JobCast e-mail service.

Job seekers and hiring companies can find articles of interest on Career Central's Web site. The service is free to members.

Finally, a worry-free site for employed job seekers! Completely confidential—you can even block certain companies from receiving your résumé. ➜

Heroes come in all sizes, and you don't have to be a giant hero. You can be a very small hero. It's just as important to understand that accepting self-responsibility for the things you do, having good manners, caring about other people—these are heroic acts. Everybody has the choice of being a hero or not being a hero every day of their lives.
George Lucas, *Star Wars* film director, as quoted in *Time* magazine, April 26, 1999

Great Big Classified Ads ➜

http://www.careerpath.com/
CAREERPATH
Published by the *Los Angeles Times*, CareerPath.Com is a mammoth job-hunting website containing on average over 120,000 current help-wanted ads from newspapers across the country. Just click on *Jobs* and you'll be presented with a list of 50 or so U.S. newspapers to search. Then enter the job category desired and click *Search* to see listings. You will also find Employer Profiles in a searchable database of "mini-homepages" which provide background information about some of America's leading employers.

Emphasizes jobs and job hunting in the Pacific ➜ Northwest.

http://www.todays-careers.com
TODAY'S CAREERS—THE EMPLOYMENT PAPER
Today's Careers is an online employment newspaper published weekly. It offers a regular source of job-hunting advice as well as a limited database of employment opportunities. *Today's Careers* offers a strong collection of job opportunities via its online database. To do a quick search of job opportunities listed in *Today's Careers*, click on *Job Search*. Users can also review the *Hot Jobs* section to review the premium jobs available through the site. If you're looking in a specific community, click on the city icons located on the left hand side of the homepage. As such its content tends to reflect the computing and electronics industries that have clustered in this region of the country. The newspaper's real value lies in its collection of online feature articles and advice columns on job hunting and career development.

This one is IT ➜

http://beast.monster.com/home.html
MONSTER BOARD
The Monster Board claims to be the largest career opportunities site on the Net, with 50,000 job opportunities in all fields available at any given time. Look for a job in *Career Search*, submit your resume, or take a virtual tour of companies in *Employer Profiles*. You can search the database in one of three ways: (1) by career location, discipline, or company; (2) by specific skills or job titles; and (3) by using a linked listing of job-related newsgroups. Also contains *Folios*, pages that feature leading companies in various industries.

http://www.compuserve.com
CAREER FORUM
In addition to job postings and an electronic resume bank, this site provides good career counseling and practical advice for career development. Begin your visit to the Career Forum by reviewing the Forum Notices for an overview of the site's resources. There is a special guide for new members that is worth reviewing. Also, review the Sysop roster to familiarize yourself with the sources of online support available.

www.careers.org
CAREER RESOURCE CENTER
This valuable megalist contains more than 7,500 hyperlinks to jobs, employers, business opportunities, education indices and associations, and career service professionals. It also features more than 6,000 other resources, including bibliographies, software lists, publications, and resource evaluations. Whenever possible, Career Resource Center thoughtfully cross-references its resources geographically and alphabetically.

International Jobs ➜

www.cweb.com
CAREERWEB
A premier global career recruitment and resource service, CareerWEB offers a wide range of products, including free access to its database of international job postings and company information for job seekers and employers. Tips, topic-related articles, and an online bookstore also are available.

www.careercity.com
CAREER CITY
Career City provides a great combination of employment search tools and useful content. You can search more than 125,000 job listings by employment category, state, keyword, description, or any combination of these. Plus, you will find helpful feature articles, advice about how to get the interview, and much more. You also can search more than 100 job newsgroups and check links to more than 650 corporate employment sites.

www.jobdirect.com
JOB DIRECT
With too many graduates chasing what seems like too few entry-level positions, young job seekers need help. Start with Job Direct, the site for newcomers to the world of work. Eye-catching cartoons and graphic designs spread the word about the Job Direct roving job fairs, online resume builder, and job search engine. Employing

new grads? Job Direct offers focused and targeted recruitment, plus online extensive searches of posted resumes. Job Direct, which was founded by college students, can be a student's or new graduate's best online friend.

Telecommuting Jobs

http://www.tjobs.com
TELECOMMUTING JOBS
If you've fantasized about working out of the house, this website is for you. The Telecommuting Jobs site describes telecommuting employment opportunities for job-hunters and offers a place for human resource specialists to recruit outstanding employees based all over the world. Job listings on the Telecommuting Jobs site are provided under *Job Seekers*. The jobs available emphasize the type of work you would expect could be conducted from a remote location, particularly writing and computer programming.

Part 6: Start up Businesses/ Franchises/ Family Businesses

http://www.franchise1.com
FRANCHISE HANDBOOK: ONLINE
For entrepreneurs shopping for a potentially profitable franchise, this online handbook is your first stop. Not only will you find articles offering advice on franchising, a directory of funding sources, and a list of worldwide franchise associations, by clicking on *Featured Franchises*, you'll find a listing of intriguing franchising opportunities from printing, copying services and painting to upholstery repair and automobile products and services

http://fambiz.com
FAMBIZ.COM
This mid-sized but focused resource for family business executives and owners includes articles such as one titled "Which comes first, the family or the business?" —in addition to an online library of 300 relevant articles and a directory of family business websites.

Small Business –not too much job search competitiion here. Happy to hear from you! ➜

www.isbc.com
ISBC
The International Small Business Consortium (ISBC) provides extensive information for small- and medium-sized businesses worldwide. You can join a discussion group, read about issues of interest, or follow hyperlinks to related websites.

www.nextwavestocks.com
NEXT WAVE STOCKS
Although historically, small-cap stocks have been responsible for some pretty big returns, these types of investments aren't for the faint of heart. Next Wave Stocks specializes in small-cap stocks, buying into companies with market values of up to $1 billion. These companies, many of them technology oriented, are mostly emerging companies. Great for exploring smaller business job opportunities.

www.webcom.com/seaquest/sbrc/welcome.html
SMALL BUSINESS RESOURCE CENTER
This Small Business Resource Center has a handy list of articles that cover the basic questions you need to ask yourself before starting a business or buying a franchise. What sets this site apart from the rest is its coverage of specific industries. For example, it has articles such as "How to start your own day care center," "How to start a home-based secretarial service," and many more.

www.lowe.org/smbiznet
smallbizNet
The smallbizNet website will not only help you get your business started, but it will also help you develop it. SmallbizNet also boasts a search engine that combs through a library of more than 3,000 articles and government publications, though viewing some may cost a fee.

www.sbaonline.sba.gov
U.S. SMALL BUSINESS ADMINISTRATION
This site provides information about the entire array of services offered by the Small Business Administration (SBA), including several loan programs, numerous services for economically and socially disadvantaged business persons, and many programs to help small companies compete in foreign markets. Bargain hunters will also want to check out the link to the list of properties and capital equipment obtained in SBA loan foreclosures.

Section Two: Materials in Print

**compiled and annotated by
Wendy Alfus Rothman**

Introduction

During your job search there will be moments when "I don't know" may seem to be your constant refrain. You will say to yourself, "I don't know what industry to target" or "I don't know how many companies are in my target" or "I don't know what to ask my networking contacts" or "I don't know how to write a compelling letter" or "I don't know how to prepare for this interview." When you hear those words in your head, remember that the answers lie in research. Look for research resources right here in this annotated bibliography.

There are a great many books and databases listed on these next pages. Incredibly, this is only a sampling of what is available! I have organized the print bibliography for easy accessibility. Some of the materials are also available on disk and I have indicated when that is the case.

You will find five categories in the pages that follow:

1:   a guide to guides, directories and business information sources;

2:   a list of sources for investigating industry trends and outlooks;

3:   describes guides and directories across an array of industries;

4:   describes even more focused directories, geared for specific industries. They are divided into the following sections:

A. Advertising	M. Non-Profit/Fund-Raising
B. Environment	N. Public Relations
C. Finance	O. Publishing
D. Health Care	P. Sales and Marketing
E. High Technology	Q. Services
F. Human Resources	R. Small/Private Business
G. Importing, Exporting	S. Events/Trade Shows
H. Information Industry	T. Transportation
I. International Markets	U. Travel and Hospitality
J. Law and Government	V. Real Estate
K. Management Consulting	W. Education
L. Media	

5:   gives information on people and their backgrounds.

There are some universal laws to remember when conducting research:

1. **Call the library in advance of your visit.** Ask them what their hours are, the quietest times for using computer databases, and whether there is anything else that you need to know (e.g., charges for printing, time constraints for terminals). If necessary, ask to make an appointment to review how to use electronic information. You will be far better off than if you walk in at the busiest time and hope to get someone to help you.

2. **Prepare a list of questions you want to have answered for each session**. If you don't go with an agenda, it will be very easy to get distracted.

3. **When locating resources, always go to the primary source**. Some of these resources may not be in your local library. Call the library first and ask whether the volume or database you want is there. If it is not, perhaps the library has an alternative that would be just as valuable. If they do not, this is what I do: I call the publisher, I tell them what I want and where I am, and ask them what convenient library or facility they could refer me to. (The most prolific of these publishers is Gale Research in Detroit, Michigan. Their catalog of available resources is mind-boggling.)

4. **Use the locating of directories as a networking device.** Many people get frustrated when they can't find a particular reference book. In fact, the act of locating the information can itself be used as a powerful networking tool. For example, if you are looking for a directory of major financial institutions, you can network with someone in a financial institution, and ask if they have access to that directory. If they do, you can use it. If they don't, you can still talk about why you need it, which can lead into a discussion about your job search. Either way, you have nothing to lose.

5. **Don't just use books and databases in your own industry**. If you want to know who the experts are in your field, think about using the *Experts Contact Directory*. If you want to get a sense of a particular company, try looking it up in the *PR News Casebook*. Look up a company in *The Corporate Giving Directory* and see where they make charitable contributions. Get creative!

6. **Recontact people**. As you are researching, you will come across information that will be of interest to your networking contacts. Copy the articles and send them to appreciative people. See how much that will add to the "give" part of the give and take relationships you develop.

SECTION TWO: MATERIALS IN PRINT

1. Guide to Guides, Directories, and Business Information Sources

• **Directory of Industry Data Sources**. Ballinger Publishing Company, Harper & Row Publishers, Inc. Lists 3,000 publishers of industry data sources including bibliographic and source databases, indexing and abstracting services, and market research firms; describes monographs, surveys, periodical special issues, market studies, etc., covering 65 industries. Lists company names, addresses and phone numbers. Arranged alphabetically and by type of publication service. Three volumes cover the United States and Canada. Two volumes cover Western Europe.

• **Directories in Print.** Annual. Gale Research. Charles Montney, editor. Contains over 13,000 detailed and up-to-date entries, including international, all conveniently arranged in 26 subject chapters. An Alternative Formats Index lists directories published in non-traditional formats, such as on-line databases, CD-ROM, diskettes, microfiche, and mailing labels and lists. It is easy to scan columns and find alternative format titles. Directories in Print is also available on-line through DIALOG.

One stop ➔
shopping for
information on up-
to-date subjects, with
tables, graphs and
charts and where-to-
go for more info.
Check it out.

• **Encyclopedia of Business**. Gale Research. Provides in-depth coverage on an expansive selection of business issues. Includes over 700 signed articles written by subject matter specialists, covering major business disciplines, concepts and timely topics. Subjects include: business ethics, accounting, finance, public relations, valuation, home office, World Bank, ergonomics, robotics, family leave, and more. Most entries include a section listing sources of additional information.

• **Encyclopedia of Business Information Sources**. Gale Research. James Woy, ed. Wide range of business information sources listed under 1,000 alphabetically arranged business subjects. For each subject, you can quickly identify key live, print, and electronic sources of information. Provides title of the publication; database or organization; publisher of the information source; address, phone, and price/availability.

Covers basic business subjects as well as subjects of current interest, new technologies, and new industries. These include business policy trends like AIDS Policy, technological developments like facsimile systems, current issues like business innovation, and health industry material like Employee Wellness Programs.

2. General: Industry Trends, Forecasts, and Outlooks

• **Encyclopedia of Associations**. Annual. Gale Research. Guide to 22,000 national nonprofit organizations of all types, purposes and interests. Gives contact names, headquarters addresses, phone numbers, chief officials, number of members and chapters, description of membership, aims and activities. Includes lists of special committees and departments, publications, and a 4-year convention schedule. Arranged by subject, and cross-referenced by name of chief executive and geographic location, as well as by organization name.

➔ A powerful,
resource. Use this!

Though it is often
overlooked, I
personally love this
book. It tells me ➔
exactly where to go
to get concise and
precise market
research on any
topic that I am
interested in.

• **Findex: The Directory of Market Research Reports, Studies, and Surveys**. Cambridge Information Group Directories, Inc., JoAnne DuChez and Sharon J. Marcus. editors. An annotated bibliography of published business and market research reports, U.S. and foreign. These research reports come from many sources, and concern both domestic and foreign economies. The focus is on the operations of individual companies and on industries and their specific products. Also contains research reports on corporate management. The profile of each market report includes the title, publication date, publisher, summary, number of pages, price, and a report identification number. This is a major source for identifying commercially available market research reports and for learning where to obtain copies. Available online.

• **Manufacturing USA**. Gale Research. Arsen J. Darnay, editor. Gives profiles and top company rankings for about 460 manufacturing industries, organized by 1987 four-digit SIC codes. Manufacturing USA synthesizes relevant data from the Census of Manufacturers, the Annual Survey of Manufacturers, the County of Business Patterns, the U.S. Industrial Outlook, and the Industrial-Occupational Matrix produced by the U.S. Department of Labor.

Profiles provide industry statistics: indices of change, selected ratios; product share; statistical analyses by states and regions; occupations employed by various industries; fuel and other resource consumption data; and more. Product, Company Name, Occupations Employed, and 1987 four-digit SIC indexes.

*Self-respect is the fruit of discipline; the sense of dignity grows
with the ability to say no to oneself.*
Abraham J. Heschel, quoted in Ruth M. Goodhill ed., *The Wisdom of Heschel*

Another great way to get your hands on ➜ research reports for any field, including international areas; available on-line as well.

If you want to learn industry jargon, names of key ➜ players, hot topics, and important companies, this is your resource. Many newsletters will send you free sample copies. Ask!

➜ Great books, with the added benefit of being available in most libraries.

Terrific source of information on industry growth projections. Particularly great for those of you with a focus on numbers, ➜ graphs, and tables.

➜ Big, fat book with short and sweet descriptions. Not too in-depth, but very useful for quick forecasts.

This is a spectacular book that is a great supplement to the book of Associations and the U.S. Industry Profiles. ➜

New, thorough, and worth reading in print! Historic ➜ performance,

• **Market Share Reporter 2000**. Gale Research, 10th edition. Arsen J. Darnay, editor. MSR compiles producer and product share-of-market reports from a wide range of published sources including thousands of consumer, trade, and industrial publications. It also contains reports from foreign publications to offer coverage of world trade, international products, and global competitiveness.

Arranged by 4-digit SIC code, each of MSR's 2,000 entries includes: descriptive title of report; data and market description; remarks on the history, scope, and other characteristics of the study; list of producers/ products along with their assigned market share; and source citation. Brand Name, Source, Place Names, Companies, Products, Services, and Issues Indexes. MSR is also available on-line through NEXIS.

• **Newsletters in Print**. Annual. Gale Research. John Krol, editor. Newsletters in Print details more than 10,000 authoritative sources of information on a wide range of high-interest topics. Entries are arranged under seven broad categories comprising 33 specific subjects. Topics include business and industry; family and everyday living; information and communications; community and world affairs; science and technology; and more. Newsletters in Print is also available on-line.

• **Service Industries USA**. Gale Research. Arsen Darnay, editor. A comprehensive source of vital statistics on more than 150 U.S. service industries, as well as more than 4,000 leading public and private corporations and nonprofit institutions active in those industries. Service Industries USA (SIUSA) organizes widely scattered and difficult-to-use federal economic information into a usable and easy-to-read graphic format.

The first part of SIUSA lists industries by SIC code and provides industry data for the U.S. and the states, using various federal statistics for service industries. The format and content of information closely follows that of MUSA (with no overlapping entries), and contains: brief industry description; general statistics; indices of change; selected ratios; statistical analyses by state and region; occupations employed; leading companies; employment; and institutional involvement within an industry.

The second part contains Metro Area Statistics, arranged alphabetically by metro area and by SIC code, for more than 600 metropolitan areas of the United States. Tables include such valuable data as: numbers of establishments, total employment, revenues, and ownership patterns for each service industry in that metro area. SIC, Services, Metro Area Index, Company/Nonprofit Organization and Occupation Indexes.

• **Standard & Poor's Industry Surveys.** Quarterly. Standard & Poor's Corporation. Two volumes of up-to-date data for all major domestic industries. Prospects for a particular industry are followed by a historical presentation of trends and problems.. Tables and charts accompany the text. Sales, earnings, and market data for the leading companies in an industry are provided. This title is updated on a quarterly basis.

• **Statistical Forecasts of the United States**. Gale Research. James E. Person, Jr., editor. Population, employment, labor, crime, education, health care—all the key areas of American life are covered in SFUS.

SFUS goes beyond standard demographic data to provide in-depth coverage of "hot topics" such as the environment and health-care costs. Statistics are compiled from a diverse range of periodicals and research journals, industry reports, books, government documents, association reports, and other print sources. Data are presented in hundreds of charts, graphs, tables, and other statistical illustrations portraying both long- and short-term forecasts of future developments in the U.S.

SFUS is generously indexed to aid user access to information. In addition to the Subject Index, an Index of Forecast by Year allows users to find, for example, all predictions for the year 2005.

• **U.S. Industrial Outlook.** Annual. U.S. Department of Commerce. Describes prospects for over 350 manufacturing and service industries. An annual source of industry information, this title analyzes recent trends and forecasts for hundreds of industries. Data are presented in both narrative and tabular form. A list of additional references is included at the end of each chapter.

• **U.S. Industry Profiles**. Gale Research. Contains over 100 articles that analyze the most lucrative industries, including agriculture, construction, manufacturing, transportation, entertainment, wholesale and retail trade and others. Articles provide info on the size and impact of the industry, current trends and future forecasts, leading companies, size and nature of the work force, international influence, technological and legal developments, and major industry associations and publications..

• **U.S. Market Trends and Forecasts.** Gale Research. 1st Ed. 1999.U.S. Market Trends and Forecasts is an annual publication that provides market data for each of 400 industries with an overview of each industry

predicted future performance, and trends for over 30 broad industry categories.

and projections for industry performance including: market size, market sectors, competitive analysis, and market forecasts including projected performance of the market segment for six years in the future and an accompanying table with specific figures. There is a section on historical industry performance as well as an introductory essay that synthesizes trends and notes the fastest growing and slowest growing industries, as well as those projected to grow most and least quickly.

3. General: Company Information Guides and Directories

• **Business Rankings Annual**. Gale Research. A guide to published lists and rankings excerpted from major business publications. Has an easy-to-use subject arrangement, a listing of the top ten names in each ranking, a source list, and one master index to every name in every list. In addition to giving the top ten names in each list, each entry gives the ranking criteria; the number listed in the original ranking; and the name, date, and page of the source. The 1999 edition lists some 4,500 "top ten" businesses.

D&B's books are all-time standbys. Use for determining the size of your target, and collecting vital statistics on the ➜ companies in your target.

• **Dun & Bradstreet's Million Dollar Directory**. Annual. Dun's Marketing Services. Information on some 160,000 private and public U.S. businesses that have indicated net worth of more than $500,000. Each company listing includes the name, address, and telephone number of the company, the titles and names of key executives, a brief product or service description, approximate annual sales, and number of employees. All listings are cross-referenced geographically as well as by Standard Industrial Classification (SIC) code.

Another concise ➜ and succinct update on robust industry info from Gale. Find your industry and know it all!

• **Dun & Bradstreet and Gale Industry Reference Handbooks**. Gale Research. 1st Ed. 1998-1999. This is a new line of industry-specific Reference Handbooks that provides the following information: industry statistics and performance indicators; financial norms and ratios; key companies in the industry; ranked list of key companies; mergers and acquisitions; associations relevant to the industry; consultants that provide consulting services relevant to the industry; directory of important trade information sources; and trade shows and conferences important to the industry.

What a terrific resource. Here is a description of the history and events that have shaped major companies in a variety of fields. ➜ You want to impress people with your knowledge? You need to come up with good questions for networking and/or interviewing? Look no more—here is the resource to use.

• **International Directory of Company Histories**. Gale Research. Accurate and detailed information on the development of the world's 1,200 largest and most influential companies. This multi-volume work is the first major reference to bring together histories of companies that are a leading influence in a particular industry or geographic location.

Each two- to four-page entry is meticulously detailed, with facts gathered from popular magazines, academic periodicals, books, annual reports, and the archives of the companies themselves. Entries provide information on founders, expansions and losses, labor/management actions, and other significant mile-stones—all prepared with statistics, dates, and names of key players.

Organized alphabetically by industry; includes Cumulative Index to companies and personal names.
Volume 1: Advertising, Aerospace, Airlines, Automotive, Beverages, Chemicals, Conglomerates, Construction, and Drugs.
Volume 2: Electrical & Electronics, Entertainment & Leisure, Financial Services, Food Products, Food Service and Retailers.
Volume 3: Health and Personal Care Products, Health Care Services, Hotels, Information Technology, Insurance, Manufacturing and Materials.
Volume 4: Mining and Metals, Paper and Forestry, Petroleum, Publishing and Printing and Real Estate.
Volume 5: Retail and Wholesale, Rubber and Tire, Telecommunications, Textiles and Apparel, Tobacco, Transport Services, Utilities, and Waste Services.
Volume 6: Service Industries.
Volume 7 and 8 will be published later this year, thus continuing this interesting and informative series.

➜ All of Moody's books are classics, especially for financial info.

• **Moody's Manuals**. Moody's Investors Service. This set of eight manuals, plus index and updates, reports current financial and other information on publicly held companies, banks, utilities, and governments (federal, state, and local). The component manuals, arranged by type of organization, are: Bank and Finance Manual; Industrial Manual; International Manual; Municipal and Government Manual; OTC Industrial Manual; OTC Unlisted Manual; Public Utilities Manual; and Transportation Manual.

Includes financial-statement data and narrative reviews. The information was obtained from corporations, Securities and Exchange Commission reports, reports to stockholders, and other sources. The scope includes thousands of companies and government bond-issuing agencies. There are four levels of coverage in the profiles, depending on the level that was purchased. Descriptions are arranged by coverage level and, in some of these titles, by geographic location or type of company. A blue section in the center provides special features that are usually summary statistics or special lists, depending on the manual's subject.

• **National Directory of Minority Owned Business Firms.** Business Research Services. 47,000 minority business enterprises are listed including all vital company statistics.

• **National Directory of Women-Owned Business Firms.** Business Research Services. 28,000 entries with 17 points of data including company name and contact information

• **Notable Corporate Chronologies.** Gale Research. A two-volume set presents concise chronologies for over 1,150 of the most significant corporations currently operating in the U.S. and abroad. Coverage on both established companies, as well newcomers.

• **Walkers The Corporate Directory of U.S. Public Companies.** Annual. Gale Research. The Corporate Directory gives you all the essential facts on more than 9,500 publicly traded firms having at least $5 million in assets. Entries are arranged alphabetically by parent company name and provide: company name and contact data; general information such as incorporation and fiscal year end, legal counsel, etc.; stock data: price range for a 52-week period, closing price at last sale; summary of the company's areas of business, primary SIC; additional SICs; major subsidiaries; and more. Eight indexes.

• **Ward's Business Directory of U.S. Private and Public Companies.** Annual. Gale Research. Profiles of some 100,000 private and public companies. The information provided for each company resembles in both style and content that which is found in the sources discussed above. All companies profiled may be accessed geographically and by SIC code. A special feature of Ward's is that companies are ranked by sales within 4-digit SIC code categories. Available online.

• **Ward's Private Company Profiles.** Gale Research. Articles from over 150 sources including investment reports and company brochures about this significant and often elusive segment of the American economy. Find big companies, recognized names, as well as cutting edge firms and small aggressive companies.

4. Specific Industry Trends and Company Information

A. Advertising and Public Relations

• **Standard Directory of Advertising Agencies: The Agency Red Book**. National Register Publishing Company. An international guide to the advertising industry. Lists advertising agencies alphabetically and profiles each agency by reporting its address, telephone number, specialization, annual gross billings by media, names of accounts, names of management and account executives, and other information. Also provides a geographical index of agencies.

• **Vault.Com's Guide to Advertising**. Provides the inside scoop, what it's like working in the industry, who the players are in the industry, how to get ahead in the industry, and how to get hired in the industry. Reviews America's top employers in the advertising industry, including Bozell Worldwide, Grey Advertising, Leo Burnett, Ogilvy & Mather, TBWAChiat/Day, and many more!

B. Environment

Companies in this industry are listed; so are articles on trends and outlooks. A must for anyone targeting the environment. ➔

• **Environmental Encyclopedia**. Gale Research. William P. Cunningham, Terence Ball, et al., editors. Comprehensive, multidisciplinary approach to the study of the environment. Over 1,200 articles provide in-depth, worldwide coverage of all aspects of the environment in a convenient encyclopedic format. Included are articles on air, water, and noise pollution, climate, prominent personalities, biology, political science, economics, organizations, legislation, regulation and compliance, and more.

Each article is written in a non-technical style by an authority from an academic or professional post and compiled under the direction of Professor William P. Cunningham, author of *Environmental Science: A Global Concern*, and associates from the University of Minnesota representing a broad spectrum of interests and experiences in environmental sciences. Articles analyze major issues and events, provide insight on current status and problems, and suggest potential solutions.

A where-to-go for info in this field. Unbelievable for learning the environmental industry quickly and accurately. ➔

• **Encyclopedia of Environmental Information Sources**. Gale Research. Sarojini Balachandran editor. Information on hazardous materials, acid rain, endangered species, global warming, recycling, alternative

> *The opposite of love is not hate, it's indifference. The opposite of art is not ugliness,*
> *it's indifference. The opposite of faith is not heresy, it's indifference.*
> *And the opposite of life is not death, it's indifference.*
> Elie Wiesel

energy, and many other environmental topics. The subject-specific approach allows you to quickly identify more than 20,000 up-to-date citations to printed, electronic, and live information in more than 800 subject areas, including: abstracting and indexing services; bibliographies; directories; encyclopedias and dictionaries; on-line databases; periodicals and newsletters; associations and societies. Alphabetically arranged sections allow easy searching for specific information. This is a "source of sources," providing researchers with a convenient method to compile subject-specific lists for further research.

➜ Look! Not just info on the environmental industry, but from an international perspective.

• **World Guide to Environmental Issues and Organizations**. Gale Research. Peter Brackley, editor. Comprehensive, international coverage of 250 key environmental issues and organizations including government organizations, public and private research projects, and regulatory and campaign organizations. Some of the topics covered include global warming, acid rain, marine pollution, ozone depletion, forest loss, nuclear issues, water quality, and more.

C. Finance

➜ You want banks? Here are banks.

• **American Bank Directory.** Lists over 18,000 banks. Names of executives, addresses, and phone numbers.

➜ Oh, you said insurance? No problem.

• **Best's Insurance Reports, Property and Casualty.** Annual. A.M. Best Co. In-depth analyses, operating statistics, financial data and ratings, and names of officers in over 1,300 major stock and mutual property-casualty insurance companies. In addition, provides summary data on over 2,000 smaller mutual companies and on 300 casualty companies operating in Canada.

• **Business and Finance Career Directory.** Gale Research. Bradley J. Morgan; editor. Insider information from industry professionals. Essays cover topics such as working as a certified public accountant; what it's like to be a securities analyst or trader; becoming a financial planner; management information consulting as a career; and the facts about banking and insurance.

➜ Relevant and timely...and updated, too!

• **Cases in Corporate Acquisitions: Buyouts, Mergers & Takeovers.** Gale Research. 1st Ed. September 1999. Presents significant examples and analysis of mergers and acquisitions activity, covering both major successes and failures. Approximately 300 entries are arranged alphabetically by the name of the resulting company. The focus is on this century's merger and acquisitions activity where at least one participant is a U.S.-based corporation. Each entry contains three basic parts: brief background information; a summary of major players; and the main essay with background information on the companies involved, financial details such as stock prices, bond ratings, revenue and market share; how the merger/acquisition happened and the activity's driving market forces; resulting industry changes; and a review of the outcome.

• **Vault.Com's Guide to Investment Banking**. Provides the inside scoop, what itís like working in the industry, who the players are in the industry, how to get ahead in the industry, and how to get hired in the industry. Reviews America's top employers in the investment banking industry, including Bankers Trust, Goldman Sachs, JP Morgan, Morgan Stanley, and many more!

• **Financial 1,000 Yellow Book.** Commercial banks, insurance companies, Wall Street firms, and thrifts.

• **Financial Planners and Planning Organizations Directory.** Over 4,000 planners/organizations profiled.

➜ More insurance companies, this time international as well.

• **Financial Times World Insurance.** Annual. Gale Research. This complete guide to the insurance industry and more than 1,150 insurance companies around the world provides background information on recent developments in the insurance industry, currency tables, and definitions of key financial terms, as well as detailed summaries of individual companies.

• **Moody's Bank and Finance Manual**. Moody's Investors Service. Profiles institutions in the U.S. finance industry: banks, savings and loan associations, investment companies, insurance companies, real estate companies, real estate investment trusts, unit investment trusts, and other financial enterprises.

Includes history; location; names of officers and directors; consolidated financial statement; financial and operating ratio; debt structure; letters to shareholders; list of securities held in trust; record of income and principal distribution; and other financial information that is appropriate to the type of financial institution.

- **Pratt's Guide to Venture Capital Sources**. Venture Economics, Inc., Stanley E. Pratt and Jane K. Morris, editors. Venture capital firms and individuals in the U.S. and Canada. Brief description of each source that includes address, telephone number, industry and project preferences, and other related information. Also includes a list of firms that underwrite public offerings for equity capital in small businesses.

- **St. James Mutual Fund Directory**. Gale Research. More than 2,500 mutual funds operating in the U.S. Easy-to-use volume. Explains what funds are, how they are operated and regulated, and how to read a prospectus. Answers the most commonly asked questions.

    Organized by mutual fund types, its 22 chapters cover virtually every mutual fund in America, providing addressees and phone/fax numbers, years in operation, names of investment advisors, asset size, minimum initial and subsequent investment requirements and where shares can be purchased.

- **Standard & Poor's Bond Guide.** American and some foreign bonds, including S&P quality ratings.

- **Standard & Poor's Corporation Records.** Similar to Moody's manuals, but covers companies not listed on any stock exchange.

- **Value Line Investment Survey.** Lists 1,700 companies, with statistics and key investment factors. Ratings, prospects, charts and brief explanatory texts. Revised quarterly.

D. Health Care

- **Dun's Guide to Healthcare Companies.** Annual. Dun's Marketing Services. Detailed information on more than 15,000 companies which provide products or services in the health-care industry. Standard directory-type information is provided for each company. All listings are cross-referenced geographically, by SIC code, by medical/diagnostic device, and by brand name.

- **Encyclopedia of Medical Organizations & Agencies.** Gale Research. Karen Backus, editor. This encyclopedia gives you instant access to the more than 12,000 public and private organizations and agencies concerned with medical information, funding, research, education, planning, advocacy, advice, and service. Entries in 69 subject chapters include the organization's name, address, telephone number, key officials, founding year, number of members, number of employees, publications and their frequency, as well as a brief description of the group's purpose.

- **Industrial Biotechnology International.** Contains an overview of major advances in biochemistry and biotechnology that are of commercial significance. Also included are financial reports of biotechnology corporations and pharmaceutical companies, discussions of specific companies involved in biotechnology, and a review of recent patents.

→ Great resource for info on topics in health care.

- **Medical & Health Information Directory**. Gale Research. Karen Backus, editor. Comprehensive guide to organizations, agencies, institutions, services, and information sources in medicine and health-related fields. in three volumes. Volume 1 has descriptive information on more than 16,400 organizations, agencies, and institutions. Volume 2 has contact data and descriptive details on over 9,700 libraries, publications, and institutions. Volume 3 has current data on over 23,000 health services. Also available on diskette.

- **Vault.Com's Guide to Healthcare**. Provides the inside scoop, what it's like working in the industry, who the players are in the industry, how to get ahead in the industry, and how to get hired in the industry. Reviews America's top employers in the healthcare industry, including Magen, Eli Lilly, Johnson & Johnson, Oxford, Pfizer, Schering-Plough, and many more!

E. High Technology

→ This is the where-to-go for info for high tech.

- **Computers and Computing Information Resources Directory**. Gale Research, edited by Martin Connors. A comprehensive directory of print and nonprint sources of information on all aspects of computers, computing, and data processing. It is a guide to finding sources of computer-related information. These sources include user groups, trade and professional associations, consultants, university computer facilities and research organizations, trade shows, professional exhibits, computer related association conventions, on-line database vendors and teleprocessing networks worldwide. The sources also include special libraries and information centers with an emphasis on computers or computer science, as well as journals, newsletters, and computer-oriented directories. Each entry contains the name, address, telephone number, purpose or activities, and other descriptive information for each source. Also contains a directory of some persons in the computer-information field, listing their addresses and telephone numbers.

• **Corporate Technology Directory**. Corporate Technology Information Services, Inc. Public and private U.S. firms and U.S. operating units of foreign companies that manufacture or develop high-technology products, including: advanced materials, automation, biotech, chemicals, computers, software, energy, manufacturing, medical, pharmaceuticals, telecommunications, and others. Company profiles include company name, other or former company name(s), address, telephone number, telex, fax, ownership of the company, ticker symbol, year founded, description of the business activity, annual sales revenue, number of employees, names of executives with their titles and areas of responsibility, product descriptions, SIC codes, detailed Corp Tech product codes, and other information. Through the elaborate indexing system, companies can be identified by name, location, parent name, and their high-tech products.

• **Data Sources: Data Comm/Telecomm**. Ziff-Davis Publishing Company. A guide to data communications and telecommunications hardware. Directory of data/telecommunications company profiles. Gives a description of each product. These products include network processor/network management systems, modems, multiplexors, emulation/conversion equipment, security equipment, PBX/CBX equipment, telephone call-accounting systems, facsimile machines, teleconferencing systems and services, and other telecommunication equipment. Some of the data are displayed in charts that facilitate product comparisons.

• **Telecommunications Directory**. Lists national and international organizations involved in telecommunications. Includes voice and data communications services, local area networks, teleconferencing facilities, videotex and teletext operations, and companies providing electronic mail, facsimile, telegram and telex, voice processing/response, satellite, and telecom-related associations, consultants, law firms, publishers, regulatory bodies, and seminar/training organizations.

• **Vault.Com's Guide to High Tech**. Provides the inside scoop, what it's like working in the industry, who the players are in the industry, how to get ahead in the industry, and how to get hired in the industry. Reviews America's top employers in the high tech industry, including Broderbund, Cisco Systems, Hewlett-Packard, Intel, Microsoft, Sun Microsystems, and many more!

F. Human Resources

• **Directory of Executive Recruiters**. Consultant News, Kennedy Publications, New Hampshire. James H. Kennedy, editor. A directory of more than 2,500 executive search firms. These are executive recruiters who are paid by management, not job hunters. Provides the name of the executive- search firm, address, contact person, field of specialization, and other information.

• **Personnel Executives Contact Book**. Annual.Gale Research. Cindy Spomer, editor. Complete contact information for key personnel officers at 30,000 companies across the U.S. Arranged alphabetically by company name, listings contain information most frequently requested by job hunters: company name, address, and phone number; SIC code; number of employees; annual revenues; the name of the key personnel executive (highlighted for easy discovery); and the names of other human resources staff.

• **Training and Development Organizations Directory**. Gale Research. Janice McLean, editor. Guide to companies that produce workshops, seminars, videos, and other training programs that can enhance skills and personal development. Fully describes more than 10,000 such training programs.

Detailed contact information is provided for the training organization, including full name, address, phone number, fax, toll-free number, date founded, names of principals, staff size, areas of course emphasis, typical clients/target audience, course titles and fees, and packaged training programs. Geographic, Personal Name, and Subject Indexes. Directory is also available on-line.

Sidebar notes:

Global high tech! What's going on around the world in high tech and in ➜ specific industries that are related to high tech? Check it out.

➜ Very good info on all aspects of the high-growth field of telecommunications.

➜ Use this directory if you need to locate headhunters who specialize in specific industries, or if you are in the search business and need to identify companies in your target. Kennedy Publications has a wide variety of guides for the staffing and consulting industries.

We have come out of the time when obedience, the acceptance of discipline, intelligent courage and resolution were most important, into that more difficult time when it is a person's duty to understand the world rather than simply fight for it.
Ernest Hemingway

G. Importing / Exporting / Trading

• **Directory of United States Importers**. Journal of Commerce. A directory of importers with a profile of each firm. Cites name, address, telephone and telex numbers, cable address, year established, names of principal officers, custom-house broker, port of entry, products imported, and the source nations for the imports. Reviews the U.S. Customs Service regulations and importing procedures. Lists products that are imported and their respective importers. Also cites U.S. and foreign embassies and consulates, international banks in the U.S., trade associations, and ports of the world.

• **Exporters Directory/U.S. Buying Guid**. Journal of Commerce. A directory of American exporters. Lists firms alphabetically and by product. Also contains a brand-name index. Profiles of exporting firms include name, address, telephone number, telex number, cable address, names of key officers, number of employees, year established, ports of exit, products exported, countries served, and international freight forwarder. Also describes export-related services provided by the U.S. Department of Commerce. Lists U.S. and foreign embassies/consulates, international banks in the U.S., trade associations, and ports of the world.

• **World Business Directory**. Gale Research, edited by Meghan A. O'Meara and Kimberley A. Peterson. Lists over 105,000 trade-oriented businesses of all sizes from more than 190 countries (even the smallest) including: top trading firms from each country or market region; small and medium-sized companies not listed elsewhere; international trade/import leaders.

Contains vital details for exploring and evaluating international markets, finding potential trading partners, identifying which firms compete internationally, and contacting executives or consultants in specific industries. The entries give readers the data they need to achieve the desired goal.

A typical entry lists: company name and contact names; contact information: address, phone, fax, telex; business activities; product details; WTC affiliation and NETWORK access code; company type (holding company subsidiary, etc.); import/export designation; revenue figures; parent company name; year established.

First three volumes contain company listings arranged geographically, then by company; fourth volume consists of three indexes (Alphabetical, Industry, and Product). Also available on CD-ROM.

→ A directory of trading firms—both big and small—across the globe. Includes their areas of specialization.

• **World Trade Resources Guide**. Gale Research. Kenneth Estell, editor. *WTRG* brings together in one convenient, easy-to-use source a wide range of resource information for anyone interested in import/export opportunities around the world. WTRG includes 80 of the world's largest trading nations as well as many smaller countries which play an important part in world trade.

Countries are arranged alphabetically in chapters, providing complete contact data for government organizations, shipping lines of registry, principal ports, free trade zones, nonprofit or trade associations, sources of foreign trade statistics, and publications concerned with foreign trade.

Each country chapter opens with a profile that provides vital statistics on that country's population, currency exchange rates, GNP/GDP, import/export/trade balance figures, major trading partners, principal commodities imported and exported, and memberships in international organizations.

H. Information Industry

NOTE: Information Industry here refers to Information Services & Retrieval. Other aspects of the broader Information & Communication industry can be found under High Technology, Publishing and Media and Broadcasting

Use this guide in case you want to explore the incredible field of research services; you can also identify companies that, for a fee, will help you do your own research in some other target! →

• **Directory of Fee-Based Information Services**. Burwell Enterprises, edited by Helen P. Burwell. Directory of information specialists who provide services for a fee. Includes information brokers, free-lance librarians, fee-based services of public and academic libraries, and information packagers, U.S. and abroad. Includes name of the firm or individual, address, telephone number, telex and fax numbers, contact person, subject specialization areas, and types of information services provided (e.g., research, on-line retrieval, and report writing). Each profile concludes with a descriptive summary.

• **Prentice Hall Directory of Online Business Information**, 1998.
This tome tells you where to go for immediate online info: it reviews over 1,500 online business sources, and it includes a glossary of Internet terms and concepts.

• **Vault.Com's Guide to Internet and New Media.** Provides the inside scoop, what it's like working in the industry, who the players are in the industry, how to get ahead in the industry, and how to get hired in the industry. Reviews America's top employers in the Internet and new media industry, including Amazon.com, CDNow, DoubleClick, Excite, Netscape, Yahoo!, and many more.

I. International Markets

• **America's Corporate Families and International Affiliates**. Dun's Marketing Services. A directory of U.S. corporations and their foreign subsidiaries, arranged by corporate family. Also lists foreign parent companies with their U.S. subsidiaries. Excludes companies that are based either exclusively in the U.S. or totally outside of the U.S. Provides a cross-reference index between subsidiaries and their parent companies. Publishes a profile of corporations that reports the location's telephone number, nature of business, officers, sales volume, export/import activity, and other descriptive information for each.

• **Dun's Europa.** Dun & Bradstreet Europe. Annual. Details on 45,000 leading European companies. All 12 countries of the European Community are represented, along with Austria and Switzerland. Listed alphabetically by country. Includes rankings by sales and indexing by line of business.

• **Eastern Europe: A Directory and Sourcebook**. Gale Research. Economic background information, business information sources, profiles of leading companies, and current market and consumer trends. Includes Bulgaria, Germany, Hungary, Poland, Romania, and the former states of Czechoslovakia, Yugoslavia, and the Soviet Republics. Five sections: the first gives an overview of the categories; the second discusses economics; the third lists major state-owned and private companies; the fourth provides business information sources; and the fifth gives comparative data tables in such areas as demography, energy, retail sales, and more.

• **Eastern European Business Directory**. Gale Research, edited by Frank X. Didik. More than 7,000 companies and organizations providing close to 9,000 distinct products in the countries of Bulgaria, Hungary, Poland, Romania, the former Czechoslovakia and western Soviet Union. Arranged by product/service, geographic location, and company name.

• **Encyclopedia of Business Information Sources: Europe**. Gale Research, edited by M. Balachandran. Covers a wide range of business information sources from 32 Eastern and Western European countries and lists them under approximately 1,000 alphabetically arranged business subjects. From Accounting to the Video Recording Industry, *EBIS: Europe* includes the most up-to-date topics relevant to today's researcher. Within each topic category, entries are divided geographically and then by type of resource.

125 vital international industries exposed! ➜

• **Encyclopedia of Global Industries**, Gale Research. Covers industries with significant global trade and interdependence covering a broad spectrum of topics for each industry including size & economic/social impact of the industry, how it is organized and how it functions, history & development, current economic status, size & nature of the work force.

It's simply amazing to have, in one volume, the names and specialized markets for 5,000 European consultants. This is a great way to tap into the global marketplace. ➜

• **European Advertising, Marketing and Media Data**. Gale Research. Comprehensive and detailed look at European marketing statistics: economic indicators, demographics, geographic location, and market size of 16 major Western European markets. Indispensable to marketing directors, sales and export directors, corporate planners, advertising executives, media and management consultants, students, and job hunters.

• **European Consultants Directory**. Gale Research, edited by Karin Koek. Helps users find consultants to advise them in management, finance, and other business affairs as well as agriculture, engineering, education, and political and social issues. The more than 5,000 consultants are grouped by country, by broad subject terms, and then alphabetically by consulting organization. The directory also lists additional addresses for almost 2,500 branch offices, so you can contact nearly 7,500 consultants throughout Europe. Three indexes: Consulting Activities Reference List, Consulting Firms, and Personnel Listings.

Offers qualitative information about market share and ➜ *recent company developments.*

• **European Major Companies Directory**, 1998. Euromonitor. Provides information on 6,000 leading companies of all types in 16 European countries. Each entry details company activity, ownership, subsidiaries, key personnel, main operations, main products and brand names, number of employees and financial data for the last four years. Includes company news and recent company developments.

The only joy in the world is to begin.
Cesare Pavese, Italian writer

→ European MSR will instruct you on how to find any information in the EEC

Most global → directories cover only the largest firms. This volume helps you identify the mid-sized growth companies of Europe, where so much job opportunity exists.

You will find all → the answers to the big picture questions here: international trends, forecasts and outlooks; areas growing and areas declining. Think of how this can help you design really powerful questions for networking!

• **European Market Share Reporter**. Gale Research, edited by Oksana Newman and Allen Foster. As the planned economic alliance of the European nations creates the world's largest single market, related information needs will grow. Helps locate market share information for companies, products, industries, and markets within the European Economic Community. Coverage, format, and organization are similar to the U.S.-focused *Market Share Reporter*. 1,400 entries are arranged by 4-digit U.S. SIC codes.

• **Europe's Medium-Sized Companies Directory**, 1998, Euromonitor. Over 6500 of the most important medium-sized companies in Western Europe. All types of companies from all the main sectors of the economy are featured including manufacturing, trading, banking, consumer products, and so on.

• **International Marketing Handbook**. Gale Research. Detailed marketing profiles for 141 nations. Country reports—averaging 31 pages in length and complemented by maps, tables, and charts—have been developed by the International Trade Administration of the U.S. Department of Commerce. Includes authoritative information on such areas as: foreign trade outlook; industry trends; government contracting; employment and wages; trade regulations; foreign investment; sources of economic and commercial information; more.

Includes trade guides and international marketing briefs concerning the European Common Market, the Near East and North Africa, the Middle East situation, East-West trade, and other related topics of interest to international business.

• **Major Financial Institutions of Continental Europe**. Gale Research. Profiles more than 1,100 leading financial institutions of Europe, arranged within country chapters, providing name of firm, address and telephone number, telex and fax numbers, name of chairman, name of board members, principal business activities, number of employees, and more. Company and Geographic Indexes.

• **Medium Companies of Europe**. Gale Research. Describes Europe's many privately owned and growing medium-sized firms. Three volumes bring you information on over 7,000 rising European businesses.

• **Principal International Business**. Dun's Marketing Services. The most prominent and largest businesses in countries around the world. Lists firms alphabetically within country and in a composite list for all countries. Also organizes them by line of business (SIC code). Entry profiles include address, SIC code, name of parent company, name of senior operating officer, and other information.

• **International Directory of Corporate Affiliations**. Register Publishing Company. A directory of foreign parent companies with their domestic and international holdings and of U.S. parent companies with their foreign subsidiaries, affiliates, and divisions. Lists companies by country. Also provides addresses and telephone numbers of foreign consulates in the U.S., U.S. embassies, American Chambers of Commerce abroad, and foreign trade commissions and Chambers of Commerce.

→ How much more current could you get than a volume called "The World's Emerging Markets"? Even if this is not your target, thinking of how this kind of information could impact your target will lead to very powerful interviews.

• **The World's Emerging Markets**. Gale Research. This major new data book draws together a wide variety of statistics and analyses, providing a clear assessment of business opportunities in the world's fastest-growing markets.

Up-to-date, usable information about industries, regions, and particular companies. Included are market prospects, demand characteristics, and policy environment in most of the world's emerging economies. Markets are ranked by size, wealth, stability, and future potential. *The World's Emerging Markets* also contains an extensive compilation of up-to-date statistical data covering socio-economic activity, external trade and investment, standard of living indicators, consumer expenditures, retail distribution, advertising, marketing, and household composition.

Chapters include comprehensive information on the economies and prospects of countries within the following regions: Eastern Europe and the former USSR, Southern Europe, The Pacific Rim, Central Asia, South America, Africa, and the Middle East.

→ Worldwide high tech.

• **World Technology Policies**. Gale Research. Offers an authoritative and comprehensive look at science and technology worldwide. Included are an overview of key trends and reviews of four key areas of growth: new materials, information technology, biotechnology, and defense. The status of science and technology in the major nations of the world is presented, including details of important national and international organizations.

Many are stubborn in pursuit of the path they have chosen,
few in pursuit of the goal.
Friedrich Nietzsche

• **Worldwide Branch Locations of Multinational Companies**. Gale Research, edited by David S. Hoopes. More than 500 top multinational companies, and nearly 20,000 plants, branches and subsidiaries located worldwide. Covers companies that are not headquartered in the U.S. in addition to those that are. Divided geographically by country. Branch, plant, and subsidiary entries are listed alphabetically within each country section. Each listing has an entry number to accommodate references for the indexes.

J. Law and Government

In addition to identifying opportunities for lobbyists and government-relations people, this book is a fabulous way to identify the issues particular ➔ companies are lobbying for. This provides new insight into company values and company problems. Very clever!

• **American Lobbyists Directory**. Gale Research, ed: Robert Wilson. A complete guide to federal and state lobbyists. Listings include 57,000 lobbyists and 25,000 organizations in state-by-state sections, 8,000 registered federal lobbyists, and 4,000 represented organizations. Descriptive entries provide complete contact information, including phone numbers, for the organizations and lobbyists involved in particular issues. Lobbyists Index, Organizations Index, and Subject/Specialty Indexes.

• **Encyclopedia of Governmental Advisory Organizations. Annual**. Gale Research, edited by Donna Batten. Over 6,000 entries describing the activities and personnel of groups and committees that function to advise the President and various departments and bureaus of the federal government, as well as giving detailed information about historically significant committees.

Includes information about White House Conferences and other conferences sponsored by the federal government, groups under contract doing studies for the federal government, and congressional committees doing studies of current topical interest. Complete contact information provided when available. Five indexes provide easy access: Alphabetical and Keyword, Personnel, Publications and Reports, Organizations by Federal Department or Agency, and Organizations by Presidential Administration.

• **Law and Legal Information Directory**. Gale Research, edited by Steven Wassermann and Jacqueline Wasserman O'Brien. Descriptions and contact information for 30,500 institutions, services, and facilities arranged in 25 chapters, including National and International Organizations, Bar Associations, Federal Court System, Law Schools, Scholarships and Grants, Legal Periodicals, Lawyer Referral Services, Legal Aid Offices, Public Defender Offices, Small Claims Courts, and more.

Twenty-five chapters help you find information on a particular area of law; discover the status of a bill in progress at the state level through a quick phone call; locate nearby law schools and schools for continuing legal education or paralegal training; and much more.

• **Worldwide Government Directory**. Gale Research, annual. This directory provides current contact information on 173 countries, their leaders, and major government offices. For each country listed, following general background facts—such as official language, capital, currency exchange rates, and telephone codes—you'll find names, titles, addresses, and telephone numbers for its head of state, cabinet members, ambassadors, key officials, state agencies, ministries, embassies, and other government offices. This new edition's comprehensive coverage includes more than 50,000 entries, and reflects recent changes in Eastern Europe, unified Germany, and the former Soviet Republics.

K. Management Consulting

New book that addresses so many of the failures and successes in business strategy today. Truly an amazing wealth of do's and don'ts for consultants.

• **Cases in Corporate Innovation**. Gale Research. Contains approximately 300 entries arranged alphabetically by company name. Each entry has contact and financial information, followed by a major essay addressing the following components:
  - A review of the organization before the management practice was adopted
  - The forces driving the implementation of the new practice
  - How the management practice was implemented at the company
  - The effect of the practice on the company
  - How these management principles have been implemented elsewhere
  - How these principles have affected the industry
  - Further research covering 10-15 relevant and annotated sources
Primarily covers American companies, with approximately 25% coverage of international companies from

the 20th century, including restructurings, team and matrix management and corporate strategic changes. You'll find both successful and failed management practices from industry leaders for domestic entries and companies listed on the London, Hong Kong and Japanese stock exchanges for international entries.

• **Vault.Com's Guide to Management Consulting**. Provides the inside scoop: what it's like working in the industry, who the players are in the industry, how to get ahead in the industry, and how to get hired in the industry. Reviews America's top employers in the management consulting industry, including Andersen Consulting, Boston Consulting Group, McKinsey, PricewaterhouseCoopers, and many more!

L. Media & Broadcasting

• **Gale Directory of Publications and Broadcast Media. Annual**. Gale Research. Julie Winklepleck, editor. Over 36,000 entries, including listings for radio and television stations, and cable companies. For each state, province, and city in the U.S. and Canada, you can quickly identify its magazines, newspapers, radio and television stations, and cable companies.

→ Includes radio, TV, and cable.

Entries are arranged by state or province, and then by city. Brief demographics are given for each city. Television and radio station entries contain: station call letters and channel; Area of Dominant Influence (ADI); name of owner network affiliation; top three local programs; advertising rates; and more. Master Alphabetical/Keyword and Classification Indexes. Also available on-line.

• **Gale's Guide to the Media: A Gale Ready Reference Handbook.** Gale Research, 1st Ed., Spring 2000 Features associations, directories, periodicals, databases and online services, leading companies and organizations and supplier companies relevant to the media industry. This edition also has sections particular to the media industry, including publicity organizations and agencies and major cable and network TV stations.

• **Radio and Television Career Directory**. Gale Research, Bradley J. Morgan, editor. Discover on-air and behind-the-scenes opportunities in radio, TV news, broadcast meteorology, radio programming, radio marketing, writing for television, cable TV, and other specialties through insightful essays written by noted professionals within the industry.

• **Spot Radio Rates and Data**. Standard Rate and Data Service. A directory of the radio industry, with an alphabetical listing, by state and U.S. possession, of radio stations. The station profiles include address, telephone number, call letters, names of key personnel, advertising contract terms and spot rates, and other information about the station. Reports descriptions and rankings of television market areas. Contains a listing of program syndicators and firms that represent radio stations.

• **Vault.Com's Guide to Media and Entertainment.** Provides the inside scoop: what it's like working in the industry, who the players are in the industry, how to get ahead in the industry, and how to get hired in the industry. Reviews America's top employers in the media and entertainment industry, including AOL, Blockbuster, CNN, Dreamworks, Gannett, National Public Radio, Time Warner, and many more!

M. Not-for-Profit / Fund-Raising

• **America's New Foundations. Annual**. Gale Research. Many new foundations are emerging every year and *ANF* helps fundraisers find them. Provides current contact information on more than 3,400 private, corporate, and community foundations created since 1987—including 250 new funding organizations.

→ *ANF* is a brilliant resource, especially valuable for people searching for information on smaller foundations, where much opportunity lies. It is updated annually.

These newly established foundations—with assets or annual giving of $100,000 or more—offer unique opportunities, as smaller foundations with brief giving histories are often overlooked. The funding organizations profiled here have combined assets of at least $4.4 billion—and total giving of more than $382 million. *ANF* provides a constant flow of new and changing information.

• **Charitable Organizations of the U.S.** Gale Research, 2nd edition, edited by Doris Morris Maxfield. Nearly 800 entries describe groups active in soliciting funds from the American public—their history and purpose, the nature and extent of their activities, their leadership, spokespersons, and sponsors.

Of special interest is this volume's detailed coverage of each charity's fundraising activities and expenses. Profiles include data on sources of income; expenses for administration, fund-raising, and program payout based on total income. Geographic Location, Keyword, Subject, and Personal Name Indexes.

• **Corporate 500**. Gale Research. A convenient source of factual information on the funding programs of the 580 American corporations with the most active programs. Provides a clear picture of each corporation, including address, phone number, contact person, eligibility, number of grants made, application process, sample grants that tell who got them, why and how much, and other pertinent information. Each part of the main entry is separately indexed for quick data retrieval. Indexes.

• **Corporate and Foundation Grants**. Gale Research. Comprehensive guide to more than 95,000 recently awarded grants from private foundations, corporate foundations, and corporate direct-giving programs. Includes grants from hard-to-identify corporate direct givers. Awards are arranged by recipient's actual location. Provides access to grantmakers with a demonstrated history of activity in a particular geographic or interest area.

Volume One, Grants by Category, lists recipients by eight major subject areas and by the state and city in which they are located. Volume Two, Guide to Funding Organizations, lists more than 5,500 corporate and private grantmakers, and includes application procedures, deadlines, and restrictions for the programs listed. In addition, grant recipients are indexed alphabetically by name, and funding organizations are indexed alphabetically by recipient type and by grant recipient location.

• **Taft's Corporate Giving Directory. Annual**. Gale Research. A classic reference that identifies 607 companies that collectively donate $2.75 billion in cash and non-monetary support annually—more than 50 percent of all corporate giving. Provides up-to-date contact names, deadlines, total assets, average grant size, and names of recent front recipients. The new edition profiles 35 corporate givers never before featured.

Approximately 60 percent of the profiles in this edition cover difficult-to-find corporate-giving programs—information not available from the IRS, corporate annual reports, or similar directories. Also provides practical insights—biographical data on decision makers, analyses of priorities, corporate philosophy, etc.

• **Corporate Giving Yellow Pages. Annual**. Gale Research. Easy-to-use guide to the people to contact at the leading corporate-giving programs and corporate foundations in America. Over 3,900 listings: contact name, title, address, and phone number. The directory provides the most current contract data available.

• **Taft's Directory of International Corporate Giving in America and Abroad. Annual**. Gale Research. In this age of global markets, a great many of the world's most powerful multinational corporations have set up international philanthropies. Profiles more than 450 companies that give in the U.S. and overseas.

Section 1 provides fundraisers with the most current information available on the funding activities in the U.S. of 350 companies; Section 2 provides up-to-date information on international funding activities of 105 U.S.-headquartered companies.

This is the only directory on U.S. companies that give internationally and the only one that profiles foreign multinationals giving in the United States. More than 75 percent of the entries profiled maintain direct giving programs, providing information not available from public records. All profiles have been updated since the last edition—and 30 new profiles have been added. Multiple indexes allow you to uncover networks and connections between companies, countries, and philanthropic interests.

• **Finding a Job in the Nonprofit Sector**. Gale Research. A combined career advisory guide and employment directory, this volume helps experienced nonprofit professionals as well as newcomers to the nonprofit field assess their potential and find their niche within this vast and potentially lucrative job market. In addition, career counselors, librarians, recruiters and others seeking information on employment opportunities in the "third sector" would be wise to tap into this useful publication.

Finding a Job in the Nonprofit Sector first presents two insightful essays on job hunting, an analysis of employment trends in the sector, and detailed listing of nonprofit employers. The essays, "Forty-Two Action Steps for Seeking NPO Jobs" and "What If? Approaching NPOs from Where Your Are," give job seekers tips on search strategy, interview preparations, skills inventory, and more. An additional feature, "The Nonprofit Sector: An Overview of Employment Trends," summarizes facts from recent annual National Nonprofit Wage and Benefit Surveys published by the Technical Assistance Center in Denver.

The guide also lists nearly 5,000 nonprofit organizations from across America, all with estimated annual incomes of more than $10 million. Approximately 1,000 full descriptive profiles are provided.

➜ All these books—*Corporate 500, Taft's*, all of them—are useful not just for those in the not-for-profit sector, but for people who want to get a "fresh angle" on companies in their target area. If you want to understand what really drives a company— its values, its Board of Directors, its vision, its "behind-the-scenes" stuff—take a look at to whom they give money, or even *whether* they give money to anyone.

This kind of knowledge will give you an added insight and valuable understanding. And of course, very few people think to do it.

➜ International giving.

Job hunters, career changers, and career counselors, take note of this surprising statistic: as of 1987, employment in the nonprofit sector ➜ totaled 12,449,000—almost 10 percent of total U.S. employment.

If you live in New York City, use the Center as well as their directory. It is dedicated to the not-for-profit industry. If you don't live in ➜ the city, call them and ask for help. The people are terrific and incredibly knowledgeable.

• **The Foundation Directory**. Foundation Center. Loren Renz and Stan Olson, editors. Lists foundations alphabetically by state. Reports for each foundation its address, telephone number, purpose, types of projects funded, financial data, application information, whom to write, and the names of officers and trustees. Foundations are indexed by subject area of giving, geographical location, type of support awarded, and alphabetically. Specifies the geographical scope of a foundation's activities.

• **National Directory of Nonprofit Organizations 2000**. Gale Research, 4th edition. Provides the annual income figures, names, addresses, and phone numbers of more than 256,000 organizations—175,000 of which have incomes in excess of $100,000. An indispensable aid to professionals who search in the nonprofit sector. Volume 1 (in two parts) lists organizations with annual revenues of $100,000 or more. Volume 2 covers organizations with annual reviews between $25,000 and $99,999.

In addition, two step-saving indexes—Geographic/Income and Activity—allow users to access organizations by the state and the ZIP codes in which they are located, and by their principal areas of activity.

Inside stories on managing image under siege. ➜

M. Public Relations

• **Crisis Response**, Visible Ink Press. 25 chapters written by media professionals who handled crises such as Love Canal or the Perrier recall. Summaries provided of the crisis and understanding of each incident.

• **O'Dwyer's Directory of Public Relations Firms.** J.R. O'Dwyer Co. Found here are directory entries of over 1,900 U.S. and Canadian public relations firms, listed alphabetically, including overseas offices, clients, and billings. Indexed by firm specialty, client and geography, including a list of top 50 public relations firms.

• **Public Relations Career Directory.** Gale Research, Bradley J. Morgan, editor. In this resource, the pros offer advice to you on international public relations, the differences in beginning your career at a large vs. a small PR firm, opportunities in corporate communications, community affairs, media relations, and public relations for associations, financial and sports organizations.

Here is another ➜ example of creative use of research tools. Don't just use this book if you are in advertising! It is like a window into major faux pas that companies have had to handle. You learn a lot by seeing how firms have dealt with problems and/or public perceptions of those problems. This is a <u>fantastic</u> book.

• **The PR News Casebook**. Gale Research, edited by David Bianco. From the pages of *PR News*—the world's most widely read public relations weekly—comes this collection of 1,000 case studies covering major PR campaigns and events from the publication's nearly 50-year history. Based on personal interviews conducted by *PR News* founder and former publisher Ms. Denny Griswold, each case study analyzes how the most important businesses, government agencies, and other organizations from around the world have handled issues such as: boycotts, downsizing, industrial achievements, minority relations, new product introductions, plant closings, product tampering, stockholder relations, and many others.

Each one-page entry begins with a brief overview of the background leading up to the campaign, then deals with the company's planning for the event, the public's reaction to it, and the methods they used to respond to it. The analysis includes a review of how effective the company was (or was not) in handling the event.

*We're a society that's not about perfection, but about rectifying mistakes.
We're about second chances.*
Harry Edwards, in "Hardline," *Detroit Free Press,* May 1988

O. Publishing

• **National Directory of Magazines.** Annual. Oxbridge Communications. Information on 20,000 North American magazines. Entries include details on staffing, advertising, and production details.

• **National Directory of Mailing Lists**. Annual. Oxbridge Communications. Organizes & describes magazines, journals, newsletters, catalogues, directories, newspapers, tabloids, looseleafs, bulletins, indices, and all other periodically produced publications-over 15,000 lists. Entries arranged within specific subject categories.

• **Publishers Directory. Annual**. Gale Research, 21st edition, 2000, Detailed information on more than 20,000 U.S. and Canadian publishers and small, independent presses.

→ As the publishing industry grows, new kinds of products and new kinds of companies are continually created. This resource captures many of those opportunities and includes novel ways of contacting them.

Makes it easy for you to research or contact virtually all the publishing firms listed in *Literary Market Place* as well as the independent and hard-to-find firms.

In one soft-cover volume, *Publishers Directory* gives you such key facts on each publisher as: complete contact information; founding date; ISBN; discounts and returns policies; description of subject specialties; imprints; a breakdown of sales to libraries, bookstores, non-book retail outlets and individuals; a list of representative titles and more. Publishers, Subject, and Geographic Indexes.

P. Sales and Marketing

→ Here they are: International market research companies.

• **The GreenBook: International Directory of Marketing Research Companies and Services**. American Marketing Association. Names firms in 53 countries that provide market research services. Lists address, telephone number, names of principal officers, and a description of services offered. Indexed by service, geographically, and alphabetically, including advertising research, concept development and testing, consumer research, interviewing service, name development, package development, and product testing.

Have you ever wondered how marketing campaigns such as → Microsoft's "Where do you want to go today?" came to be? Find the answers in this new book that describes successes and failures of market trends, strategies and initiatives.

• **Encyclopedia of Major Marketing Campaigns**. Gale Research 1st Ed. 1999. The *Encyclopedia of Major Marketing Campaigns* looks at 500 major marketing and advertising campaigns of the 20th century from a historical perspective and several related initiatives of earlier years that developed the basis for present day advertising.

Entry articles look at the advertising campaign's or market initiative's historical context, target market, expected outcomes, competition, marketing strategy and development hurdles and the outcome of the campaign—what worked, what didn't and why.

• **Vault.Com's Guide to Marketing and Brand Management**. Provides the inside scoop, what it's like working in the industry, who the players are in the industry, how to get ahead in the industry, and how to get hired in the industry. Reviews America's top employers in the marketing and brand management industry, including General Mills, Procter & Gamble, Nike, Coca-Cola, and many more!

• **Marketing and Sales Career Directory**. Gale Research, Bradley Morgan, editor. Tells effective ways to reach customers and consumers. Includes direct sales, industrial sales, business-to-business marketing, consulting, services marketing, retail marketing, database marketing, and market research.

Q. Services

→ Everyone says they want to be a consultant—check it out with the pros.

• **Consultants and Consulting Organizations Directory. Annual**. Gale Research, edited by Janice McLean. Here you can find important details, like services offered, typical clients, full contact information, date founded, principals, and more.

The nearly 18,000 firms and individuals listed in the new edition are arranged alphabetically under 14 general fields of consulting activity ranging from Agriculture to Marketing. Over 400 specialties are represented including finance, computers, fundraising, job hunting, and more. Location, Specialization, Personal Name, and Company Name Indexes enable users to pinpoint the best source for expert advice. Consultants and Consulting Organizations Directory is available on-line.

• **Dun's Directory of Service Companies.** Dun's Marketing Services. Annual. Profiles of some 50,000 companies, both public and private, deriving their primary revenue from a service activity and employing 50 or more people. Very little overlap exists between this and other titles. Indexing by geography and by industry.

Change does not roll in on the wheels of inevitability, but comes through continuous struggle.
And so we must straighten our backs and work for our freedom.
A man can't ride you unless your back is bent.
Martin Luther King Jr., "The Death of Evil upon the Seashore,"
sermon given at the Cathedral of St. John the Divine, New York City, May 17, 1956

R. Small / Private Business

• **Small Business Sourcebook**. Gale Research, edited by Carol A. Schwartz. Look to *SBS* to find 30 new small business profiles as well as broader coverage of audiovisual media; expanded listings of newsletters; increased coverage of Canadian resources.

SBS's convenient arrangement and special features, such as an appendix of Standard Industrial Classification (SIC) codes used to profile small businesses, as well as a glossary of small business terms, make locating information easy.

• **MacMillan Directory of Leading Private Companies.** Lists 12,500 companies and wholly-owned subsidiaries with sales of $10,000,000.

• **Over the Counter 1,000 Yellow Book.** Has the leading growth companies quoted on NASDAQ; comprehensive directory introducing leading, dynamic, younger growth companies in the U.S. Gives address, phone, titles of 20,000 executives who manage these smaller companies on the cutting edge of innovation.

• **The Top 1,500 Private Companies.** Listing with brief information and ranking by sales, products, employees, and number of locations.

• **Small Business Administration.**

• **Small Business Development Corporations.**

• **Chambers of Commerce.**

Following are lists from magazines. Updated annually.

• **Business Week 100 Best Small Companies.**

• **Business Week Top 1,000.**

• **Crain's Lists.**

• **Forbes 200 Best Small Companies in America.**

• **Forbes 400 Largest Private Companies in the United States.**

• **Inc. Magazine's 500 America's Fastest Growing Private Companies.**

• **Inc. Magazine's 100 Fastest Growing Small Public Companies.**

• **Ward's Private Company Profiles,** Gale Research. Articles from over 150 sources including investment reports and company brochures about this significant and often elusive segment of the American economy. Find big companies, recognized names, as well as cutting edge firms and small aggressive companies.

• **Small Business Profiles,** Gale Research. A guide to top opportunities for entrepreneurs. Covers start up business issues and opportunities. Issues include marketing, advertising, licensing and insurance, computer systems and programs, costs and profits, financing, location, layout, staffing, and more.

S. Special Events / Trade Shows

• **Trade Shows and Professional Exhibits Directory**. Gale Research, edited by Robert J. Elster. A directory of exhibitions, trade shows, conventions, and other types of meetings designed to foster direct sales/trade contacts. Lists these meetings by general subject categories. Each entry includes such information as the name, address, and telephone number of the sponsor; name of the exhibits manager; co-sponsors; expected attendance; targeted participants; charges to exhibitors; and dates and locations of the meetings.

• **Trade Shows Worldwide**. Gale Research, edited by Valerie J. Webster. *TSW* provides profiles of 5,796 trade shows—2,400 more than competing directories and over 700 more than the previous edition. *TSW* lists more than 4,600 trade show organizers and sponsors throughout the world and provides complete contact information and events descriptions.

This new edition covers 723 convention centers worldwide and provides listings of 431 exhibit builders, transportation firms, and other industry suppliers. Information about professional associations, consultants, and published sources of industry information is also included in this essential reference source.

Here's a tool for those hard to research smaller companies where opportunities abound. →

Find the information you seek on that elusive segment of industry in the private arena. →

For people investigating starting their own business, this is a terrific resource. →

→ I talk to so many people who are interested in this field, but have no idea how to find out names of possible companies.

T. Transportation

• **Directory of Consultants.** National Association of Regulatory Utility Commissioners. Annual. Lists 190 consultants and consulting firms active in utility and transportation industries. Includes firm or individual name, address, and phone; names of regulatory agencies by which engaged in the past; purpose and dates of past engagements; areas of specialization; qualifications and experience.

• **Moody's Transportation Manual.** Moody's Investors Service. One of the eight Moody's Manuals, it profiles companies in the transportation industry. These include railroads, airlines, trucking, steamships, automobile/truck leasing and rental companies, oil pipelines, and bridge companies. The level of coverage for each company depends on the coverage purchased.

➜ Here's a guide to trends, forecasts, and histories of companies in the transportation industry. Something for everyone!

The information usually includes corporate history, company business activities, annual report to stockholders, address and telephone number, names of officers and directors, consolidated income account, consolidated balance sheet, notes to financial statements, structure of long-term debt and bond ratings, and other information. For some of the major companies, a map of their routes is displayed. A "Special Features" section presents summary statistics of the transportation industry.

U. Travel and Hospitality

• **Travel and Hospitality Career Directory.** Gale Research, Bradley J. Morgan, editor. Find out about the wide variety of career options this industry has to offer. Essays discuss breaking into the hotel and motel industry, working for a local travel and tourism board, becoming a travel agent, getting started in car rental, convention and meeting planning, working for an airline, and more.

• **Financial Times International Yearbook: World Hotel Directory. Annual.** Gale Research. Directory of over 3,200 hotels in 140 countries around the world. Lists hotels by geographic region, allowing users to quickly identify business in an easy-to-use, country-by-country format.

Includes the hotel address; telephone, fax, and telex number; reservation system; style; location; and manager's name. Information on rooms, fees, service, and facilities is also available. Additional sections list hotel incentive programs, foreign currency exchange rates, major airports worldwide, and airlines.

V. Real Estate

• **The Directory of Real Estate Investors.** National Register Publishing Co. International directory of brokers, investors, and developers of commercial property who have at least $1 million of equity funds to invest. Reports the kind of income-producing properties in which they are interested and the geographic region(s) of their preference. Each company is described by reporting the address, telephone number, names of contact persons, size of portfolio, investment structure, total funds available, and other relevant information.

W. Education

• **The World of Learning.** An international directory of educational, cultural, and scientific institutions with contact information of over 150,000 people—chief personnel involved in higher education worldwide. Also provides information on over 400 international organizations.

5. Information on Executives and Management

• **Experts Contact Directory.** Gale Research, edited by Nora Paul. This directory is a compilation of contact information for 25,000 academics in the U.S. who are recognized authorities in their fields. This comprehensive and timely reference is designed to help users locate speakers, expert witnesses, network contacts, interview subjects, and others.

This is simply a brilliant and novel approach to networking and ➜ asking true experts about their field. Even if you don't talk to them, knowing who they are is in itself pretty impressive knowledge.

Arranged by subject with names of experts listed alphabetically under appropriate subheadings, each entry contains the expert's name, title, position, university, specialty, and phone number(s). Geographic, University Name, and Personal Name Indexes.

• **How to Find Information About Executives.** Washington Researchers Publishing. A guide to how and where to find information about executives in the business community. Explains procedures and places. Targets may be the competitor's business manager, plant manager, or others. Useful for locating information about prospective customers or clients, prospective employees, suppliers, the CEO of a company in which an investment is being considered, and other persons.

The sources of information are governmental agencies, the Securities and Exchange Commission, courts, trade and professional associations, labor unions, publications, databases, and other references. Also explains how to conduct telephone interviews when seeking information about people.

As a splendid palace deserted by its inmates looks like a ruin, so does a man
without character, all his material belongings notwithstanding.
Mohandas Gandhi

• **International Who's Who**. Europa Publications Ltd. Biographical dictionary profiles notable persons from around the world and in most areas of endeavor. Biographical sketches include the biographee's nationality, birth date, education, names of parents, marriage, career information, awards, publications, office address, home address, telephone number (home and/or office), and other biographical data.

• **Medical Sciences International Who's Who**. Gale Research. Turn to this global resource when you need to get in touch with medical scientists and researchers from around the world. Detailed professional biographies are provided for approximately 8,000 senior biomedical scientists and their researchers in over 90 countries worldwide. All subject areas are covered, including biochemistry; dental sciences; immunology and transplantation; clinical medicine; molecular biology; neoplasia; pharmacology and therapeutics; psychiatry; clinical psychology; and surgery and anesthesia. Entries include full contact data, education, career information, memberships, publications, and more. Fully indexed.

• **Taft's Owners and Officers of Private Companies**. Gale Research. An annually updated source of hard-to find data on the people who form the backbone of American business.

Volume 1 provides entries on more than 105,000 owners and officers of private American companies with annual sales over $5 million. Volume 2 contains Personal Name, Company Name, Standard Industrial Classification (SIC) and Geographic Indexes.

• **Reference Book of Corporate Managements**. Dun's Marketing Services. Annual. Biographical data and work history for tens of thousands of people who are officers and directors of more than 12,000 companies.

➜ If you want to be in corporate America, it surely would be important to know who owns what. Talk about seeing the connections and links...

• **Who Owns Corporate America. Annual**. Gale Research. Offers comprehensive listings of "insider" stockholders-the officers, directors and 10 percent principal stockholders who own securities registered with the U.S. Securities and Exchange Commission (SEC). Lists approximately 75,600 stockholders by last name—along with detailed information on the list's stock ownership—thus facilitating biographical research.

Annual updating ensures that you get the latest information on wealthy stockholders. Entries include: insider's name; name of the security/issuing company; stock symbol; number of shares held by listee; date of last transaction; "type" of security held; ownership; and market value in dollars of the holdings.

• **Who's Who in Business and Industry in the UK. Annual**. Gale Research, edited by Juliet Margetts. Provides biographies of the 10,000 most important people in British industry, including managers, executives and directors of Britain's top 1,000 companies as well as those involved in distribution, advertising, consulting, civil service, trade associations, unions, journalism, and academic pursuits.

Each entry includes the entrant's responsibilities, career, education and recreations, as well as biographical facts. Also includes three indexes: the Company Index provides address and telephone as well as names of top managers; the Business Sector Index arranges company names by 80 subject categories; and the Geographic Index lists companies by nearly 100 areas, from Aberdeen to York.

• **Who's Who in Finance and Industry**. Marquis Who's Who/Macmillan Directory Division. Biographical dictionary of notable persons in finance and industry. Biographies are of corporate executives and people from professional and trade associations, business research, stock exchanges, labor unions, government agencies, and other organizations. Includes occupation, home and business addresses, date and place of birth, marriage data, education, professional certifications, memberships, avocations, and other information.

➜ Pretty interesting reading!

• **Taft's Who's Wealthy in America. Annual**. Gale Research. More than 100,000 of America's most wealthy. Each new edition contains information on hundreds of new prospects, plus information on previous listees—such as political contributions made in elections. Up-to-date, valuable prospect information, designed to put you in touch with new donors—America's top-tier wealth holders and consumers. Contact information, plus critical data on political contributions, insider stock holdings, education, and lifestyle indicators (Rolls-Royce owner, art collector, etc.). Additional references will lead you to further information.

• **Who's Who in Venture Capital**. John Wiley & Sons. A directory of venture capitalists: their address, telephone number, investment interests, names of principals with their educational and business experience, size of investment fund, and average amount per investment. Includes venture capitalists in the U.S., U.K., and Canada. Discusses criteria often used by venture capitalists when contemplating an investment decision.

• **Standard & Poor's Register of Corporations, Directors and Executives.** Directors and Executives volume. Annual. An alphabetical list of over 70,000 individuals serving as officers, directors, trustees, partners, etc. Provides principal business affiliations with business addresses, residence addresses, and where available, year and place of birth, and college.

The
Five
O'Clock
Club®

PART SIX

WHAT IS THE
FIVE O'CLOCK CLUB?

"AMERICA'S PREMIER CAREER COUNSELING NETWORK"

How to Join the Club

The Five O'Clock Club:

- Job-Search Strategy Groups
  - Private Coaching
- Membership Information

The Five O'Clock Club was founded
by Kate Wendleton in 1978 to provide
thoughtful career-development help
for busy people of all levels.
The programs and materials have helped
thousands take control of their careers
and find good jobs fast.

*The original Five O'Clock Club was formed in
Philadelphia in 1883. It was made up of the
leaders of the day, who shared their experiences
"in a spirit of fellowship and good humor."*

There *is* a Five O'Clock Club near you!
**For more information on becoming a member,
please fill out the
Membership Application Form in this book,
sign up on our Website at:
http://www.FiveOClockClub.com
or call:
1-800-538-6645, ext. 600**

**Note: Counseling session fees are in addition
to membership fees.**

*The median number of years men have been with their
current employer fell between 1983 and 1996 for most
ages, the Bureau of Labor Statistics reports: from 7.3
to 6.1 years for ages 35 to 44 and from 15.3 to 10.5
years for ages 55 to 64. But the overall median held at
about four years on the job, as the work force aged.
For women, the median tenure rose overall.*
Albert Karr, *The Wall Street Journal,*
February 11, 1997

The Five O'Clock Club Search Process

The Five O'Clock Club process, as outlined in Kate
Wendleton's books, is a targeted, strategic approach
to career development and job search. Five O'Clock
Club members become proficient at skills which
prove invaluable during their *entire working live*s.

We train our members to *manage their careers,* and
always look ahead to their *next* job search. Research
shows that an average worker spends only four years
in a job—and will have 12 jobs, in as many as 5
career fields—during his or her working life.

Five O'Clock Club members find *better jobs,
faster.* The average job search for a managerial
position is now estimated at 8.1 months. The average Five O'Clock Club member who regularly
attends weekly sessions finds a job by his or her
tenth session. Even the discouraged, long-term job
searcher can find immediate help.

The keystone to The Five O'Clock Club process
is in teaching our members an understanding of the
entire job-hiring process. A first interview is only a
time for exchanging critical information. The real
work starts after the interview. We teach our members *how to turn job interviews into offers,* and to
negotiate the best possible employment package.

The Five O'Clock Club is *action-oriented.* **We'll
help you decide what you should do this very
next week to move your search along**. By their
third session, our members have set definite job
targets by industry or company size, position,
and geographic location, and are out in the field,
gathering information and making the contacts
which will lead to interviews with hiring managers.

Our approach evolves with the changing job market.
We're able to synthesize information from hundreds
of Five O'Clock Club members, and come up with
new approaches for our members. For example, we
now discuss temporary placement for executives,
how to handle voice mail, and how to network
when doors are slamming shut all over town.

The Job-Search Strategy Group

The Five O'Clock Club meeting is a carefully
planned *job-search strategy session.* We provide members with the tools and tricks necessary to get a good
job fast—even in a tight market. Networking and emo-

194

Let us consider how we may spur one another on toward love and good deeds.
Let us not give up meeting together, as some are in the habit of doing, but let us encourage one another.
Hebrews 10:24-25

tional support are also included in the meeting.

Each week, you will **listen to a lecture** on some aspect of the Five O'Clock Club methodology. Then you will **join a small group strategy session** led by a trained Five O'Clock Club career consultant.

Hear one lecture per week via one of 16 audiotaped lectures by Kate Wendleton. (The boxed lecture set is $150 or comes FREE with the purchase of 10 Virtual Branch sessions.)

Join the *weekly small group strategy session* with a senior Five O'Clock Club career consultant via teleconference from the convenience of your home, or anywhere else. Your *small group* is your chance to get feedback and advice on your own search, listen to and learn from others, and build your business network. All groups are led by trained career consultants who bring years of experience to your search. The teleconferenced small group is generally no more than six people, so everyone gets the chance to speak up.

Members are urged to attend at least 10 meetings in a row to develop momentum and perhaps land an appropriate position. Our research proves that those who attend on a regular basis get jobs faster and at higher rates of pay than those who attend sporadically, search on their own or even those who see a coach privately throughout the process.

(optional) Virtual Branch members: Enjoy the Five O'Clock Club website and private message boards for your small group.

FEES: Our competitors charge $5000 to $7000 up front. The Five O'Clock Club costs less than ten percent of that! See our website for the counseling staff, the full offerings and the fees at the branch of your choice.

Private Coaching

Club Members: we will review your background and refer you to appropriate certified Five O'Clock Club career counselors. Fill out the Coach Request Form on FiveOClockClub.com, or meet with your group head between meetings for *private coaching*. Individual sessions help you answer specific questions, prepare your résumé, or take an in-depth look at your career path. Please pay the consultant directly, as *private coaching is **not** included in The Five O'Clock Club seminar or membership fee.*

From the Club history, written in the 1890s

At The Five O'Clock Club, [people] of all shades of political belief—as might be said of all trades and creeds—have met together. . . The variety continues almost to a monotony. . . [The Club's] good fellowship and geniality—not to say hospitality—has reached them all.

It has been remarked of clubs that they serve to level rank. If that were possible in this country, it would probably be true, if leveling rank means the appreciation of people of equal abilities as equals; but in The Five O'Clock Club it has been a most gratifying and noteworthy fact that no lines have ever been drawn save those which are essential to the honor and good name of any association. Strangers are invited by the club or by any members, [as gentlepeople], irrespective of aristocracy, plutocracy or occupation, and are so treated always. Nor does the thought of a [person's] social position ever enter into the meetings. People of wealth and people of moderate means sit side by side, finding in each other much to praise and admire and little to justify snarlishness or adverse criticism. People meet as people—not as the representatives of a set— and having so met, dwell not in worlds of envy or distrust, but in union and collegiality, forming kindly thoughts of each other in their heart of hearts.

In its methods, The Five O'Clock Club is plain, easy-going and unconventional. It has its "isms" and some peculiarities of procedure, but simplicity characterizes them all. The sense of propriety, rather than rules of order, governs its meetings, and that informality which carries with it sincerity of motive and spontaneity of effort, prevails within it. Its very name indicates informality, and, indeed, one of the reasons said to have induced its adoption was the fact that members or guests need not don their dress suits to attend the meetings, if they so desired. This informality, however, must be distinguished from the informality of Bohemianism. For The Five O'Clock Club, informality, above convenience, means sobriety, refinement of thought and speech, good breeding and good order. To this sort of informality much of its success is due.

Questions You May Have About the Weekly Job-Search Strategy Group

The Weekly Job-Search Strategy Group

is a Professional Career-Counseling Program presented at branches of The Five O'Clock Club.
"America's Premier Career Counseling Network"

Job hunters are not always the best judges of what they need during a search. For example, most are interested in lectures on answering ads or working with search firms. We will cover those topics, but, strategically, they are relatively unimportant in an effective job search.

At The Five O'Clock Club, you get the information you *really* need in your search—such as *how to target more effectively, how to get more interviews, and how to turn job interviews into offers.*

What's more, you will work in a small group with some of the best counselors available. In these strategy sessions, your group will help you decide what to do, this week and every week, to move your search along. And you will learn by coaching and being coached by others in your group.

Here are a few other points:
- For best results, attend on a regular basis. Your group gets to know you and will coach you to eliminate whatever you may be doing wrong—or refine what you are doing right.
- Those who think they need to come to a session only to ask a quick question are usually wrong. Often the problem started weeks before the job hunter realized it. Or the problem may be more complex than the job hunter realizes and requires a few sessions to straighten out.
- <u>You must be a member to attend the strategy sessions</u>. To get started in the small group sessions, you must purchase a minimum of 10 sessions, which *includes* the set of 16 audiotaped presentations on Five O'Clock Club methodology.
- After that, you may purchase five or ten sessions.
- <u>If you miss a session</u>, you may make it up at any time. You may even transfer unused sessions to a friend! (or use it during your next search).
- Carefully read all of the material in the Beginner's Kit that you get with your Five O'Clock Club membership. It will help you decide whether or not to attend.

- Although many people find jobs quickly (even people who have been unemployed a long time), others have more difficult searches. Plan to be in it for the long haul and you'll do better.
- The first week, pay attention to the strategies used by the others in your group. Soak up all the information you can. We will work on your search the *second* week.
- *Read the books and listen to the lecture before you come in the second week.* They will help you move your search along.

To register
1. For an application and pricing information, visit our website or call 1-800-538-6645 ext. 600.
2. Become a member and get your Beginner's Kit; then reserve a space by calling 212-286-9332.
3. You will get instructions on how to attend your first small-group teleconferencing session.

To assign you to a small group counselor, we need to know:
- your current (or last) field or industry,
- the kind of job you would like next (if you know),
- your desired salary range in general terms.
- your time zone/geographic location.

If you would rather see a private counselor, fill out the Coach Request Form on our website.

What Happens at the Meetings?
Each week, job searchers from various industries and professions attend. Some branches specialize in professionals and managers; others in those earning more than $100,00 per year; still others in recent college graduates, or those who have yet reached the professional or managerial ranks. Usually, half are employed; half unemployed.

Before the meeting, listen to the tape on a Five O'Clock Club job-hunting topic. Then, job hunters meet weekly in small groups headed by senior full-time, professional counselors.

The first week, you get the textbooks, listen to the lecture, are assigned to your small group, and *listen to the others in your group.* You learn a lot by listening to how your peers are strategizing their searches.

By the second week, you will have read the materials. Now we can start to work on your search

We find ourselves not independently of other people and institutions but through them. We never get to the bottom of our selves on our own. We discover who we are face to face and side by side with others in work, love, and learning.
Robert N. Bellah, et al, *Habits of the Heart*

strategy and help you decide what to do next to move your search along. For example, we'll help you figure out how to get more interviews in your target area, or how to turn an interview into a job offer.

In the third week, you will see major progress in the other members of your group, and you may notice major progress in your own search as well.

By the third or fourth week, most members are conducting a full and effective search. Over the remaining weeks, you will tend to keep up a full search rather than go after only one possibility. You will regularly aim to have six to ten things in the works at all times. These will generally be in specific target areas that you have identified, will keep your search on target, and increase your chances of getting multiple job offers to choose from.

Those who stick with the process find that it works.

Some people prefer to just observe for a few weeks before they start their job search, and that's okay, too.

How Much Does it Cost?

The fees vary by salary level and location. A typical fee is 10 sessions for $400 for those earning under $100,000 per year, and 10 sessions for $600 for those who have earned $100,000 and over. The average person purchases only 10 sessions, although those with difficult searches may need more time.

You must have the materials so you can review them before the second session. Otherwise, you will tend to waste the time of the others in the group by asking questions that are covered in the texts.

Is The Club right for me?

The Five O'Clock Club process is for you if:

• You are looking for a job or consulting work.
• You are a professional, manager or executive. (Most attendees earn between $30,000 and $300,000 a year, although some earn more and others earn less than those amounts.)
• You want to participate in a group process on a regular basis.
• You realize that finding or changing jobs and careers is hard work . . . which you are absolutely willing and able to do.

If you have no idea about the kind of job you want next, attend the first session, get the assessment assignment from your counselor, see the counselor privately for one or two sessions to develop tentative job targets, and come back to the group with tentative targets in place. Since you don't participate the first week, it is usually best to join the group immediately and get your assignment. If you would prefer to see privately a counselor other than your group head, just fill out the "Coach Request Form" on our site.

How long will it take me to get a job?

Although our members tend to be from difficult fields or industries, the average person who attends regularly finds a new position within just ten sessions. Some take less time, and others take more. One thing we know for sure: *Those who get regular group coaching during their searches get jobs faster and at higher rates of pay than those who search on their own, simply take a course, or even those who choose to see a counselor privately throughout their searches.* This makes sense. If a person comes only when they think they have a problem, they are usually wrong. They probably had a problem a few weeks ago, but didn't realize it. Or the problem may be different from what they thought. Those who come regularly benefit from the observations others make about their searches. Problems are solved before they become severe, or are prevented altogether.

Those who attend regularly also learn a lot by paying attention and helping others in the group. This "vicarious" learning can cut weeks from your search. When you hear the problems of others who are ahead of you in the search, you can avoid those problems completely. People in your group will come to know you, and will point out subtleties you may not have noticed and interviewers will never tell you.

Will I be with others from my same field/industry?

Probably, but it's not that important. If you were a salesperson, for example, would you want to be with seven other salespeople?

Probably not. The search techniques are the same for the level handled by your branch. You will learn a lot and have a much more creative search if you are in a group with people who are in your general salary range but not exactly like you. Our clients are from virtually every field and industry. The process is what will help you. You will love the small group.

We've been doing this since 1978, and under-

The Five O'Clock Club is plain, easy-going and unconventional. . . .
Members or guests need not don their dress suits to attend the meetings.
(From the Club History, written in the 1890s)

stand your needs. That's why the mix we provide is the best you can get.

How can you charge such a small session fee?

1. We have no advertising costs because 90 percent of those who attend have been referred by other members.

We need a certain number of people to cover expenses. When lots of people get jobs quickly and leave us, we could go into the red. But so long as members refer others, we will continue to provide this service at a fair price.

2. We focus strictly on job search strategy, and encourage our clients to attend free support groups if they need emotional support. We focus on getting jobs, which reduces the time clients spend with us and the amount they pay.

3. We attract the best counselors, and our clients make more progress per session than they would elsewhere, which also reduces their costs.

4. We have expert administrators and a sophisticated computer system that reduces our overhead and increases our ability to track your progress.

May I change counselors?

Yes. Some care is taken in assigning you to your initial counselor. However, if you want to change once for any reason, you may do it. We don't encourage group hopping: It is better for you to stick with a group so that everyone gets to know you. On the other hand, we want you to feel comfortable. So if you tell us that you prefer a different group, you will be transferred immediately.

What if I have questions outside of the group?

Some people prefer to see their group counselor privately. Others prefer to meet with a different counselor to get another point of view. Whatever you decide, remember that the group fee does not cover counselor time outside of the group session. Therefore, if you want to be able to ask a counselor a "quick question" in between sessions, you would normally meet with the counselor first (usually by phone) for a private session so he or she gets to know you better. "Easy, quick questions" are often more complicated than they appear on the surface. After your first private session, some counselors will allow you to establish an account by paying in advance for one hour of counsel-

ing time, which you can then use for quick questions (usually a 15-minute minimum is charged). Since each counselor has an individual way of operating, find out how the counselor arranges these things.

What if I want to start my own business?

The process of becoming a consultant is essentially the same as job hunting, and lots of consultants attend regular Five O'Clock Club meetings. However, if you want to buy a franchise or an existing business or start a growth business, you should see a private counselor who specializes in entrepreneurial counseling.

What if I'm still not sure what to do.

Members may sometimes be allowed to pay for a single session before signing up for the entire package.

Whatever you decide, just remember that it has been proven that those who receive regular small group help during their searches get a job faster and at higher rates of pay than those who search on their own or simply attend a course.

If you get a job just one or two weeks faster because of this program, it will more than have paid for itself. And you may transfer unused sessions to anyone you choose (who must become a member of the Club and pay for the remaining sessions).

What if I need help negotiating my severance or outplacement services?

If you are a professional, manager or executive and think you are about to lose your job, we can help you to negotiate your severance with your employer. *We have even helped consultants, part-timers and short-timers negotiate severance packages* well in excess of what they expected. **An outplacement firm cannot advise you** (since they are hired by your employer), but we can.

Just visit our website for helpful information -- including **letters you can actually hand to your employer**. In addition, we can assign you a career counselor to help in your negotiation -- for a modest hourly fee.

Fortune 500 as well as smaller **corporations and not-for-profits have paid for their employees to use The Five O'Clock Club's services**. Maybe you can get your employer to give you the same kind of help. Take a look at our website: **www.FiveOClockClub.com**.

The Way We Are

The Five O'Clock Club means sobriety, refinement of thought and speech,
good breeding and good order. To this, much of its success is due.
The Five O'Clock Club is easy-going and unconventional.
A sense of propriety, rather than rules of order, governs its meetings.

J. Hampton Moore, *History of The Five O'Clock Club*
(written in the 1890s)

Just like the members of the original Five O'Clock Club, today's members want an ongoing relationship. George Vaillant, in his seminal work on successful people, found that "what makes or breaks our luck seems to be . . . our sustained relationships with other people." (George E. Vaillant, *Adaptation to Life*) Five O'Clock Club members know that much of the program's benefit comes from simply showing up. Showing up will encourage you to do what you need to do when you are not here. And over the course of several weeks, certain things will become evident that are not evident now.

Five O'Clock Club members learn from each other: The group leader is not the only one with answers. The leader brings factual information to the meetings, and keeps the discussion in line. But the answers to some problems may lie within you, or with others in the group.

Five O'Clock Club members encourage each other. They listen, see similarities with their own situations, and learn from that. And they listen to see how they may help others. You may come across information or a contact that will help someone else in the group. Passing on that information is what we're all about.

If you are a new member here, listen to others to learn the process. And read the books so you will know the basics that others already know. When everyone understands the basics, this keeps the meetings on a high level, interesting, and helpful to everyone.

Five O'Clock Club members are in this together, but they know that ultimately they are each responsible for solving their own problems with God's help. Take the time to learn the process, and you will become better at analyzing your own situation, as well as the situations of others. You will be learning a method that will serve you the rest of your life, and in areas of your life apart from your career.

Five O'Clock Club members are kind to each other. They control their frustrations—because venting helps no one. Because many may be stressed, be kind and go the extra length to keep this place calm and happy. It is your respite from the world outside and a place for you to find comfort and FUN. Relax and enjoy yourself, learn what you can, and help where you can. And have a ball doing it.

There arises from the hearts of busy [people] a love of variety,
a yearning for relaxation of thought as well as of body,
and a craving for a generous and spontaneous fraternity.

J. Hampton Moore
History of The Five O'Clock Club

The original Five O'Clock Club was formed in Philadelphia in 1883. It was made up of the leaders
of the day, who shared their experiences "in a spirit of fellowship and good humor."

The
Five
O'Clock
Club®

Lexicon Used at
The Five O'Clock Club

Use The Five O'Clock Club lexicon as a shorthand to express where you are in your job search. It will focus you and those in your group.

I. Overview and Assessment

How many hours a week are you spending on your search? Spend 35 hours on a full-time search; 15 hours on a part-time search.

What are your job targets?
Tell the group. A target includes industry or company size, position, and geographic area.
The group can help assess how good your targets are. Take a look at "Measuring Your Targets."

How does your résumé position you?
The summary and body should make you look appropriate to your target.

What are your back-up targets?
Decide at the beginning of the search before the first campaign. Then you won't get stuck.

Have you done the Assessment? If your targets are wrong, everything is wrong. (Do the Assessment in *Targeting the Job You Want.*) Or a counselor can help you privately to determine possible job targets.

II. Getting Interviews

How large is your target (e.g., thirty companies)? How many of them have you contacted? Contact them all.

How can you get (more) leads?
You will not get a job through search firms, ads, networking or direct contact. Those are techniques for getting interviews—job leads. Use the right terminology, especially after a person gets a job. Do not say, "How did you get the job?" if you really want to know, "Where did you get the lead for that job?"

Do you have six to ten things in the works?
You may want the group to help you land one job. After they help you with your strategy, they should ask, "How many other things do you have in the works?" If "none," the group can brainstorm how you can get more things going: through search firms, ads, networking, or direct contact. Then you are more likely to turn the interview into an offer because you will seem more valuable. What's more,

five will fall away through no fault of your own. Don't go after only one job.

How's your Two-Minute Pitch?
Practice a *tailored* Two-Minute Pitch. Tell the group the job title and industry of the hiring manager they should pretend they are for a role-playing exercise.
You will be surprised how good the group is at critiquing pitches. (Practice a few weeks in a row.) Use your pitch to separate you from your competition.

You seem to be in Stage One (or Stage Two or Stage Three) of your search. Know where you are. This is the key measure of your search.

Are you seen as insider or outsider?
See "How to Change Careers" for becoming an insider. If people are saying, "I wish I had an opening for someone like you," you are doing well in meetings. If the industry is strong, then it's only a matter of time before you get a job.

III. Turning Interviews into Offers

Do you want this job?
If you do not want the job, perhaps you want an offer, if only for practice. If you are not willing to go for it, the group's suggestions will not work.

Who are your likely competitors and how can you outshine and outlast them? You will not get a job simply because "they liked me." The issues are deeper. Ask the interviewer: "Where are you in the hiring process? What kind of person would be your ideal candidate? How do I stack up?"

What are your next steps? What are *you* planning to do if the hiring manager doesn't call by a certain date, or what are you planning to do to assure that the hiring manager *does* call you?

Can you prove you can do the job? Don't just take the "Trust me" approach. Consider your competition.

Which job positions you best for the long run? Which job is the best fit? Don't decide only on the basis of salary. You will most likely have another job after this. See which job looks best on your résumé, and will make you stronger for the next time.
In addition, find a fit for your personality. If you don't "fit," it is unlikely you will do well there. The group can help you turn interviews into offers, and give you feedback on which job is best for you.

The
Five
O'Clock
Club®

Dear Prospective Five O'Clock Clubber:

The Five O'Clock Club has helped thousands find jobs, change, or manage their careers!

At The Five O'Clock Club, we focus your search with real-world information that tells you exactly what you need to get more interviews . . . **and turn those interviews into offers.**

As a member, you also get—

❏ An attractive **membership card** and a **Beginner's Kit** containing information based on 12 years of research regarding who gets jobs and why, that will enable you to improve your job-search technqiues . . . immediately.

❏ A **subscription to *The Five O'Clock News***, ten issues filled with information on career development and job-search techniques— information to help you thrive in your career.

❏ **Access to reasonably priced weekly seminars** featuring individualized attention to your specific needs in small groups supervised by our senior counselors.

❏ Access to **one-on-one counselor matching**.

❏ Access to **members-only Bulletin Boards** to exchange ideas, experiences, and even role-play with other job searchers and career changers.

All that access, all that information, for the nominal membership fee of only $49.

The sooner you become a member, the sooner you can begin working on having a career that truly meets your financial, emotional, creative and intellectual needs.

Believe me, with self-examination and a lot of hard work with our counselors, you **can** find the job . . . you **can** have the career . . . you **can** live the life you always wanted!

The best of luck, whatever you may decide.

Sincerely,
Kate Wendleton, President

❏ Yes! I want access to the most effective methods for developing and managing my career, as well as for finding jobs.

. . . .

I enclose ❏ $49.00 for one year ❏ $75.00 for two years.
(foreign membership: $59 for one year; $85.00 for two)
I will receive ✓ a Beginner's Kit, ✓ a membership card, ✓ a subscription to *The Five O'Clock News*, ✓ a listing of current branches of The Five O'Clock Club, ✓ access to a network of career counselors (fees vary); ✓ to reasonably priced seminars at branches of The Five O'Clock Club in the U.S. and Canada; and ✓ to the members-only section of www.FiveOClockClub.com.
✓ other benefits listed on our website: www.FiveOClockClub.com.

Name _____

Address _____

City _____ State/Prov. _____ Zip/Postal _____

Work Phone _____ Home _____

Email address _____

Today's Date: _____

How I heard about you: _____

Targeting the Job You Want

. . . .

Method of payment:

❏ I enclose my check made out to The Five O'Clock Club, 300 E. 40th St., Suite 6L, NY, NY 10016.

❏ MasterCard, VISA or American Express:
(This form can be faxed to 212-286-9571)

Account Number: _____

Exp. Date: _____ Signature: _____

. . . .

The following information is for statistical purposes. Thanks for your help.

Salary range:

❏ under $30,000   ❏ $30-$49,999   ❏ $50-$74,999

❏ $75-$99,999   ❏ $100-$125,000   ❏ over $125,000

Age: ❏ 20-29   ❏ 30-39   ❏ 40-49   ❏ 50+

Gender: ❏ Male   ❏ Female

Current or most recent position/title: _____

_____

. . . .

The original Five O'Clock Club® was formed in Philadelphia in 1883. It was made up of the leaders of the day, who shared their experiences "in a spirit of fellowship and good humor."

Index

About the Author

Kate Wendleton is a nationally syndicated careers columnist and recognized authority on career development, having appeared on the *Today* Show, CNN, CNBC, Larry King, National Public Radio and CBS, and in *The New York Times, The Chicago Tribune, The Wall Street Journal, Fortune* magazine, *Business Week* and other national media.

She has been a career coach since 1978, when she founded The Five O'Clock Club® and developed its methodology to help job hunters and career changers of all levels in job-search-strategy groups. This methodology is now used by Affiliates of The Five O'Clock Club, which meet weekly in the United States and Canada.

Kate also founded Workforce America®, a not-for-profit Affiliate of The Five O'Clock Club, serving adults in Harlem who are not yet in the professional or managerial ranks. Workforce America helps each person move into better-paying, higher-level positions as each improves in educational level and work experience.

Kate founded, and directed for seven years, The Career Center at The New School for Social Research in New York. She also advises major corporations about employee career-development programs, and coaches senior executives.

A former CFO of two small companies, she has twenty years of business-management experience in both manufacturing and service businesses.

Kate attended Chestnut Hill College in Philadelphia and received her MBA from Drexel University. She is a popular speaker with groups that include the Wharton Business School Club, the Yale Club and the Columbia Business School Club.

While living in Philadelphia, Kate did long-term volunteer work for the Philadelphia Museum of Art, the Walnut Street Theatre Art Gallery, United Way, and the YMCA. Kate currently lives in Manhattan.

Kate Wendleton is the author of The Five O'Clock Club's four-part career-development and job-hunting series: *Targeting the Job You Want, Getting Interviews, Interviewing and Salary Negotiation* and *Building a Great Résumé.*

The original Five O'Clock Club was formed in Philadelphia in 1883.
It was made up of the leaders of the day, who shared their experiences
"in a spirit of fellowship and good humor."

About the Five O'Clock Club and the "Fruytagie" Canvas

Five O'Clock Club members are special. We attract upbeat, ambitious, dynamic, intelligent people—and that makes it fun for all of us. Most of our members are professionals, managers, executives, consultants and freelancers. We also include recent college grads and those aiming to get into the professional ranks, as well as people in their 40s, 50s and even 60s. Most members' salaries range from $25,000 to $400,000 (a third of our members earn in excess of $100,000 a year). For those who cannot attend a Club, *The Five O'Clock Club Book Series* contains all of our methodologies—and our spirit.

The Philosophy of The Five O'Clock Club

The Fruytagie Canvas by Patricia Kelly, depicted here, symbolizes our philosophy. The original, which is actually 52.5" by 69", hangs in the offices of The Five O'Clock Club in Manhattan. It is reminiscent of popular 16th century Dutch "fruytagie" or fruit tapestries which depicted abundance and prosperity.

I was attracted to this piece because it seemed to fit the spirit of our people at The Five O'Clock Club. This was confirmed when the artist, who was not aware of what I did for a living, added these words to the canvas: "The garden is abundant, prosperous and magical." Later, it took me only ten minutes to write the blank verse, "The Garden of Life," because it came from my heart. The verse reflects our philosophy and describes the kind of people who are members of the Club.

I'm always inspired by Five O'Clock Clubbers. They show others the way through their quiet behavior....their kindness....their generosity....their hard work....under God's care.

We share what we have with others. We are in this lush, exciting place together—with our brothers—and reach out for harmony. The garden is abundant. The job market is exciting. And Five O'Clock Clubbers believe that there is enough for everyone.

Part of Our Books

Because it so vividly represents our philosophy, we incorporated the Fruytagie Canvas into the covers of *The Five O'Clock Club Book Series*. The graphic element on each cover, designed by Steve Heiden, highlights a section of Kelly's canvas. *Targeting the Job You Want* contains the upper right-hand corner of the piece; *Job-Search Secrets* really is a secret—it has part of the grapes section of the tapestry, but upside-down. *Building a Great Résumé* shows part of the borders.

About the Artist's Method

To create her tapestry-like art, Kelly developed a unique style of stenciling. She hand-draws and hand-cuts each stencil, both in the negative and positive for each image. Her elaborate technique also includes a lengthy multi-layering process incorporating Dutch metal leaves and gilding, numerous transparent glazes, paints and wax pencils.

Kelly also paints the backside of the canvas using multiple washes of reds, violets and golds. She employs this technique to create a heavy vibration of color which in turn reflects the color onto the surface of the wall against which the canvas hangs.

The canvas is suspended by a heavy braided silk cord threaded into large brass grommets inserted along the top. Like a tapestry, the hemmed canvas is attached to a gold-gilded dowel with finials. The entire work is hung from a sculpted wall ornament.

Our staff is inspired every day by the tapestry and by the members of The Five O'Clock Club. We all work hard—and have FUN! The garden *is* abundant—with enough for everyone.

We wish you lots of success in your career. We—and your fellow members of The Five O'Clock Club—will work with you on it.

—Kate Wendleton, President

The original Five O'Clock Club was formed in Philadelphia in 1883.
It was made up of the leaders of the day, who shared their experiences
"in a spirit of fellowship and good humor."

THE GARDEN OF LIFE IS abundant, prosperous and magical. ❧ In this garden, there is enough for everyone. ❧ Share the fruit and the knowledge ❧ Our brothers and we are in this lush, exciting place together. ❧ Let's show others the way. ❧ Kindness. Generosity. ❧ Hard work. ❧ God's care.

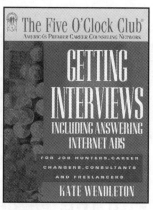

"During the time I was looking for a job I kept Kate's books by my bed. I read a little every night, a little every morning. Her common-sense advice, methodical approach, and hints for keeping the spirits up were extremely useful."
    Harold Levine, coordinator, Yale Alumni Career Resource Network

"Everyone talks about 'taking charge' of their lives; Kate Wendleton shows you how. One of the savviest and most effective career counselors that I know teaches that—even in the toughest of times—you can (and deserve to) find work that is right for you."
    Robert Mintz, director of Human Resources, Time, Inc., Magazines

"Today's job market is the toughest I've seen, and it requires the combination Kate has struck: shrewdness about the hiring process and the courage to face inner issues. Great work!"
    William Pilder, chairman, TransKey

"Kate Wendleton offers a wealth of pragmatic, uplifting advice for the job seeker. A person who follows Kate's formula would certainly get my attention, even if I'd already rejected his or her résumé."
    Carole F. St. Mark, president,
    Pitney Bowes Logistics Systems & Business Services

"Kate breaks the process into do-able steps that are easy to understand."
    Albert Prendergast, senior vice president, Human Resources, Mastercard International

"A one-woman crusade against unemployment—Kate Wendleton and The Five O'Clock Club!"
    Roberta Mell,
    vice president, National Advertising, Home Box Office

"Kate is one of the most singularly creative and energetic persons I have ever met. She is completely dedicated to the 'proposition of possibilities' in peoples' lives, and that dedication comes shining through."
    Dan Ciporin, vice president, director,
    Worldwide Brand Management, major credit card company

"The Five O'Clock Club books are 'what works now.' This indispensable, no-excuses guide to job-hunting and career building provides a step-by-step approach to organizing your search . . . targeting the job you want . . . getting in for the meetings . . . beating out the competition . . . and turning the interview into an offer."
    Jack Schlegel, New York Advertising & Communications Network

"Thank you, Kate, for all your help. I ended up with four offers and at least fifteen compliments in two months. Thanks!"
    president and CEO, large banking organization

"I have doubled my salary during the past five years by using The Five O'Clock Club techniques. Now I earn what I deserve. I think everyone needs The Five O'Clock Club."
    M. S., attorney, entertainment industry

"I'm an artistic person, and I don't think about business. Kate provided the disciplined business approach so I could practice my art. After adopting her system, I landed a role on Broadway in *Hamlet*."
    Bruce Faulk, actor,
    Manhattan (currently touring Europe in a play)

"Kate's books bring her enthusiastic, thought-provoking style to print. A must-read for every person who has a job, wants one, or may be contemplating changing it."
    Richard Schneyer, chair, Career Services Committee, Annual Convention,
    National Society of Fund Raising Executives

What They Say About Us

"One organization with a long record of success
in helping people find jobs is The Five O'Clock Club."
FORTUNE

"That's me! You have just told my story on **the** *Today Show*. Thanks for the boost. I needed it this morning. I hope others felt the same inspiration." —J.H.

"The Five O'Clock Club's arrival in D.C. reflects the growing importance of . . . career development."
The Washington Post

"Many managers left to fend for themselves are turning to the camaraderie offered by [The Five O'Clock Club]. Members share tips and advice, and hear experts."
The Wall Street Journal

"If you have been out of work for some time . . . consider The Five O'Clock Club."
The New York Times

"Wendleton has reinvented the historic gentlemen's fraternal oasis and built it into a chain of strategy clubs for job seekers."
The Philadelphia Inquirer

"[The Five O'Clock Club] will ask not what you do, but 'What do you want to do?' . . . [And] don't expect to get any great happy hour drink specials at this joint. The two-hour seminars are all business."
The Washington Times

"The Five O'Clock Club's proven philosophy is that job hunting is a learned skill like any other. The Five O'Clock Club becomes the engine that drives [your] search."
Black Enterprise

"Job hunting is a science at The Five O'Clock Club. [Members] find the discipline, direction and much-needed support that keeps a job search on track."
Modern Maturity

"Wendleton tells you how to beat the odds—even in an economy where pink slips are more common than perks. Her savvy and practical guide[s] are chockablock with sample résumés, cover letters, worksheets, negotiating tips, networking suggestions and inspirational quotes from such far-flung achievers as Abraham Lincoln, Malcolm Forbes and Lily Tomlin."
Working Woman

"On behalf of eight million New Yorkers, I commend and thank The Five O'Clock Club. Keep the faith and keep America working!"
David N. Dinkins, former Mayor,
The City of New York

"Kate Wendleton has written a sage and sensible book for the turbulent 90's."
Harvey Mackay, author of *Swim with the Sharks Without Being Eaten Alive*

"Everyone who has met Kate knows that she has a genius for caring about others."
David Rottman, vice president and manager, Career Services, Chase Manhattan Bank, New York City